1981

Morality and the Good Life

Morality and the Good Life

A Commentary on Aristotle's *Nicomachean Ethics*

Roger J. Sullivan

Memphis State University Press

Manufactured in the United States of America

Library of Congress Cataloging in Publication Data

Sullivan, Roger J   1928–
   Morality and the good life.

   Bibliography: p. 191. Includes index.
   1. Aristoteles. Ethica.   2. Ethics.   I. Title.
B430.S9   170   77–13485
ISBN 0–87870–033–1
ISBN 0–87870–111–7

The author and publisher are grateful for permission to quote from *Aristotle; Nichomachean Ethics*, translated by Martin Ostwald, copyright © 1962 by The Bobbs-Merrill Company, Inc., reprinted by permission of the publisher.

For my daughter Jenny,
with love

Contents

Preface   ix
Abbreviations   xii

1 Introduction to Aristotle   3
   Aristotle's Debt to Plato   4
   Aristotle's Writings   4
   Aristotle's View of Moral Philosophy   6
   A Look Ahead   14
   Notes to Chapter 1   16

2 The Nature of Human Action: A Matter of Contrasts   17
   First Contrast: Action vs. Passivity   18
   Second Contrast: Action vs. Process—Part 1   20
   Third Contrast: Action vs. Process—Part 2   21
   Fourth Contrast: Action vs. Thought   24
   The Nature of Action: A Summary   27
   The Two-Ply Character of Individual Actions   28
   Notes to Chapter 2   34

3 On the Outside: Kinds of Practical Activities   43
   Instrumental and Intrinsic Practical Good   43
   Pleasure and Kinds of Pleasure   47
   Poïesis and Praxis: Making and Doing   50
   Notes to Chapter 3   55

4 On the Inside: Practical Reasoning—Deliberation and
   Choice   62
   Deliberation and Choice   63
   The Logical Form of Deliberation and Choice   66
   Practical Reasoning and Theoretical Reasoning   68
   Notes to Chapter 4   72

5 On the Inside: Skillfulness, Practical Wisdom, and Moral
 Excellence 80
 Productive Skill 81
 Practical Wisdom 83
 Moral Excellence 85
 Notes to Chapter 5 91

6 The Integrity of Moral Personality 95
 The Unity of Practical Wisdom and Moral Excellence 97
 Practical Wisdom and Moral Philosophy 103
 Morality: A Synthesis of Character and of Action 112
 Notes to Chapter 6 115

7 The Political Genesis and Political Nature of Morality 124
 The State: Master Paradigm and Moral Educator 126
 Beyond the State 129
 Notes to Chapter 7 133

8 When Practice Goes Amiss 139
 Simple Error 141
 Moral Evil 142
 Moral Weakness 144
 Moral Strength 148
 Brutishness 149
 Conclusion 149
 Notes to Chapter 8 152

9 Morality and the Good Life 159
 The Good Life 159
 The Place of Nonmoral Goods in the Morally Good Life 163
 Living the Good Life 166
 A Final Problem 170
 A Personal Note 176
 Notes to Chapter 9 178

Glossary of Greek Terms 186
Works Cited 191
Index 195

Preface

This book is written, not for the philosopher or the classicist already well acquainted with Aristotle, but for the person who wants to get to know Aristotle's moral philosophy. The *Nicomachean Ethics* is surely the most widely read of all Aristotle's writings, but, strangely enough, there is no commentary available which presents in an organized and detailed way the fundamental tenets of Aristotle's ethics, at least no such commentary for the nonexpert.

The book proceeds on three different levels. The first level consists of the exposition proper, and there I have tried to present Aristotle's doctrines as coherently and sympathetically as I could. The time for criticism is after a person first has appreciated the nature of the problems which have preoccupied a philosopher and the ways in which he has approached and tried to resolve those problems. A person just beginning to study Aristotle's ethical philosophy, therefore, can stay mainly with the text of the commentary.

The second level consists in a very large number of references to the *Ethics* and to other writings of Aristotle. These references are meant to perform two functions. First, they are meant to encourage the reader not to take this commentary as a substitute for reading Aristotle himself. Secondly, they are meant to help readers interested in particular topics by guiding them to relevant passages in the Aristotelian corpus. Students wishing to write papers on topics discussed in this book will find the Index helpful in arranging their papers and the footnote references a reliable guide to most of the relevant passages both in the *Ethics* and in other works of Aristotle.

The third level consists in my own comments on and criticisms of Aristotle's presentation. The majority of these comments occur only in the footnotes, but there seemed no way in which to avoid placing some in the text itself, and these occur primarily in the beginning of Chapter 6 and in the final sections of Chapter 9. I have not tried to make my criticisms exhaustive; they are intended only to indicate some ways in which Aristotle might be questioned. In the notes I have also occasionally referred to other commentaries, but I have done so only when it seemed to clarify my own presentation of Aristotle's doctrines as I now understand them.

The organization of materials in this book is largely the product of my attempts to teach an introductory course in ethical theory. In such a course, students commonly experience great difficulty evaluating and comparing the various theories they have studied. When, however, students have organized their thoughts, using the conceptual framework provided here or one similar, they have been able to achieve substantial clarity about the elements involved in the construction of an ethical theory; they have been able to analyze both the similarities and differences between various ethical theories; and they have achieved a fairly sophisticated view of their own moral life. The gains from the use of this approach have been sufficiently great that this present volume is projected as the first part of a trilogy which will include also commentaries on the moral philosophies of Immanuel Kant and of John Dewey.

No knowledge of Greek has been presupposed, but some key Greek terms used by Aristotle are included, transliterated, in the text, partly because different scholars translate them differently and partly because no English translation catches their meaning accurately. Further, a reader who wishes to continue his reading of Aristotle will be helped by having a minimal acquaintance with Aristotle's technical vocabulary. A glossary of some of these terms can be found in the back of the book.

References which are not otherwise identified in the notes are always to the *Nicomachean Ethics*, and all references follow the standard Bekker numbers for page, column (a or b) and line, so that the reader can use almost any translation available. Occasionally I have used my own translation of a text, but in general I have tried to use standard, accessible translations. Most of the citations I have used are from the *Nicomachean Ethics* and are taken from *Aristotle: NICOMACHEAN ETHICS*, translated by Martin Ostwald, copyright © 1962 by The Bobbs-Merrill Company, Inc., and are reprinted by permission of the publisher. The translators of other, scattered texts are noted in the footnotes. From the twelve-volume Oxford translation, *The Works of Aristotle*, I have used citations from Benjamin Jowett (*Politics*), J. Solomon (*Eudemian Ethics*), J. A. Smith (*On the Soul*), and W. Rhys Roberts (*Rhetoric*). From the twenty-three volume translation of Aristotle in the Loeb Classical Library, published by Harvard University Press, I have used citations from translations by H. Rackham (*Nicomachean Ethics*), A. L. Peck (*On the Parts of Animals* and *On the Generation of Animals*), W. S. Hett (*On the Soul*), and E. S. Forster (*On the Movements of Animals*). Quotations from the *Metaphysics* have been taken from Richard Hope's *Aristotle's Metaphysics*, published by Columbia University Press.

I hope that women readers will not be offended by the fact that I usually have followed Aristotle's grammatical form in using such expressions as "the man of practical wisdom" and "the morally good man." Although Aristotle himself accepted the chauvinistic values of Athenian society, he does not offer any cogent reasons for not extending his analysis of moral personality to women. Consequently, referents such as "he" and "man" can and should be understood as applying to human beings of either sex.

For their criticisms and suggestions I wish to thank Professors Rosamond Kent Sprague and L. Shannon DuBose of the University of South Carolina. Richard Ruta helped me make some decisions about the contents of the Greek Glossary. I also want to acknowledge the encouragement and support given me by Eugene Thomas Long, Chairman of the Department of Philosophy, University of South Carolina, and by Irwin C. Lieb, Vice-President and Dean of Graduate Studies, The University of Texas at Austin.

The writing and typing of the final draft of the manuscript were supported in part by a grant from the University of South Carolina Research and Productive Scholarship Fund.

Abbreviations

An. post.	*Analytica posteriora*
An. pr.	*Analytica priora*
Cat.	*Categoriae*
De an.	*De anima*
Eth. Eud.	*Ethica Eudemia*
Eth. Nic.	*Ethica Nicomachea*
Gen. an.	*De generatione animalium*
Hist. an.	*Historia animalium*
In. an.	*De incessu animalium*
Mem.	*De memoria*
Metaph.	*Metaphysica*
Motu an.	*De motu animalium*
Part. an.	*De partibus animalium*
Ph.	*Physica*
Poet.	*Poetica*
Pol.	*Politica*
Rh.	*Rhetorica*
Sens.	*De sensu*
Top.	*Topica*

Morality and the Good Life

1

Introduction to Aristotle

The main known facts of Aristotle's life can be told quickly.[1] He was born about 384 B.C. in Stagira, a city in northern Greece. His father Nicomachus was physician to the Macedonian king, Amyntas II, father of Philip the Great. Nicomachus died when Aristotle was about 17 years old, and Aristotle then went to Athens where he joined the Academy of Plato. There he remained for over twenty years, until shortly before the death of Plato in 348 B.C. Aristotle then spent several years in Assos, a city on the coast of Asia Minor across the Aegean Sea from Greece. There he taught in a branch of the Academy and there he married Pythias, the daughter of Hermias the ruler of Assos, who had studied for a time the Academy in Athens.

Aristotle had left Assos to do biological research in Lesbos, an island in the Aegean whose people were noted both for their masonry work and their sensualities, when he is said to have accepted an invitation from Philip to tutor his thirteen year old son Alexander.

Aristotle's tutorship ceased in 335 B.C. when Alexander became king at the age of nineteen. Many stories circulated about Aristotle's stay at the palace in Pella, but scholars today are virtually unanimous in agreeing that Aristotle did not greatly influence the political thinking of the future world conqueror. Aristotle returned to Athens where his philosophic differences with some of the members of the Academy were sufficiently great that he founded his own school.[2] Since he was a *metic*, a resident alien without the right to own property, he held his classes in the Lyceum, a public gymnasium with an adjoining park called the *Peripatos* or "covered walk." (Aristotle's students came to be known as Peripatetics.)

For twelve years the school grew in fame and numbers. Besides regular lectures, its activities included biological and political research. But in 323 B.C., the death of Alexander led to an anti-Macedonian revolt in Athens. Because he had performed many diplomatic services for both Philip and Alexander, Aristotle was charged with the capital crime of impiety. He fled Athens before the trial, tradition has it, saying that he would not give Athens another chance to sin against philosophy as it had in condemning Socrates on the same count (and Anaxagoras and Protagoras as well). He returned to his mother's birthplace, Chalcis in Euboea, where he died a year later at the age of sixty-two or -three.

ARISTOTLE'S DEBT TO PLATO

Although we are not concerned here with a detailed examination of Aristotle's intellectual development, some mention needs to be made of Aristotle's great debt to Plato. Aristotle would not have remained at the Academy for twenty years had he not believed there was no philosopher superior to Plato. And Plato's decisive influence on his student can be seen on virtually every page Aristotle wrote. Certainly that is true of both the *Nicomachean Ethics* and the *Politics*.

Aristotle is not merely an echo of Plato, for he gradually came to disagree with fundamental Platonic doctrines such as the theory of Forms. Yet the influence of Plato remains pervasive. As G. E. R. Lloyd wrote: "Not only did [Aristotle] inherit many of his problems from Plato, but his criticisms of Plato often provide the starting-point and foundation of his own theories."[3]

What is important for our purposes is the fact that the tensions between Aristotle the student of Plato and Aristotle the independent thinker were never completely resolved. These tensions create difficulties in his ethical theory which will be discussed later but which can only be understood fully within the context of his effort to emancipate his thinking from what he saw as fatal defects in the Platonic position.

ARISTOTLE'S WRITINGS

Like Plato, Aristotle published a number of dialogues, which he called his 'exoteric' or public works; tragically, only fragments of these works have survived. What have survived are a large number of unpublished works on a wide variety of topics—natural science, social science, ethics, logic, rhetoric, composition, and constitutional law among others. Today scholars generally accept them as substantially Aristotle's own lecture notes, which apparently were kept at the Lyceum after Aristotle's death and were edited into the order in which we now have them in the first century B.C. by Andronicus of Rhodes, the tenth or eleventh head of the Lyceum. They were brought to Rome by Sulla about 86 B.C.

Besides these manuscripts, other survivals include most of an early work entitled the *Protrepticus*, meaning "exhortation to the intellectual life," a eulogy of a friend (used in the charge of impiety), and an essay entitled "The Constitution of Athens."

With a very few exceptions, then, the Aristotelian writings as we now have them were not intended for publication. They are best understood as work in progress. For this reason, the *Nicomachean Ethics* is not a finished, polished book. It is filled with repetitions, incomplete arguments, hesitancy on some points, and an obvious reworking of materials resulting in different approaches to the same doctrines and some problematic inconsistencies.

There is another Aristotelian work on ethics, called the *Eudemian Ethics*, which most scholars now believe to be an earlier set of notes, perhaps written at Assos. Three of its eight "books" are missing. Apparently they were revised by Aristotle and included as Books 6, 7, and 8 of the *Nicomachean Ethics*. Perhaps as a consequence, *Eth. Nic.* contains two separate discussions of pleasure, one in Book 7 and another in Book 10.

A third treatise on ethics, called the *Magna Moralia*, was included by Andronicus, but the general opinion today is that the work is not Aristotle's but was written by some member of the Aristotelian school.

Strangely enough, we do not owe the Aristotelian corpus we now have either to Athens or to Rome, for when the Emperor Justinian became a Christian, he closed all schools of philosophy in his empire. The writings of Aristotle that have survived, were saved primarily by Arabic scholars and philosophers.[4] When Latin translations of the Arabic texts and commentaries by Arabian thinkers began to be circulated in Europe in the twelfth century, they were again seen as a threat to Christian belief and were banned.

Within two centuries, however, largely as a result of the efforts of Thomas Aquinas and of European contact with Eastern thought through the Crusades, the influence of Aristotle became so strong that his writings could be treated as a final authority, unchallengable and unalterable. This was diametrically opposed to Aristotle's own view; he thought of his writings as provisional, constantly open to challenge and, if necessary, to revision. In the *Generation of Animals*, for example, he had noted that the facts about the generation of bees had not yet been "sufficiently ascertained; and if at any future time they are ascertained, then credence must be given to the direct evidence of the senses more than to theories, —and to theories too provided that the results which they show agree with what is observed [*ta phainomena*]."[5]

The dogmatizing of Aristotle's thinking eventually led to a widespread reaction; men like Bacon, Galileo, and Boyle thought of Aristotle as the chief enemy of scientific progress. For the next four centuries Aristotle was read mainly by classicists and theologians, and only within the past hundred years has his reputation regained some of its former brilliance. Among his writings, no book is read more often today than his *Nicomachean Ethics*.

ARISTOTLE'S VIEW OF MORAL PHILOSOPHY

Different people read the *Ethics* for different reasons. Many regard it as one of the world's pieces of great literature, though it cannot compare stylistically with Plato's *Republic*. Others see Aristotle as offering us insights about our own lives which have as much validity today as they had over two millenia ago. Still others believe that it is impossible to understand the present apart from the past, and they look to great thinkers like Aristotle to help illuminate the present.

Aristotle is neither the first nor the last word in ethical philosophy (although he is the first to study ethics as a separate inquiry), but he is a man who thought deeply and sensitively about what it means to live a life of specifically human quality. He is genius enough to understand us better than we often do ourselves. Even when we disagree with him, he is still immensely valuable in discerning and discussing many of the most critical questions in ethics. In doing so, he helps us focus more clearly on our own thoughts and lives.

As Aristotle saw it, we live in a world filled with power and with agents, ourselves included, exercising power on and interacting with one another. The most fundamental ways we are in the world are as agent and as patient, and our personal history consists mainly of what others have done to, for, against, with, or through us, and of what we have done to, for, against, with, or through them.

We are also thinkers, and sometimes we think only to know, to understand. But thinking of this sort, usually called theoretical or speculative, is only episodic; we can, and we often do, put off satisfying our curiosity and wonderment. What we cannot cease doing is acting. The world and our own desires and needs press upon us, and we cannot be still. Because we have power, we always have it. We cannot renounce it, nor can other agents, whether persons or natural forces, cease to act on us.

The most obvious criterion for power and its use is sheer effectiveness. But, and this is the most basic claim underlying any moral philosophy, the description and assessment of our power in terms of effectiveness is only a partial judgment. Other—moral—questions remain: questions about what actions are worth doing and what goals are worth pursuing.

The same point can be made from another perspective. Our very survival demands that our loves and aversions have some minimally consistent shape or orientation. This complex of attitudes is our character. Our character does not consist only in our abilities and skills—what we are able to do (although that is not irrelevant to our character), but also in the use we make of our abilities. Because our moral values determine how we use our abilities, moral philosophy is a *doctrine of power*, a more or less systematic argument for how we should develop and use the power we have.

What enables us to be moral agents is our ability to think about how to arrange our priorities and our ability to act on the basis of our thinking. It is this ability to reason practically which makes our actions distinctively different from other physical events, such as chemical reactions and the actions of animals, and also prevents our character from consisting only in behavioral patterns. Practical reasoning is not something added on to our actions; rather, it is our way of acting effectively and selectively. Because moral philosophy is concerned with rational norms for conduct and because it is itself an exercise of our power to think about how to act, moral philosophy is not only a doctrine of power; it is also a *doctrine of practical reason*.

We have another dimension to our agency besides power and rationality. We are ineluctably social beings. From conception on, our life is interwoven with the lives of others. We do not only need them to satisfy our needs; the love and friendship of others are among the best pleasures of human life. This social dimension to the exercise of human power means that there is no sharp division between moral and social concerns. Moral philosophy is inseparable from politics and from economics, education, and sociology as well. Because it concerns the whole of our practical life, moral philosophy is preeminently *a doctrine of political practice*.

Moral philosophizing, finally, aims to help us achieve clarity about the most ultimate and general norms for human life. But clarity is not the main goal, at least not as Aristotle understood moral philosophy. The purpose of this inquiry is practical: to help us become better persons, to help us to live our lives as well as possible. That means, above all else, that we develop an integrated, coherent life, one minimizing conflicts whether within (between what we see as right and what we want) or between the inner and outer dimensions of our life (between our character and our actions), between the individual and the sociopolitical aspects of our life. As we will see, Aristotle does not think we can achieve this integrity merely by thinking; character is developed primarily by what we do. Nevertheless, moral philosophy does consider how the best life for men should be understood, and for that reason it is *a doctrine of the good life*.

Aristotle's view of moral philosophy may seem to omit the most important aspect of ethics. Many of us have been raised to think of morality only as an aspect of religion: morality is God's legislation. Clearly, a person's religious commitment can and often does influence his morality. But because people without a religious commitment still possess power and still are affected by the power of others, they too must worry about how power should be used. Consequently, morality and its norms are more fundamental than religious belief; and morality need not presuppose a belief in the existence of God.

There is another way in which Aristotle's notion of moral philosophy may seem strange. There is a widespread tendency to think of morality only or primarily in terms of a person's motivation, while practicality is equated with effectiveness. In ordinary language, then, the word "practical" is frequently contrasted, not equated, with the word "moral": "Forget your moral ideals! Be practical!" But Aristotle argues that morality and practicality cannot be separated. Intentions can have moral significance only because they normally affect the ways in which we act.

For Aristotle, the single most crucial and pressing question is: what kind of human life is most worth living? Unlike other living beings which operate largely on instinct, man cannot help but think about how to live his life. He is a self-conscious being, aware of his need to choose between alternatives. Whether or not a person ever studies moral philosophy in a formal way, he cannot avoid doing moral philosophizing; in contemporary terms, we are all obsessed with the problem of meaning, of finding or of giving meaning to life. Our choice, then, is not between doing and not doing moral thinking, but between doing it haphazardly and trying to do it well.

Buckminster Fuller once commented that man's main problem is that the world came without an instruction manual. Many agree with him, and they become either moral skeptics or moral relativists. Skeptics generally argue that claims for morality are illusory; relativists, that all moral claims are merely conventional, contingent only on the desires of those who make such claims. Both find support in the fact that men have held the most extraordinarily diverse views about morality and its rules.

Aristotle argues strongly against all three views—against Fuller's, against moral skepticism, and against moral relativism. Skepticism is futile, he in effect tells us, because it tries to discourage us from thinking about decisions we cannot avoid making. Because we cannot "turn off" the power we have, we cannot stop thinking practically about how to live and act. We cannot cease to be moral

agents. Relativism can take different forms, and relativists themselves are not always clear about what it is they are claiming. For our
present purposes we can take Fuller's comment as the basis for a
common form of relativism. Against it Aristotle argues that we can
indeed be instructed by the nature of things in the world. His
doctrine concerning the methodology proper to ethics is complex
and will be discussed in more detail later.[6] Briefly, his contention is
that through experience we can learn both our limits and our
opportunities. Men have learned, for example, that they cannot live
satisfactorily by trying to live a kind of life inappropriate to their
fundamental nature: we cannot live like beasts nor can we live as
gods. Through both personal experience and the cumulative experience of others, then, we learn what it is to have a specifically
human nature, and the potentialities and needs of this nature
provide an objective basis for understanding how best to live as a
human being.

Moral norms and claims always have a generality about them
which is lacking in statements about purely personal likes and
dislikes, and they have this characteristic because men are fundamentally alike—agents with power, with sufficient rationality to
reflect on themselves and their lives, and with social drives and
needs. The fact that we can read Aristotle and other Greek
philosophers and dramatists, not as extra-terrestrial aliens far removed from us and our lives, but as fellow human beings from
whom we can learn much about human life, is strong evidence that
Aristotle's view is not implausible. The classical Greek authors are
distant from us in time, but not in nature; their experiences with
human living are not utterly different from our own.

It would be a serious mistake, however, to think that Aristotle
is a dogmatic absolutist in moral matters. He avoids the extremes
both of those who would have us believe that man is totally plastic
and those who would hold that human nature is rigidly set at birth.
Although we have specifically human potentialities, both our nature and the structure of human society can be developed in many
different but legitimate ways, depending on the varying possibilities of the world and the varying talents of individuals.

Aristotle therefore offers us a way to avoid the extremes of both
moral absolutism and moral relativism. The moral ideal (what he

calls the *kalon*) is absolute and apodictic, yet the rules for acting morally well and for achieving the good life do not and cannot have genuine universality. Too much depends upon the ways in which individual persons differ and the ways in which circumstances and situations vary. Too much also depends on our other beliefs about the world—cultural differences, scientific theories, and religious convictions; for moral beliefs and rules are not formulated in splendid isolation from other, nonmoral aspects of human living. We are still not forced into a kind of relativism which would license every kind of conduct and offer no way in which to arbitrate between differences except by brute force. What is morally right, Aristotle argues, can be determined in general terms which will hold for the most part, and what is morally right in the individual situations of life depends both on those general truths and on the facts of the particular case, which can be determined objectively. If this means that there are limitations to the extent to which an ethical theory can hope to offer us guidance, it also means that the morally mature person cannot avoid accepting the responsibility for deciding how to act in the particular situations of his life.

There is another important aspect of moral philosophizing, as Aristotle sees it, which needs to be mentioned at this point. We have seen that his methodological touchstones are reality (the nature of things) and man's cumulative experience with reality. This experience *and* our reflections about it are, Aristotle argues, never purely intellectual but also ineluctably emotional. This is not a popular view among most contemporary ethicists. They regard their enterprise as purely theoretical, a purely logical analysis of moral language, with few or no practical implications for how men ought to live. But Aristotle appeals to experience to claim that none of us can approach discussions about the nature and meaning of life in a totally disinterested, detached way. Our present thinking is too much a product of our past—the loves we have learned to cherish, the concerns to which we are committed, and the habits which have become our second nature. Our most fundamental values are at stake, under scrutiny, and no person can reflect on fundamental commitments of his own life in a totally detached manner.

Like other Greeks before him, for example, Aristotle sees the universe and life within it as beautiful, exciting, good, and pleasurable. The universe and the world are man's home, and when their laws and man's own nature are respected we can, he says, expect to find life fulfilling, rich, and meaningful.[7] There is no way, Aristotle thinks, that we can seriously discuss this view or competing views without our own commitments intruding, however subtly.

Aristotle's observations convinced him the kind of a life a person lives depends on what that person sees as his predominant value or "good"—whether it be physical pleasure, production and economic gain, honors and the approval of others, moral goodness, or theoretical wisdom. Discussions about the relative value of various kinds of life are difficult precisely because every person has already made some commitment, at least to some degree, to one or the other kind of life. To restate a point already made, moral philosophy is not only about reasoning practically; it is itself an exercise of practical reason.

For the same reason Aristotle insists that the purpose of ethical philosophy is practical and not merely theoretical; it is not simply to help us achieve clarity but to help us to live well.[8] Because our emotions may prevent us from pursuing what we recognize intellectually to be the best way to live, Aristotle also insists on the limited efficacy of reading, discussing, and thinking about moral philosophy. Rational insights can be warped and frustrated by a person's character, and a person's character, Aristotle writes, depends not on philosophizing but on the ways in which he has acted and does act.

Just as Aristotle's view of the nature of moral philosophy differs from the view held by many modern ethicists, so his view of man differs from views now prevalent. Contrary to many sociologists and psychologists today, he argues that human life and action do not consist only in observable behavior, but that we have both surface and depth, both an inner and an outer dimension. Consequently education and growth are not attained solely through the mediation of outside influences; growth must also come from within. Contrary also to a related tendency to model the social sciences on the methodologies used in the physical sciences, Aristotle argues that different kinds of inquiries need different methodologies, depending on the kind of subject and the purpose of each kind of inquiry. Scientific knowledge of the interactions of things, for example, is different from knowledge of human actions, and moral knowledge is different from the kind of knowledge involved in the various skills and arts.

Against the common Christian conviction that every man has an irreducible core of evil, Aristotle sees us as having a nature which is initially neither morally good nor evil; our moral destiny depends upon the way in which our self is shaped, first by others, then by ourselves. And in contrast to those who see us either as radical individuals or as completely creatures of our environment, Aristotle sees man as both individual and social in nature. Against those who claim that man is only corrupted by society, he argues that we cannot achieve humanity apart from others, nor can we live a fully human life divorced from the society of our fellow man. Likewise, while many people today tend to separate politics from morality, to the detriment of both, Aristotle stresses the essentially moral character of the state and the great importance of the political arrangements within a state to the moral education and the quality of life of its citizens.

Not all of contemporary thought lies outside the Aristotelian view. Much of Aristotle's moral philosophy is echoed today in the writings of psychologists such as Erich Fromm, Jean Piaget, Eric Berne, Carl Rogers, Erik Erikson, Abraham Maslow, and Rollo May. For Aristotle as for these men the best life for man is a pleasurable, healthy, meaningful life of personal growth and integrity, a life in which human needs and aspirations are honestly recognized and met. There is no great gulf between Maslow's "self-actualizing" person and Aristotle's man of "moral excellence," for norms such as freedom, self-respect, dignity, and community are ideals equally important to morality and to psychological health and fulfillment.

Aristotle's best person, the man of moral excellence, embodies human nature at its best. He is a person who enjoys internal harmony, an integrity of mind and emotions. In character he has a permanent commitment to living rightly and well, a character constituted of sensitive, intelligent habits. Aristotle's ideal person is sometimes summed up by the aphorism that "a good race horse is one that wins races."[9] The point is not badly taken. Aristotle has no room in his ethical theory for the well-meaning fool; the good person is one who shows his good will by both his sensitivity and his competence.

The integrity of the good man extends also to the social and political aspects of his life. He seeks and does what is in his own best interest, but this does not mean he is selfish in a morally derogatory way. Aristotle argues that the distinction between egoism and altruism often is badly drawn; that is not the way in which to distinguish between morally good and morally defective character. Because there is no great chasm between the personal and social aspects of human life, the man who genuinely loves and esteems himself is the person best able to love and esteem others. The good man takes the greatest pleasure in acting well toward others because he sees this is a natural expression of a morally good life.

A Look Ahead

There are several good reasons for not trying to follow the organization of the *Nicomachean Ethics* as the text has come to us. One reason, already mentioned, is that treatise was never edited by Aristotle for publication. It is filled with incomplete remarks which Aristotle must have amplified while lecturing; it has puzzling repetitions; crucial points are often stated in very compressed form, while other less important topics are discussed at length. A commentary which organizes important topics systematically cannot replace the original but can help those reading Aristotle for the first time to think through Aristotle's views for themselves.

Trying to achieve precision and clarity of thought, philosophers commonly develop their own technical vocabulary. Aristotle is no exception. While it is not necessary for a person to read Greek in order to read Aristotle, it is necessary to understand that there are a number of key terms which have a technical meaning for Aristotle and which can be misread, either because no English word catches their meaning accurately or because the usual English translation now carries connotations not intended by Aristotle. For example, the Greek word *eudaimonia* is traditionally translated as "happiness," and a reader can easily project his own meaning into the word and, by doing so, seriously misread Aristotle.[10]

Moreover, philosophers do not always agree on the meanings of terms. So the meaning of Aristotle's 'happiness' (or *eudaimonia*) is very different from the meaning of Kant's 'happiness' (for *die Glückseligkeit*). A reader who wishes to compare the moral theories of these two men would misrepresent both if he thought the two terms synonymous. For this reason, *eudaimonia* is translated, in a less misleading way, in this book as "the good life," although some citations from translations by others still use the word "happiness."

As a rule, the original Greek word is included, transliterated, along with a translation, when these key technical terms occur. A glossary of these terms can be found in the back of the book. There the words are written in both English transliteration and in the Greek alphabet, but, as an aid to the non–Greek reader, the words are listed according to the English rather than the Greek alphabet.

The exposition of Aristotle's fundamental doctrines begins in the next chapter with an analysis of his theory of human action—what, in his view, makes human agents and human actions distinctive and ultimately susceptible to moral judgment. In the following chapter we examine the way in which he distinguishes between activities which are only instrumentally good and those which are intrinsically and morally good.

The fourth through the sixth chapters explain in depth Aristotle's analysis of the inner dimension of our agency: the nature of practical reason in general (deliberation and choice), the differences between practical and theoretical thought, and the differences between moral and nonmoral kinds of practical reasoning. They conclude with his delineation of moral excellence.

Chapter 7 considers Aristotle's doctrine of the nature of the state and its role in moral education. Chapter 8 is an exposition of kinds of practical mistakes and kinds of defective moral character. The ninth and final chapter summarizes Aristotle's doctrines concerning the nature of the good life for man and the place of morality within that life.

Notes to Chapter 1

1. See Anton-Hermann Chroust, *Aristotle: New Light on his Life and on Some of his Lost Works*.

2. See John Patrick Lynch, *Aristotle's School: A Study of a Greek Educational Institution*.

3. G. E. R. Lloyd, *Aristotle: The Growth and Structure of his Thought*, p. 41. See also Sir Alexander Grant, *The Ethics of Aristotle*, 1: 179–219.

4. See F. E. Peters, *Aristotle and the Arabs*, esp. pp. 221–237.

5. *Gen. an.* 3. 10. 760b30-33 (Peck's translation). As John Burnet wrote, "the spirit of the Platonic dialogue with its tentative arguments and provisional conclusions still lives in [Aristotle's] procedure. He is seeking the truth along with his hearers and not expounding a ready-made system;" see *The Ethics of Aristotle*, p. xiv.

6. See chap. 6.

7. See 9. 9. 1170a26-b15; unless otherwise identified, all references are to *Eth. Nic.*

8. See, e.g., 10. 9. 1179a33-b19.

9. 2. 6. 1106a19-21.

10. See note 5 in chap. 9.

2

The Nature of Human Action:
A Matter of Contrasts

When we make moral assessments, we are judging either human actions—what men have done, or are doing, or might do—or men themselves, the initiators of their own behavior, or both. There are other kinds of agents and other kinds of behavior, e.g., chemical agents and animal behavior, but these are not usually considered to be susceptible to moral appraisal. An adequate moral theory, then, must include some view on what there is about human agency and human actions which makes them morally significant. To put the same point another way, an adequate theory of action must underlie any moral theory, and without this as a foundation and framework, any attempt to analyze morality will be haphazard and confused.

In this chapter we will set out in a provisional way Aristotle's theory of human action and agency, and this exposition will gradually be strengthened later when we examine Aristotle's thoughts about how men and their actions should be sorted out by specifically moral criteria and how those criteria can be discovered and used.

Aristotle understood the importance of a clear and adequate doctrine concerning the nature of human action, and his methodology for presenting that doctrine follows a procedure he often uses to clarify the meaning of terms and, when it is appropriate, the range of their referents.[1] Because the meaningfulness of terms frequently depends on contrasts, he begins by looking for other terms with which 'action' can be contrasted.[2] If different contrasts can be found, then it follows that the term 'action' can be used in different senses. This in fact turns out to be the case; the notion of 'action' can be drawn more or less restrictively.[3] In ordinary conversations we often use action-verbs in casually imprecise ways, and we cause no problems or confusions by doing so; but when matters of great

17

importance will be decided partly by the ways in which we define
the notions of 'action' and 'agency', then we need to constrain our
language to exactness.

Through the use of various contrasts, then, Aristotle develops
a view of the nature of action which defines the necessary and
sufficient conditions for human action in the strictest sense. This
analysis will also introduce his doctrines concerning the nature of
rationality and the role of reasoning in action. While that analysis
will have to be developed and tightened in the following chapters,
this introduction provides the context within which further precision and clarity will be possible.

First Contrast: Action vs. Passivity

The most fundamental way in which Aristotle elucidates the nature
of action is by contrasting it with passive states, considered either as
the actual undergoing of changes as a result of something else that
has happened or as the capacity to be affected.[4] When "the initiative
or source of motion comes from without. . . . [and] the person acted
upon contributes nothing," a case of physical constraint occurs; it is
an event in the history of an agent, but it is not his action.[5]

The mere fact that we know what is happening to us does not
necessarily alter our condition. We may be only too well aware of
our states as we live through them, 'affections' such as feeling
uncomfortably hot, or aging, or dying. When natural processes (*ta
phusei huparkonta*, literally, "things existing by nature") are not
within our control, occurring according to physical laws of nature
or because of chance, they simply happen to us, with or without our
consent. We are spectators to what is occurring and such events can
be welcome or unwelcome, frustrating or serendipitous, and so on.[6]

By contrast, the most fundamental way of exercising agency is
to be the cause of one's own behavior, "the source [*archē*] and
begetter [*gennētēs*] of his actions as a father is of his children."[7] A
movement is an action when the efficacy which brings about the
change lies primarily in and with the agent, who then can be said to
act voluntarily or willingly (*hekōn*).[8]

Two comments need to be made here. First, underlying this
primitive notion of agency is the notion of power (*dunamis*).[9] When

he suggests that we think of our bodies as instruments by and through which our agency is expressed, Aristotle is insisting on the physical, outward character of action, its nature as an expression of force and might.[10] Although Aristotle does not believe in a universal determinism,[11] he sees the world filled with active things, constantly exerting pressures on each other; this is a world in which one either coerces or is coerced. Whether changes are only events or are also actions, things are constantly interacting with one another, and even our own past history influences and shapes our present self.[12] When we act, other agencies cooperate with or resist us, and thereby limit, channel, support, or qualify our agency.

The second comment concerns one important reason for making the distinction between mere events and actions: the assigning of responsibilities.[13] Here we need not pursue the rationale for engaging in this sort of ascription. It is sufficient to point out that our activities of encouraging and persuading, of commanding, requesting, and forbidding, of praising and blaming, of honoring and punishing are usually inappropriate if what has happened or will happen is not the addressee's except in the sense of his being affected by someone or something. Aristotle writes:

> Nobody encourages us to perform what is not within our power or what is not voluntary: there would be no point in trying to stop by persuasion a man from feeling hot, in pain, or hungry, and so forth, because we will go on feeling these conditions no less for that.[14]

The topic of responsibility-assignment is extremely complex, and these remarks will have to be qualified and sharpened later. There are cases, for example, when we may hold that a man did do a particular action but we still do not hold him responsible for it. But frequently, what is important is only the fact that an agent *did* do something, regardless of other qualifications which could be made. This is often the case in games, in legal matters, and in situations in which the consequences of an action are or could be catastrophic. For example, an injustice can come under legal norms of rectification even when no agent has meant to act unjustly. In these cases, the additional characterization of the doing as "intentional" often is used to indicate a particularly blatant offense. Aristotle's analysis of the term "intentional" is the substance of the next contrast.

SECOND CONTRAST: ACTION VS. PROCESS—PART 1[15]

Saying that the initiative for an event must lie in and with an agent specifies a necessary but often not a sufficient condition for our considering an event to be a man's action. There are many things which agents do which we are not willing to call their actions, at least not without some qualification. A second condition is this: the agent must not only initiate his own behavior, he also must be aware of what he is doing. He must mean to do it; he must do it intentionally.

If, for example, a man talks in his sleep and thereby happens to frighten away a burglar, this second condition rules out our saying that he performed the *action* of frightening away the burglar, even though that was, in fact, a consequence of his talking. If a man accidentally steps on another's foot, that is clearly something he did, but it is not his action.[16] We show this in our ordinary conversations when we attribute an event to an agent (he did it) but then quickly add that he did it unintentionally, he didn't mean to do it. Individual actions are complexes of particular facts, and if an agent misapprehends one or more of these, there can be discrepancy between what he means to do and what he actually does. Whether we are willing to attribute "what he actually did" to him as his action depends on the extent of, and his culpability for, his ignorance.[17]

If an agent is to be aware of what he is doing, he obviously must be capable of some mental activity. He must be able to receive sensations and perceive objects as unities (*aisthēsis*) and he must have memory (*mnēmē*) so as to be able to retain and recall what he has perceived. Finally, percepts and mental images need to be combined into patterns, and this is the task of the 'sensitive imagination' (*phantasia*).[18] Aristotle believes that this kind of mental activity is possible for at least some animals, for children, and for adult humans alike.[19]

Aristotle's doctrine concerning the first two conditions necessary for an agent's behavior to be considered his action in the full sense is summarized in this passage:

Since an action is involuntary [*akousion*][20] when it is performed under constraint or through ignorance [*di' agnoian*], a voluntary action would seem to be one in which the initiative lies with the agent who knows the particular circumstances in which the action is performed.[21]

The first condition concerned the power by virtue of which an action is produced; the second concerns the awareness which we often demand of an agent before we consider his conduct to be his action in an unqualified sense.

THIRD CONTRAST: ACTION VS. PROCESS—PART 2

In cases of undergoings, we may notice what is happening to us; but our awareness, our knowing, does not by itself necessarily lead us to action. For one thing, the process affecting us may not be alterable, and then there would be no point in trying to affect it.[22] For another, we may not *want* to try to stop what is happening. Aristotle therefore concludes that "thought alone moves nothing; only thought which is directed to some end and concerned with action can do so."[23]

Actions are not just movements or processes; they are movements arising out of some kind of desiring, and a being capable of acting must be capable of desiring what he does not now have, "the realizable good."[24] Since agents act out of their interest in securing whatever it is they desire, because "all appetite is for an end," actions also are always purposeful.[25]

The notion of goal-directed behavior must be drawn with care, for it is possible to describe many physical events teleologically even though we would not also classify them as actions. We can, and Aristotle did, describe many physical systems in terms of laws specifying a particular direction in which those systems tend to develop.[26] Most scientists and philosophers of science today argue that all such descriptions can and should be replaced by non-teleological accounts. But action, Aristotle argues, is not merely behavior which generally converges toward and has a certain terminating point or end-condition if it is not frustrated. Behavior which is action not only *has* a given direction but *is directed to* a particular end by its agent; the agent determines his goal and he acts for the sake of it.[27]

Only when behavior satisfies this strong teleological criterion do we have grounds to speak literally of attempts, failures, and achievements. So critical is the forward-looking character of action that Aristotle begins the *Nicomachean Ethics* by stating that "every action and choice seem to aim at some good."[28] We cannot understand an action unless we know its "final cause," that for the sake of which the action is done, for that provides the rationale for the action.[29] The goal of an action not only defines the nature of that action; it also determines what must be done to reach it:

> The physician or the builder sets before himself something quite definite . . . and once he has got this, each of them can tell you the causes and the rational grounds for everything he does, and why it must be done and he does it.[30]

Because they are appetitive beings, animals and children can and do perform actions. They can be aware of their own needs and desires as well as stimuli from their environment, and much of their behavior is purposeful.[31] But all such actions are nonrational, for they arise out of sheer appetite (*epithumia*).[32] This kind of agency can be exercised only under appropriate conditions of sensuous need and sensory stimulation, and it is limited to ends which are perceived as sensually pleasurable (or at least not painful).[33]

Human adults sometimes act irrationally too, when they act impulsively. But man possesses a source of self-initiated activity other than desire alone, namely desire united to and directed by intelligence (*logos*) and the extent of human agency is thereby enlarged and its flexibility and power increased. Because of his intelligence, man is not limited to ends presented sensuously; he has the radically superior ability to rise above the restrictions of a particular spatiotemporal setting. He can be self-conscious, he can form concepts which are universals, and he can apprehend and use general principles by which to direct his agency. He can deliberately frustrate sensual desires for the sake of other goals of which lower kinds of agents are not conscious. All this is built into the notion of "intelligently directed behavior." Because human agency is made distinctive by man's ability to reason practically, men can engage in kinds of activities and pursue goals which simply are not open to animals and only potentially to children.[34] (Understanding the nature of practical reason and its role in action is one of our main concerns, but that aim is best served now by completing the outline of Aristotle's analysis of action.)

Whether an agent possesses one or two principles of action, that is, whether he acts out of desire alone or whether he acts out of a complex of reason and appetition, Aristotle takes any behavior originating in and with an agent and done intentionally by him to be his action.[35] But only rational agents are capable of action (*praxis*) in the more restrictive sense of rational and morally significant conduct.[36] While we can describe many of the movements of animals and children as actions, we do not hold them responsible for what they do in the same way in which we often hold adults responsible.[37]

How can actions be voluntary when they arise out of an agent's attraction to things outside himself?[38] Aristotle argues that voluntary action consists in an exercise of power which is not forced or compelled from the outside; to be attracted by what is pleasant and/or noble is not contrary to and so not coercive against the springs of action *within* a man.[39] The Socratic analysis of practical error ended in the contention that, since every man seeks what he sees as good, moral faults must be due to inculpable ignorance. Against this, Aristotle argues that it is wrong to hold that no one is ever responsible for his mistakes; the source (*aitia*) of both right and mistaken practice is the same—a human agent.[40] Among voluntary actions, those based on reason (*meta logou*) are the most voluntary (*malista autoi kai hekousioi*)[41]; but appetites, which are the cause of wrong human practice, are just as much a part of us as our reason. As far as voluntariness is concerned, it makes no difference whether we act from one or the other.[42]

The complexity of human agency leads Aristotle to say that there are two ways in which voluntariness and compulsion can be understood. When we are concerned with agents having but one internal principle of movement—desire (*epithumia* or *thumos*), then

> it is only when something *external* moves a thing, or brings it
> to rest against its own internal tendency, that we say this
> happens by force; otherwise we do not say that it happens
> by force.[43]

In this sense, voluntariness can be defined negatively as the absence, at the moment of action, of determining coercion by external causes, though not the absence of all influence from them. Positively, an agent acts voluntarily when he acts according to the demands of his own nature.[44] In the case of agents like men, with two principles of movement, there can be internal conflict between desire and choice.[45] When conflict does occur, as in the case of moral weakness (*akrasia*), we can take two viewpoints: from the point of view of a man's psyche as a whole, a man acts voluntarily, for he is not coerced from the outside; but if his action is not sufficiently determined by his reason so that he acts against his own best considered wishes, we can say that he acts out of a sort of compulsion but not a kind of compulsion excusing him from responsibility for his action.[46]

Further, no weight should be given to the view that a man is compelled when he acts on the basis of his own deliberation; for the necessity which characterizes valid reasoning is not to be identified with the necessity of compulsion by natural forces.[47]

Finally, while no philosopher has had a deeper appreciation for the influence of both heredity and of character on the present exercise of agency, Aristotle disagrees with those who say that habituated behavior is not voluntary behavior, as long as an agent is responsible for those actions which have habituated him.[48] Even when a man's character is so set that "it is no longer possible for him not to be what he is," his actions can still be considered voluntary; the man is acting according to his own character, and he is still "in control of [his] actions from beginning to end, insofar as [he knows] the particular circumstances surrounding them."[49]

Fourth Contrast: Action (*Praxis*) vs. Thought (*Theoria*)

The exercise of a man's rationality does not always depend upon his having the sorts of interests which lead to his acting. Aristotle's argument here is simply that, since our psyche includes the power of reasoning, it is part of what it is to be a man that we can engage in thinking, even apart from the dynamic presence of desires and wishes.[50] Reason has its own *dunamis*, and when this is all that moves our thought, our thinking is disinterested; we seek to know and to understand, not to alter. Consequently Aristotle describes theoretical thinking (*theōria*) as an activity (*energeia*) which involves no change (*akinēsis*); it is "an activity of immobility."[51]

Because the meaningfulness of the term "practice" depends on the contrasts we can draw and because, following Aristotle, practice is generally contrasted with theory, we need to trace out briefly what Aristotle meant by theorizing. Originally the term *theōria* referred to that which was done by men who participated in festivals, such as the Olympic games, purely as spectators. Unlike the participants who competed for prizes and honors, theorists were simply onlookers, even when they were serving as the legates of other city states. They came only to see and to appreciate what they saw. According to Cicero, Pythagoras described the activity proper to the philosopher in terms of *theōria*.[52] Aristotle is clearly within the Pythagorean tradition; he tells us that when we philosophize we seek only wisdom, and all notions of practicality and utility are left behind.[53]

Aristotle defines theoretical knowledge (*epistēmē*) as knowledge of the fundamental explanatory principles of reality,[54] and on the basis of three kinds or aspects of reality, he distinguishes between three distinct theoretical disciplines.[55] First Philosophy (or Theology, or Philosophy in the strictest sense, or Metaphysics as it later came to be called) is the most general science, concerned with fundamental and necessary principles of being *qua* being, of all primary beings, both those which are dependent and those which are self-existent and eternally what they are.[56] Mathematics is concerned with intelligible aspects of composite being such as line, number, size, figure, and so on. Finally, the natural sciences deal with sensible reality insofar as it is composite and changeable and "has its source of movement or rest in itself."[57] Each natural science studies the principles (*archai*) governing its own kind of composite reality. Because the principles studied by the natural sciences hold only as a rule and not with strict necessity, this kind of knowledge is less perfect than the other kinds of theoretical knowledge.[58]

Theoretical wisdom (*sophia*) is the perfection of theoretical knowing, and it consists, as Joachim puts it, in the

> complete mastery of speculative truth, which includes immediate apprehension of the basal connexions (*nous*) as well as the mediate or demonstrative knowledge of the derivative connexions (*epistēmē*).[59]

The man who attains this excellence no longer strives for knowledge; he has attained it, and he contemplates it and revels in it.[60]

We cannot contrast theory with practice on the basis of one being an activity and the other not. The technical meaning Aristotle gives to activity (*energeia*) is an intelligently directed doing which contains its own end, in contrast to kinetic doings which have consummatory states distinct from the processes by which they are attained. For Aristotle, practice (*praxis* in the strict sense) and theory are both activities: both involve the actualization of man's powers. Further, the three contrasts which helped us define the nature of fully human action can be used equally well to help define the nature of theorizing. (1) Not all mental events are activities. Just as we can be affected physically, so also thoughts can merely occur to us, as they do in dreams, in daydreams, and in some cases of association; then we are passive spectators. By contrast, Aristotle's theoretical spectator is active, either seeking to know or actively contemplating the nature of things. (2) The very notion of thinking implies that a man must do it intentionally; he clearly must be aware of the objects of his thought. (3) Finally, the fact that all three kinds of speculative thought are self-contained does not mean they are done aimlessly.[61] "Not every good can excite movement, but only practical good . . . that which is capable of being otherwise."[62] Theorizing is purposive activity, aimed at the good of knowing and understanding.

So, according to Aristotle's first three criteria specifying the nature of human action, theorizing can be considered a kind of human action.[63] But when Aristotle uses the term *praxis* in its more technical sense, he does so in order to contrast practical with theoretical activities. There are good reasons for not drawing out this contrast in detail now; we need more clarity about the nature of *praxis* and of practical reason. For the present it is enough to note that Aristotle sees the differences between theory and practice as great and significant. Each has its own peculiar purpose; each has its own special objects; consequently, theoretical reasoning and practical reasoning each has its own distinctive methodology and character.[64]

THE NATURE OF ACTION: A SUMMARY

By means of four contrasts Aristotle has laid out the necessary and sufficient conditions for our behavior being our action.[65] Briefly, he has argued that the fundamental notion of action, and so also of agency, is that of power. An action is the exercise of the ability of an agent to affect other agents or things, to move them, alter them, use them, and if possible, control them. Besides power there are the notions of intentionality and purposiveness; often we do not consider an agent's doing as his action unless he knows what he is about, aiming his action at a goal he sees as good in some sense. In this fuller sense, an agent acts only when he deliberately intervenes in the world, causing a controlled change which he sees as an improvement in his situation.

There is another contrast in the teleology of human action, between the actions of animals and small children and those of adult humans. Man alone acts intelligently, and practical reasoning is a complex of thought and desire. Rational actions are not merely subsumable under generalized rules but some such rules have an efficacious role in action because, when a man acts, he acts according to his own plan or rule. The use of rules involves at least two other notions—consistency (also a demand of reason) and, in the case of actions which are regarded as instrumentalities, utility or efficiency (a recognition of causal regularities in the world).[66]

Finally, although man is a constant center of activity, not all that activity is practical; we sometimes think only to know, not because we want to change the world.

Like Aristotle, we can use the term "action" with great elasticity.[67] We sometimes talk about the actions of natural processes and attribute goals to them. (This is a way of saying that, if the initiator of an event had been an agent, we would consider this his action and that his goal.) We can and often do blur the difference between the mere doings of men and their actions. If, for example, an agent is mistaken about some of the circumstances in which he acts, we still may consider his behavior as his action; and then we distinguish between "the action he thought he was doing but didn't do" and "the action he mistakenly performed."[68]

No great harm is done as long as, in those cases in which responsibilities need to be assessed, we understand how we are using our language. It is no accident that Aristotle joins a discussion of the assignings of responsibility to his discussion of the nature of action. Our activities of praising and blaming presuppose not only norms for acting well and badly but also more fundamental criteria setting out what it is to act at all; and how we draw the notion of responsibility usually will show how narrowly or broadly we are using the notion of action. So Aristotle in effect argues that the various contrasts have helped him to develop a theory of action which is not esoteric, because it simply clarifies criteria already used both by ordinary men and by courts when they assign respon- sibilities.[69]

THE TWO-PLY CHARACTER OF INDIVIDUAL ACTIONS

One task remains before we can conclude this introduction to Aristotle's theory of action. We need to set out his analysis of what goes to make up any particular instance of human action.[70] If there are human actions, we should be able to describe them and we should be able to enumerate their components. How exact or complete a description needs to be depends upon our interests, needs, and purposes.[71] Often it is appropriate to give only a partial description, because that is all we need to know. On other occa- sions, as in court trials, we may need to mention everything which contributes to the structure of an action. What we need to do now is to set out what is meant by the term "everything."

Our actions are two-dimensional; they have an inside and an outside. (Aristotle does not himself use this terminology but adopt- ing it helps us understand his analysis.) The outer side consists in the way in which a man affects the world—how he acts on, with, against, or for other agents or things; the inner side accounts for this particular exercise of agency. As we shall see, the two are so intimately related that we risk serious mistakes if we try to describe one completely apart from the other.

I. **On the outside,** our actions are always particular (how could we perform a general action, whatever that might be?).[72] But they also are a complex, a matrix of what Aristotle calls 'ultimate particulars' (*ta kath' hekasta* or *ta eschata*).[73] Even though we can distinguish among these elements and provide a partial description of an action by attending to only some of them, we cannot *divide* an action into them. An action is more than a concatenation of these items assembled into a coherent montage; what gives it its organic singularity, however, lies mainly on the inside of the action. The outer side of an action consists of six and sometimes seven particular items:[74]

1. **The agent (Who did it?).** Every act is an act of an agent. Besides merely naming or identifying him, a description of the agent may help define his action. Whether or not a man has acted generously, for example, depends partly on what he possesses, so that we may need to identify him with a phrase, such as "that wealthy man."[75]

2. **The type of action performed (What did he do?).** The expression "kind of action" is sometimes used today to refer to the way in which muscle-twitches occur within a particular spatial-temporal sequence and are identified empirically as the physical movements of a particular animate being. But restricting ourselves to this sort of description does not allow us to distinguish significantly between human actions and events which are not human actions, and that is why, even though we can make a *distinction* between the inside and the outside of action, we cannot totally *separate* one from the other. The relation between the two dimensions of an action compels us to see the outer physical movement *as* a surface. When we group actions into types, therefore, we see them as normally purposeful undertakings which have specifiable ends at which human agents generally aim when they act in that fashion or engage in that sort of activity. Those ends help define the limits or edges (*perata*) of individual actions. The use of act-types presupposes also that we understand relevant facts about the world,

including conventional and societal norms which themselves often define kinds of activities.[76]

  3. **What persons and/or things were affected by the agent's action (To whom or with whom did he do it?).** Since an action is the expression of force in the world, when we act we always act on other persons or things, with them or against them, on them or toward them. This basic nature of an action leads Aristotle to write that, among the items which together constitute an action, "the most important factors are the thing or person affected by the action and the result."[77]

  4. **The manner in which the agent performed the action (In what manner did he do it? What were the behavioral characteristics of his action?).** Since this is an item on the outer side of an action, it refers to what we can see or hear and what usually is described by means of adverbs, e.g., violently or gently, quickly or slowly, and so on.[78]

  5. **Sometimes, the means used in the action (By what means did he do it? Did he use a tool or instrument?).**[79] This is a "sometimes" item because not every action requires the use of an object or objects (an *organon*) beyond an agent's own body.

  6. **The circumstances in which the action occurred (When did he do it? Where? For how long?).** In ordinary conversations we often elide the differences between means, manner, and circumstances when we ask, "How did he do it?" Description of the circumstances, however, localizes an action within its spatial and temporal coordinates. We cannot always describe this item apart from one or more of the other items, but it is, nonetheless, a distinct aspect of every action.

  7. **The result of the action (What did he accomplish?).** Because an action alters the world in some way, every action has some effect or result—the end state which the action causes.[80] As we have already seen, Aristotle takes this to be one of the most important defining aspects, on the outside, of an action: whether the result can or cannot be described apart from what was done to bring it about.

  These seven items together constitute the behavioral side, the outer structure of an action. Sometimes they are called "the facts," because they seem to be as observable as other things in the world.

The identification of an action-type, however, presents special problems because, as we have seen, the nature of an action depends so heavily on the aim of the person performing it; and our identification of a person's aim may also affect our description of other items, too.[81] We therefore need now to turn to the inner side of action and agency.

II. **The inner side** of an action discloses its depth, for an action is not merely a surface. What more than anything else gives it its organic unity, its nature, is the direction in which the agent orients and develops it. Actions are aimed outward only because an agent is a center of efficacy with an inside structure. Moreover, particular actions encompass only a limited span of time within the history of an agent, and what ties individual actions together as the actions of a single agent but also what prevents any single action or number of actions from being identical with an agent is the nature of our agency. We are persistent as individuals; we also are open to change and growth. Aristotle develops these notions under the rubric of character, and later we shall have to attend to that doctrine. For now, the inner side of human action and agency consists in three items.

1. **The agent's knowledge of or beliefs about the particularities involved in his action (Did he know what he was doing? What did he think he was about?).** An agent's beliefs about the particularities constituting the outer dimension of a possible action will affect the way in which he acts. If he is ignorant of one or more of them, his ignorance can be deliberate or accidental.[82]

2. **The agent's purpose (What was he trying to achieve? What was his goal?).** All action is teleological, and in intelligent action men deliberately adopt appropriate means to secure what seems good to them or to avoid what seems evil. Even in cases where the end of an action can be described apart from the action by which it was attained, a complete description of human action must include mention of the end intended by the agent. For completeness, we need to know whether he valued the action for its own sake or for the sake of something else, and we need, too, a description of his goal which tells what there was about it that led him to think it was worth pursuing or avoiding.

3. **The agent's motive(s) (What was his motive for doing that? Why did he want to do that?).** Although we do not always draw a sharp line between a man's motives and his purposes, they are distinct. Describing a person's goal does not necessarily reveal why it was that he found it attractive. Although men always act out of their interest in something, the notion of interest can be explicated either as sheer appetite or as habituated conduct or as a choice. Explanation in terms of a person's motivation is a claim based either on our general knowledge of human nature (which he shares) or on our special knowledge of that individual's personality and character.[83]

If we deny that a man's behavior can be accounted for in terms of his motives and ask for the cause of his behavior, we are regarding him, in Aristotelian terms, as a patient and not an agent; and insofar as his behavior is coerced, it should no longer be considered his action.

When we talk about the internal side of action, we are directly and immediately occupied with the nature of human agency and, in particular cases, with the nature and quality of an individual person's agency. The outside of an action manifests the efficacy of agency; it shows a person acting upon the world around him, to control and arrange it. The inside of an action explains that efficacy by understanding a person as a complex of thinking and desiring. We have only offered an outline, as it were, of man as a locus of efficacy, an outline which is unsatisfactory as it is incomplete and overly simplified; and in later chapters we will have to emend and flesh out the suggestions offered here.

So far, however, we have seen two main features of Aristotle's theory of human action: his description of the conditions necessary and sufficient for a man's behavior to be considered his action in the full sense, and his enumeration of the constituents of any instance of an action. But it will become increasingly evident as we go on that nothing is more critical to his analysis of our agency than his portrayal of action as a two dimensional reality. Men are agents because there is a lateral, outward exercise and manifestation of their power into the world around them. But this is not enough either to account for or to understand what they do. For example, on their surface two different actions may appear alike, and yet our description of each may have to differ significantly because of the way in which we assess their inner sides. So an action done out of fear may outwardly look very much like an action done because it is the right thing to do; and an action done coolly because the agent is experienced and confident that he is in control of the situation may pass for a courageous action, as also might actions done under the influence of some passion or due to ignorance or even caused by madness.[84]

Unless we take its inner side into account, we cannot understand the nature of an action—what kind of an action it is, for that nature is defined by the agent's purpose and motive. The inner side also enables us to distinguish between the actions of animals, children, and human adults, and between normal human agents, the emotionally ill, and the mentally incompetent. Further, this analysis allows us to distinguish, as we often think we need to, between actions done intentionally and those done inadvertently, between attentiveness, carelessness, absentmindedness, impetuosity, and habit. It allows us to make sense of actions which are omissions, abstinences, preventions, or negligences, and to differentiate between successes and failures, and between agents who are duped and agents who are simulating. We can sort out actions and agents in rich and sophisticated ways because the complexity of the source and inner dimension of action allows these possibilities.[85]

Notes to Chapter 2

1. The foundations of an inquiry have immense repercussions on how that inquiry is conducted. Reflecting on his methodology, Aristotle writes that the inquirer must be extremely careful about his initial definitions, "because it is of great importance for the subsequent course of the discussion. Surely, a good beginning is more than half the whole, and as it comes to light, it sheds light on many problems" (1. 7. 1098b5-7; unless otherwise identified, all references are to the *Nicomachean Ethics*).

2. See 5. 1. 1129a18-26. We can sense contrasts at the start of this inquiry because we already have some views about the nature of action, views so frequently used that they are embedded in our ordinary language and in our legal distinctions.

3. See 5. 9. 1136a27-28, b29-32.

4. See *Ph*. 3. 3. 202a13-28. It is Aristotle's doctrine that all movements within the universe are of two kinds: those caused by collision (movements of inanimate things) and those caused by animate things, namely, agents. See *Motu an*. 6. 700b6-13; *Eth. Nic*. 3. 3. 1112a31-33; 6. 4. 1140a13-16; *Ph*. 2. 6. 198al-4.

5. 3. 1. 1110a1-3; cf. b1-3, 16-17; 5. 2. 1131a1-9; 5. 8. 1135a27-28; *Part. an*. 1. 5. 645b33-646a2. Translations occasionally blur this contrast. For example, the noncommital expression *ta ginomena* (literally, "things which come into being") in 3. 1. 1109b35-1110a3 is translated as "actions" by both Ostwald and Rackham. Aristotle distinguishes between sufferings which are 'involuntary' (*akousion*) and those which are 'nonvoluntary' (*ouch hekousion*). The former occur contrary to the nature or character of the person acted upon and cause him pain or discomfort; the latter do not (see 3. 1. 1110b12-24, 1111a32-33; *Eth. Eud*. 2. 7. 1223a29-36; *Motu an*. 11. 703b2-20). Aristotle makes the same distinction when discussing actions done due to ignorance. The value of the distinction lies in the way it helps us discern differences among men; on this see chap. 8 below.

6. See 2. 5. 1105b23-1106a7; 3. 1. 1110b16-17; 5. 8. 1135a35-b3; 7. 4. 1148a23-27; *Ph*. 2. 1; *Metaph*. 5. 21, 30; 6. 3; 11. 8. Although this first contrast is significant because there are events which simply happen to us, Aristotle's doctrine of the pervasiveness of character (for which a man is responsible) indicates this set of events should not be unduly emphasized. It often is difficult, if not impossible, to draw a hard and fast line between what a man suffers, perhaps without his knowing it, but which influences his behavior, and the manner in which his character determines how outside agencies affect him and how he perceives their influence. See, e.g., 1. 10. 1100b1-1101a21; 2. 5; 2. 6. 1106b15-24; 3. 1. 1110a3-18, 23-26, b1-8; 3.

11. 1118b29-1119 a5; 3. 12. 1119a21-27; 5. 9. 1136a32-b7; 7. 2. 1146a9-16; 7. 3. 1146b13-23; 7. 4. 1148a23-29; 7. 7. 1150a17-30; *Pol.* 7. 13. 1332a18-20.

7. 3. 5. 1113b18.

8. See 3. 1. 1110a14-17, 1111a23-b3; 3. 3. 1112a32-33; 3. 5. 1113b16-29; 6. 4. 1140a13-17; *Metaph.* 9. 2. 1046a37-b3, 21-28; *Motu an.* 11. 703b3ff; *Ph.* 3. 3. 202a23-27. More precisely, actions need not be changes, for, as Aristotle recognizes, refrainings clearly can be actions; see 3. 5. 1113b8-14; 7. 7. 1150b22-24. While he does not elucidate them as a special kind of action his view is consistent with our taking them to be 'negative actions': we do not merely do something else, for that may be of virtually no significance; instead we do almost anything else but a particular action, and that not-doing-that-action constitutes this kind of action. Similar remarks can be made about omissions.

9. "Power," writes Aristotle, "means the external source of a movement or change; or, if internal, a distinct otherness in the thing moved: the building art is a power which is not present in the thing built; whereas a curative power may reside in him who is being cured, but it is a distinct capacity, not his function as a patient. In general, the beginning of a change or movement is called a power" (*Metaph.* 5. 12. 1019a16-20 (Hope); cf. *Ph.* 2. 1. 192b12-32; 3. 1. 201a19ff.; and *Motu an.* 1. 698b5-699a11). Aristotle takes the commonsense position that agents do have powers and dispositions even when they are not exercising them (see *Metaph.* 9. 3. 1046a29-1047a29).

10. See 3. 1. 1110a14-17; 7. 3. 1147a35-36; *Part. an.* 1. 1. 642a12-13; 1. 5. 645b15-20; 4. 10. 687a3-23.

11. See "Third Contrast" in this chapter.

12. See 3. 1. 1110b18-35; *Ph.* 3. 1. 200b26-201b15; 4. 10. 218a6-31; 4. 11. 219b9-220a23.

13. See 3. 1. 1109b30-34; 3. 5. 1113b22-27. The distinction is also essential to a discussion of the nature of the good life and, within that life, the nature of moral excellence.

14. 3. 5. 1113b27-29; see also 2. 5. 1105b29-1106a13; 3. 5. 1113b3-1114a3; 5. 8. 1135a15-22.

15. In this and the following section I am following the Aristotelian use of the term 'process' (*kinēsis* and, sometimes, the broader term *metabolē*) to indicate any kind of change or movement, the actualization of what is potential (see *Metaph.* 9. 6. 1048a26-b17; 11. 9. 1065b15-17; *Ph.* 3. 1. 201a7-18. Changes (*kinēseis*), as Aristotle analyzes them, can be alterations either in place, quantity (growth or diminution), or quality (see *De an.* 1. 3. 406a12ff; *Ph.* 2. 1. 192b15-16; 3. 1. 201a1-18).

16. See 3. 1. 1110b34-1111a20.

17. See 3. 5. 1113b19-25; also chap. 8 below.

18. All such 'thinking' depends upon processes within the body as conditions necessary for its possibility (see *De an.* 1. 1. 403a2-10; *Mem.* 450a25-b12, 453a14-23).

19. See 3. 1. 1111a24-26; 3. 2. 1111b8-9; 9. 9. 1170a16-19; *De an.* 3. 3. 427b27-429a9; 3. 10. 433b14-30; 3. 11. 434a5-14; *Gen. an.* 1. 23. 731a33-b1; *Part. an.* 2. 1. 647a14ff; *Metaph.* 1. 1. 980a21-b21.

20. Aristotle uses the term "voluntary" and its correlates so amply that his doctrines sometimes are very unclear. It is preferable, I think, to follow the practice of most contemporary philosophers by distinguishing between what is done (in)voluntarily and (un)intentionally. This allows us to say that voluntary behavior is not intentional at least in some cases in which an agent's awareness is limited, and some intentional behavior is not voluntary insofar as it is limited by force, fear, or neurotic compulsion.

21. 3. 1. 1111a21-23; see also 1111a3-b2; 3. 5. 1113b7-29; 5. 8. 1135a23-b2. The expression Ostwald translates as "through ignorance" is better rendered as "due to ignorance," a phrase Aristotle gives a technical meaning; see 3. 1. 1110b25-27; also note 7 in chap. 8 below. In a paper read at the 1975 meeting of the American Philosophical Association, Eastern Division, James L. Stiver pointed out that the second part of this definition is inadequate. It implies that *any* ignorance of the circumstances makes an action not voluntary; but Aristotle also holds that important classes of voluntary actions (those due to moral weakness and those caused by morally bad character) often do involve ignorance of circumstances. Stiver suggests Aristotle should have written that "an action is voluntary if and only if . . . it is neither done under constraint nor due to ignorance."

22. See chap. 7 below.

23. 6. 2. 1139a36-37.

24. *De an.* 3. 10. 433b15-16 (Smith); see also 433a8-23; 2. 3. 414b1-20; *Motu an.* 6-10.

25. *De an.* 3. 10. 433a16 (Hett); cf. *Eth. Nic.* 6. 2. 1139a21-22, b1-2; *Motu an.* 6. 700b4-35; *Ph.* 2. 8. 199a8-17. We often use the terms "intentional" and "deliberate" as synonyms for "purposeful." Whatever terminology we decide on, Aristotle insists on a distinction here. In the second contrast, the emphasis was placed on the cognitive element in agency, on an agent's awareness of what he is doing. In this contrast the emphasis is on the appetitive element in agency, on the striving for a goal.

26. See, e.g., *Part an.* 1. 1. 641b11ff; 1. 5. 645b15-20; *In. an.* 2. 704b11-17; 12. 711a17-19; *Ph.* 2. 5. 196b17-197a7; 2. 8.

27. See 1. 1. 1094a1-3; 1. 4. 1095a14-15; 1. 7. 1097a15-22; *Pol.* 1. 1. 1252a1-3. Some genuine cases of action can be described as "purposeless" in the sense that the agent has no goal beyond doing what he is doing, e.g.,

rambling through a woods on a walk. But when behavior occurs without a goal of *any* kind, then it is not a case of action.

28. 1. 1. 1094a2; 1. 6. 1097a6.

29. See 1. 12. 1102a2-3; *Ph.* 2. 2. 194a27-33; 2. 3. 194b32-195a3, 23-27; *Metaph.* 9. 8. 1050a8-15.

30. *Part. an.* 1. 1. 639b17-19 (Peck); cf. 2. 1. 646a25-b5; *Motu an.* 6. 700b13-17; *Eth. Nic.* 3. 5. 1114b15-16; 3. 7. 1115b22-23; *Eth. Eud.* 1. 8. 1218b15-18.

31. See citations in note 19. When Aristotle wrote, "Where the source of motion is within oneself, it is in one's power to act or not to act" (3. 1. 1110a17; cf. 3. 5. 1113b7-14), it is not clear whether he believed this also holds for nonrational agents such as children and animals (see *Metaph.* 9. 2). Even if it does not, their actions should be understood as responses to the stimuli of sensations. The notion of 'response' is quite different from that of 'reaction'. The former involves an agent—a center of appetition and a source of efficacy, acting in the light of a perceived situation; the latter is merely a movement caused by another movement. Although Aristotle likens the movements of animals to those of marionettes (*automata*), the analogy refers to explanation of motion only in terms of bones and muscles; he hastens to add that alteration involves and is caused by imagination, sensations, and conceptions (*ennoiai*; see *Motu an.* 7. 701b2-34). Action is always an interaction, a combination of being affected (*pathēsis*) and of affecting (*poiēsis*), of passivity and of spontaneity (see *Motu an.* 8. 702a12-21).

32. *Epithumia* is nonrational in the sense of lacking the insight of *logos*, but it is not merely blind impulse, for it is given direction by the sensitive imagination. *Epithumia* is a species of desire (*orexis*) which, whether it is rational or nonrational, consists in an agent's tendency to move in a particular way under appropriate sensory stimulation (*aisthēsis*; cf. *Motu an.* 7. 701a30ff.; *De an.* 2. 3. 414b1-20.

33. See 3. 2. 1111b4-13; 3. 12. 1119b3-11; 6. 2. 1139a18-21; 7. 3. 1147b3-5; 9. 9. 1170a16-17; *De an.* 2. 3. 414b1-5; *Gen. an.* 1. 23. 731a33-b8; *Part. an.* 2. 17. 661a7-8; *In. an.* 4. 705b8-11; *Metaph.* 1. 1. 980a26-b26; *Ph.* 2. 8. 199a20-33.

34. See 1. 7. 1097b21-1098a4; 1. 9. 1099b33-1100a3; 3. 2. 1111b4-17; 5. 8. 1135b7-8; 6. 2. 1139a18-21, 31-35; 6. 7. 1141a24-28; 7. 3. 1147b3-5, 7. 6. 1149b31-36; 9. 9. 1170a16-18, 28-b1; 10. 8. 1178b24-28; *Eth. Eud.* 2. 8. 1224a23-32; *Pol.* 1. 2. 1253a7-18; 1. 5. 1254b23-24; *De an.* 2. 3. 414a6-20; 3. 8. 431b2-18; 3. 10. 433a8-12, b27-30; 3. 11. 434a5-12; *Part. an.* 2. 10. 656a3-8; 4. 10. 687a23ff.; *Metaph.* 1. 1. 980a21-b28; 9. 5; *Ph.* 1. 5. 189a5-7; 2. 5. 196b30-197a7; 2. 6. 197b1-18.

35. See 3. 1. 1110b8-15, 1111a21-b2; 3. 5. 1113b19-21; 6. 2. 1139b4-5; *Eth. Eud.* 2. 8. 1224a21ff.; *De an.* 3. 10. 433a8-b30.

38   MORALITY AND THE GOOD LIFE

36. See 6. 2. 1139a18-21.

37. See, e.g., 7. 3. 1147b3-5.

38. "Neither Gorgias nor any other Greek of the period before Aristotle believed in a universal determinism, psychological or other. *Some* acts, all were agreed, were voluntary: the problem was to discover which, or rather to evolve a theory which should justify beliefs already held" (Arthur W. H. Adkins, *Merit and Responsibility: A Study in Greek Values*, p. 324). See also D. J. Allan, *The Philosophy of Aristotle*, 2nd ed., pp. 33-34, 131-132.

39. See 3. 1. 1110b8-15, 1111a21-b2; 3. 5. 1113b8-14.

40. See 3. 1. 1110b8-15; 3. 5. 1114b20-1115a3. Again meaningfulness depends on the possibility of contrasts: it does not make sense to claim that actions can be done well unless we also believe they can be done badly.

41. See 9. 8. 1168b36-1169a2.

42. See 3. 1. 1110b8-15, 1111a23-b3.

43. *Eth. Eud.* 2. 8. 1224b7-8 (Solomon); see also *Eth. Nic.* 3. 1. 1110a1-2, b1-17.

44. See 3. 1. 1111a35-b3; *Eth. Eud.* 2. 7. 1223a29-b5.

45. See 1. 13. 1102b12-1103a3.

46. See *Eth. Eud.* 2. 7. 1223b5-28; 2. 8. 1224b26-36.

47. See *Metaph.* 11. 8. 1064b31-1065a4. A thorough discussion of this point here is neither possible nor necessary. Aristotle's doctrine of kinds of necessity is extremely complex. There is, for example, " 'absolute' necessity, which belongs to the eternal things; and there is 'conditional' necessity which has to do with everything that is formed by the process of Nature, as well as with the products of Art" (*Part. an.* 1. 1. 639b23-27 (Peck); see also 642a2-13; *Metaph.* 5. 5; 12. 7. 1072b12-13; *Ph.* 2. 9).

48. See chap. 6 below; also 7. 6. 1149b6-13; 7. 10. 1152a30-33.

49. 3. 5. 1114a21-22 and 1114b32-33; cf. 1113b3ff.; also 1114b30-1115a3; 5. 9. 1137a6-9.

50. Pure thought is a psychic activity depending very little, if at all, on physical processes in the body. See 3. 10. 1117b27-32; 10. 7. 1177a12-18; 10. 8. 1178a13-23; *De an.* 1. 1. 403a2, b19; 2. 2. 413b24-29; 2. 3. 415a11-12; 3. 4-8.

51. 7. 14. 1154b27.

52. Cicero *Tusculan disputations* 5. 3. 8-9.

53. See 6. 2. 1139a27-30; 6. 7. 1141b4-8; 6. 12. 1143b18-21; *Pol.* 8. 3. 1338a1-29; *Metaph.* 1. 1. 981b13-25; 1. 2. 982b11-27.

54. See 6. 7. 1141a16-18; *Metaph.* 6. 1. 1025b3-4; 11. 1. 1059a18ff.; *Ph.* 1. 1. 184a9-16; 2. 3. 194b16ff.

55. See *Metaph.* 6. 1. 1025b3-1026a32; 11. 3, 4, 7; *Ph.* 2. 7. 198a30-32.

56. See 6. 1. 1025b20; 6. 3. 1139b17-24.

57. *Metaph.* 6. 1. 1025b20 (Hope); cf. *Ph.* 2. 2. 193b23-194b15; 3. 1. 200b11-14.

58. See *Metaph.* 1. 2. 982a20-b10.

59. H. H. Joachim, *Aristotle, the Nicomachean Ethics: A Commentary*, p. 201; see also 6. 3. 1139b25-35. In the *Metaphysics* Aristotle writes: "Mind is active in so far as it has the intelligible as its possession. Hence, the possession of knowledge rather than the capacity for knowledge is the divine aspect of the mind" (12. 7. 1072b23-25). Since learning is not always pleasant and since it is better to have knowledge than to be attaining it, the man of theoretical wisdom is in a superior condition to the neophyte (see 7. 12. 1153a9-15; 7. 14. 1154b17-20; 10. 7. 1177a25-27; *Pol.* 8. 5. 1339a27-31; *De an.* 2. 5.; *Metaph.* 9. 8. 1050a3-23).

60. See 3. 10. 1117b27-32; 6. 9. 1142b8-11; 10. 7. 1177a20-27.

61. Deductive thinking (*sullogismos*) is aimed at conclusions which can follow validly from premises; inductive thought (*epagōgē*) aims to abstract what is universal in individual instances; and intuitive thought (*nous*) comprehends principles so fundamental as to be unattainable by mediated thinking (*dianoia* and *logismos*). See 1. 7. 1098b1-4; 6. 3. 1139b25-35; 6. 6; 6. 11. 1143a35-b3; *Top.* 1. 12. 105a13-16; *An. pr.* 1. 1, 2; *An. post.* 1. 2-4; 2. 19. 100b5-18. See also chap. 6 below.

62. *De an.* 3. 10. 433a29-31 (Hett).

63. It is in this sense that Aristotle calls *theōria* "a life of action" (*ton praktikon*) (*Pol.* 7. 3. 1325b17).

64. See 1. 3. 1095a5-6; 2. 2. 1103b26-28; 6. 1. 1139a5-17; 6. 2. 1139a21-b13; 6. 9. 1142a32-b15; 6. 12. 1143b18-1144a6; 10. 9. 1179a35-b2.

65. In his "The Ascription of Responsibility and Rights," an article which has been responsible for much of the recent interest in philosophy of action, H. L. A. Hart argues that it is, at best, misleading to try to state the necessary and sufficient conditions for behavior being action (*Proceedings of the Aristotelian Society*, 49 [1948-1949], pp. 171-194. Reprinted in *Logic and Language*, pp. 151-174). Hart uses fundamentally the same argument often used against attempts to formulate a substantive ethical code. The statement of conditions for an action, he writes, actually functions as a summary statement of the absence of one or more of a heterogeneous range of cases in which responsibility is diminished or absent. The positive concepts of power, voluntariness, and intentionality, he goes on, are "intolerably vague"; they are understandable only in the light of pleas and defenses. While the latter can be stated very precisely, statements of necessary and sufficient conditions tend "to obscure the composite character of various defenses." They also misleadingly imply the presence of mental elements in an action.

However perceptive Hart's analysis of the role of pleas and excuses, he does not emphasize the fact that the meaningfulness of such claims depends upon the real possibility of contrasts. Saying that a man is coerced, for example, makes sense only because we think it is possible for a man to act by his own power and control his own behavior. Without the possibility of such contrasts, pleas and excuses lose their meaningfulness; that is the reason we are not tempted to say that a stone is or is not coerced when it is simply lying about.

66. See, e.g., 1. 8. 1098b11-12; 6. 12. 1144a23-29.

67. See 5. 9. 1136b29-31; Aristotle, for example, talks about the actions (*praxeis*) of plants (see *Part. an.* 2. 10. 656a3).

68. Aristotle refers to the latter as being done only 'incidentally'. If we adopt the distinction introduced in the third contrast, we need to say that not every action a man performs is his action in the tightest sense of the word.

69. See, e.g., 3. 1. 1109b30-34; 3. 5. 1113b22-1114a3.

70. Although he acknowledges no debt to Aristotle, Nicholas Rescher offers a "canonical description" of an action, which is very close to Aristotle's ("On the Characterization of Actions," in *The Nature of Human Action*, pp. 247-254; an earlier version appeared as "Aspects of Action" in *The Logic of Decision and Action*, pp. 215-219). Rescher describes his characterization as "an essentially exhaustive catalogue of the key generic elements of actions" (p. 248); he justifies his list by the same arguments used by Aristotle.

71. See 1. 7. 1098a26-34.

72. See 1. 6. 1097a11-13; 3. 1. 1110b7; 6. 7. 1141b14-20; 6. 8. 1142a24-25.

73. See 3. 1. 1110b31-1111a2, 24; 6. 7. 1141b14-22; 6. 8. 1142a24-30; 6. 11. 1143a25-35.

74. This and the following list can be found, with some variations, in many places in *Eth. Nic.*, e.g., 2. 3. 1104b21-27; 2. 6. 1106b20-23; 2. 9. 1109a27-28, b15-16; 3. 1. 1111a3-15; 3. 7. 1115b15-20; 4. 2. 1122a25-33; 4. 5. 1125b31-33.

75. See 4. 1. 1120b7ff.; 4. 2. 1122b23-32.

76. The individuation of actions is an enormously complicated business, even though it is an activity in which even children engage when, for example, they ask permissions and tell or listen to stories. We need to settle on the nature of a particular kind of action before assessing its value, before determining whether someone did in fact perform such an action, and before deciding whether we should act that way. Consequently there is no way in which to have a moral theory or a legal system without the use of act-types.

Aristotle has at least two approaches to the delineation of action-types. Often he claims that action-types can be distinguished by special characteristics they have by their very nature, apparently apart from considerations involving the agents performing them (see, e.g., 1. 1; 5. 8. 1135a6-12; 6. 5; 10. 6-7). This is the view Aristotle uses to sort out broad kinds of activities, as we will see in the next chapter. It is the view he uses when he describes education: we learn how to act by performing certain *kinds* of acts, e.g., just actions, courageous actions, competent writing, etc. (see 2. 4. 1105a17-26, b9-11). He also uses this view to talk about actions performed under coercion, due to ignorance, or for motives not obviously connected with the doing of a particular action-type (see 3. 1. 1111a7-15; 5. 8. 1135a27-34; 5. 9. 1136b26-1137a5; 6. 12. 1144a11-17; 7. 9. 1151a36-b2). There is no necessary connection between kinds of actions in this sense and kinds of character, for a person can, Aristotle argues, commit an action which is morally wrong (even knowingly and deliberately) without being the kind of person who characteristically acts in that fashion (see, e.g., 5. 4. 1132a2-7; 5. 6. 1134a17-23, 32-33; 5. 8. 1135a22-23; 6. 12. 1144a13-17). Yet it is still true, he writes, that repeated performances of a particular kind of action tend to generate corresponding qualities in an agent: morally right actions tend to produce morally good people, and practice at some art or skill tends to produce a skilled person (see 2. 1; 6. 4; 6. 12. 1144a17-20).

In many such cases, Aristotle holds that the action-type is done only "in an incidental way"; it happened to be done, but it is not done *in the way* in which people who are skilled or morally good do it (see 2. 4. 1105b5-8; 5. 8. 1135a17-19, b3-25; 5. 9. 1136a25-33, 1137a6-27; 6. 12. 1144a17-20). What is added by this "in the way" is, in the case of skills, the trained ability to know how to act skillfully and, in the case of morality, the kind of moral character which leads a person to choose to act rightly because it is the right way to act. An action-type in the full or strict sense, therefore, occurs only when, on the inside of agency, the elements of knowledge and/or stable character can fully account for what is done (see 2. 4. 1105a16-b8; 3. 1. 1111a1-23; 5. 8. 1135a15-17, 20-22, 23-27).

This double standard does not resolve all problems with the identification of actions, for in some passages Aristotle also argues that we cannot know what kind of an action has been done unless we know the agent—the extent of his knowledge, the quality of his motivation, etc. (see, e.g., 3. 8). It is difficult to see how this claim is completely compatible with his first way of describing actions.

The problems involved in delineating action-types have not been resolved yet, and they have generated an immense amount of literature in contemporary action theory. See, for example, Alvin I. Goldman, *A Theory of Human Action*, pp. 1-48.

77. 3. 1. 1111a18-19.

78. Although we often take a man's manner of acting to be our best clue, albeit not an infallible one, to his emotional state, the two are logically distinct. An agent can simulate; the same manner of acting can be related to

very different mental/emotional states; and some actions and situations offer little opportunity for the exercise and display of particular qualities on the inside of agency.

79. The text of 3. 1. 1111a4 is misleading, for it seems that the "and sometimes also" introduces three items—the means, the result, and the manner. But neither the result nor the manner can be only sometimes constitutive of an action.

80. See 1. 8. 1099a2.

81. There are other complexities here which will need to be discussed later. Aristotle claims that, because most people are not sufficiently sensitive morally, they often misapprehend what they and others are actually doing. Moreover, he thinks the role of moral character is so decisive that he does not believe argumentation will normally resolve many disputes over moral descriptions. Although he is convinced that particular actions have but one right moral description, he argues that the only person capable of getting descriptions right consistently is the thoroughly good person.

82. Ignorance can be intentional, nonintentional, or unintentional, and each kind of ignorance forms the basis for a different assessment of the character of an agent. Intentional ignorance ("acting in ignorance") involves a culpable failure to act on the right practical principle, not merely ignorance of the particularities of an action. On this, see chap. 8.

83. We generally assume that when a man engages in an activity he acts from motives typical to that activity, e.g., we eat because we are hungry. Inquiry into a man's motives, therefore, generally implies that some unusual sort of justification is needed for his action. Either his action is itself somehow unacceptable and we are unclear why, if he knew what he was doing, he acted as he did; or we suspect that the usual motive in such cases was not his motive, or at least not his chief or only motive; or we suspect that his motive was somehow unsatisfactory.

84. See 3. 8; 5. 6. 1134a16-33; 7. 9. 1151b4-8; *Eth. Eud.* 3. 1. 1229a12-31.

85. See note 8 in chap. 6.

3

On the Outside:
Kinds of Practical Activities

Aristotle has defined human practice as the intelligently directed use of our power to affect and alter, to dominate and control things and other agencies. He also has told us that, in general, the good should be defined in terms of finalities: it is that for the sake of which all else is done.[1] He now adds a third and crucial claim: the practical good "has two aspects: It is both an activity and a characteristic."[2] In this chapter we will be looking primarily at his analysis of good activity. We shall see that he argues there are fundamentally but two kinds of activities, those which are only instrumentally good and those which are intrinsically good. They are radically distinct from each other, and the latter are, by their very nature, radically superior. To classify activities, then, is also to rank them.

In the following three chapters we will investigate his analysis of the nature of the practical good on the inside of action, and what it means to say that a man has good characteristics. We will see why we can and should distinguish between good activities and good men; we will also see why we should not try to separate one from the other completely. The connection between the two will have to be made clear. What can be said now in very general terms is that there is a close correlation between the way in which we sort out kinds of activities and the way in which we sort out kinds of men. The best man will turn out to be the man who chooses to engage in the best activities because they are what they are and because he is that kind of man.[3]

INSTRUMENTAL AND INTRINSIC PRACTICAL GOOD

It is a commonly known fact that men can and do desire and take pleasure in virtually anything they can imagine to be desirable;

what rescues us from sophistic relativism and complete subjectivity is the fact that activities also have an objective nature which we can apprehend apart from the way in which any particular individual may happen to value them.[4] "What is by nature just has the same force everywhere and does not depend on what we regard or do not regard as just."[5] We always can make meaningful claims about the characteristics of kinds of action, and this is the basis for claiming that some kinds are better than others.[6]

In the last chapter we saw how the goal of an action defines the nature of an action. Aristotle now builds on that doctrine. He argues that, regardless of the great variety of activities in which men can engage, all actions are of only two fundamental kinds, distinguished by the relation between actions and their ends.[7]

Some actions are such that their ends are identifiable apart from what is done to achieve them. In these cases we can distinguish two elements: the means (*ta pros to telos*), or what is done to secure something else, the end; and the end (*telos*), the intended result or consummatory condition, which is not itself the action but which is to be produced by the action. The action is of instrumental value only, chosen only 'incidentally', and its goodness is conditional or hypothetical (*ex hupotheseōs*), for it is good insofar as it is effective in attaining a given end.[8]

Other actions are such that their ends are not extrinsic to what is done but rather the activities and their ends coalesce, and the actions are worth doing for their own sake, without regard for other possible benefits which might be attained beyond actually engaging in the activities themselves.[9] Such actions are called intrinsically or absolutely (*telos haplōs*) good, and their worth is not derived from something else. Their end consists in satisfying criteria which specify both the nature of the action and what it is to engage in that activity well.[10]

Often the same action can be described under both of these headings, because many intrinsically good activities are part of more comprehensive arts or sciences (*technai kai epistēmai*) and so a means to the more general ends of those arts or sciences.[11] But when we perform such an activity also for the sake of some further end, we still are justified in saying that the activity is itself intrinsically good; it still is worth doing for its own sake (*haireton kath'auton*).[12]

Aristotle's classification of activities depends on another distinction he makes, between *kinēsis* and *energeia*.[13] First he defines *energeia* in a wide sense, as that which is actual, in contrast to *dunamis*, that which is not yet actual but only a possibility. *Kinēsis* is the term he uses to designate any change or movement in a wide sense; it is the *energeia*, the actualization or realization, of a *dunamis* for change.[14] But he then narrows the meaning of both *kinēsis* and *energeia* so as to contrast them with each other as significantly different kinds of activities.[15] This is the contrast in which we are interested.

Instrumental activities are kinetic; they are not themselves ends but they have ends (*telē*) which also serve as limits, that is, states of affairs to which they conclude but which are distinct from the processes which produce them.[16] During the time in which a man engages in a kinetic process, he has not yet completed what he is doing, and when he does, he ceases striving because he has his goal. Kinetic processes all have a beginning (a *genesis*), a middle, and an end, and their parts and stages occupy a definite length of time—from their beginning until their end is attained. By themselves they are incomplete and so imperfect; they become 'complete' only when they succeed and then they are over and done with.[17] As examples of *kinēsis*, Aristotle lists reducing, learning, walking, weaving, rolling, house-building, doctoring, aging, being cured, and maturing.[18] Although kinetic processes always have a limit—the end to which they are the means, still the end itself has no limit, since, insofar as men consider ends to be good, their desires for them are unlimited. The man who seeks wealth cannot get too much of it, and the physician cannot make his patient too healthy.[19]

The term *energeia* designates that kind of activity which does not have an end distinct from itself but rather the end "inheres in [*enuparchein*] it" so that the doing of such an action is its own end (*eschaton*).[20] Although, for men at least, it occurs in time, such activity does not depend upon temporalities for its existence.[21] Unlike *kinēsis*, it does not have a definite stopping point, with a temporal spread marking stages of development or progress toward that end. It need not last for any particular length of time; instead it can take only a moment, or it can go on indefinitely. For whenever a person engages in *energeia*, it does not take time for him to reach his goal; nor can he possibly fail to attain it. Because the end is attained in the very act of doing, the activity is "complete in its form at any given moment."[22] *Energeia* therefore is, by its very nature, superior to *kinēsis;* it in fact is the kind of activity in which God engages.[23] Nonkinetic activities include seeing, hearing, thinking, knowing, living well and pleasurably, and contemplation.[24] Unlike kinetic processes, these activities do not suffer from the imperfection of, in a sense, destroying themselves in order to attain their ends; they are themselves perfect (*teleiai*), because they are coextensive with their ends. Only such activities can be noble (*kalon*), that is, both desirable for their own sake and also worthy of praise.[25]

Aristotle is clear about the ability of men to cut up the world in virtually any way they want and so to value instrinsic goods as instrumentalities and instrumentalities as intrinsic goods, depending, among other things, on how inexperienced, confused, or depraved they may be.[26] He is concerned here, not with all the possible and idiosyncratic psychological capabilities of men, but with the objective nature of kinds of human activities. Regardless of how some men may misapprehend them, kinetic processes are, by their very nature, imperfect and so are inferior to nonkinetic activities, which by their nature are complete and perfect.[27]

One important qualification needs to be added before concluding Aristotle's discussion of activities. He writes: "we use the word 'good' in two senses: a thing may be good in an unqualified sense [*haplōs agatha*], or good for a particular person."[28] Given Aristotle's analysis of how the particularities involved in actions can vary, this qualification could have been expected. If we always need to take into account the particularities of each situation, we should not be surprised to find that in some situations even intrinsically good activities can be bad for a person. "Even theoretical activity occasionally can be harmful to one's health," but that, of course, does not make it or other intrinsically good activities bad in themselves.[29] Likewise, most moral evils consist in pursuing physical pleasures to excess but again that does not mean physical pleasures should be considered morally evil in themselves.[30] Aristotle's discussion of this topic will be completed in the following chapters, when we discuss the inner side of agency, character.

Pleasure and Kinds of Pleasure

Pleasure and pain have so great a role in the way men live that Aristotle is willing to say that the examination of the nature of moral and political life is virtually entirely an examination of the nature and value of pleasure and pain.[31] Despite the crucial importance of the notion of 'pleasure' (*hēdonē*), however, its elucidation is notoriously difficult. But Aristotle's discussion of kinds of practical good now provides him with a way in which to develop his discussion of pleasure.[32] His entire treatment of the topic is an effort to avoid the morass of sophistic subjectivism, by connecting kinds of pleasures with kinds of activities. We can make meaningful and truth-functional claims about pleasures, he contends, because we can talk about pleasures as part of the outer side of action; we are not restricted to talking about the ways in which different men feel.

Aristotle argues that we will not understand the nature of pleasure if we begin by taking it to be a process (a *kinēsis*) or a coming-to-be (a *genesis*) of which we become aware when it happens to us.[33] For as we have seen, kinetic activity always aims at something other than itself, while men always seek pleasure as an intrinsic good.[34] We do often experience pleasure while developing our abilities, or while satisfying appetites involving some deficiency, e.g., hunger and thirst, or while undergoing remedial processes such as recuperation. But the pleasure involved in these is derived from the functioning of natural characteristics we already or still have. That such processes are only 'incidentally pleasurable' and do not disclose the essential nature of pleasure is shown by the fact that the processes are no longer pleasurable once the state of deprivation has been remedied.[35] Pleasure therefore is, by its very nature, attached primarily to the doing of nonkinetic activities, those worth doing for their own sake.[36]

When we are in good mental and physical health, pleasure normally accompanies any unimpeded, successful use (*energeia*) of all our natural abilities to perceive, to think, and to act.[37] Because it is natural for us to feel pleasure in acting, what needs explaining on any particular occasion is not that we feel pleasure but that we do not.[38] Pleasure is so intimately connected with activity that there

hardly seems to be a distinction between them: talk about a particular pleasure and talk about a particular activity can be simply
different ways of speaking of the same thing.[39] But there is this
important difference: talk about pleasure does not by itself identify
or define what one is doing, only the fact that one is doing
something for its own sake; pleasures cannot be distinguished from
one another by the sheer fact they are pleasures.

Pleasures can, however, be described and identified by refer-
ence to the activities which they normally accompany, for different
pleasures are typical of and proper to different kinds of activities.
The pleasure proper to an activity also usually contributes to the
activity in which it 'inheres', which it 'completes' or 'perfects', while
pleasures alien to an activity usually interfere with and obstruct it.
Exactly how pleasure enhances an activity depends on the activity;
pleasure may, for example, make execution more precise, or easier,
or easier to continue, or more easily understood.[40]

Because man has a complex nature, an ensouled body, his
pleasurable activities are all of two general sorts. Some are pleasures
which he "shares," in some sense, with brute animals, since he is a
sensuous being.[41] The most important of those involve the sense of
taste (pleasures involved in eating and drinking) and the sense of
touch (particularly pleasures connected with sexual activity). Because pleasurable activities involving these senses often alleviate
discomfort and because the appetites relevant to them are all subject
to deprivation and replenishment, they are particularly susceptible
to excess.[42] Somatic pleasures are an essential part of human life, for
they are necessary (*anankaia*) for life, at least to a point, and,
Aristotle thinks, most men believe there are no other pleasures.[43]
But there are other pleasurable activities, proper only to man
because of his ability to think.[44] These are activities which are not
only pleasurable but also noble and honorable, those forms of
energeia involving moral and theoretical activity.[45] Both will be
discussed in detail in later chapters.

Keeping the discussion of pleasure to the outside of action by
talking about it in relation to kinds of activities enables Aristotle to
argue for an objective basis for ranking pleasures. But we cannot
totally avoid considering pleasure from the inside perspective, and
there Aristotle faces serious problems, for all men are attracted to

what they think promises pleasure and tend to avoid what they find disagreeable, yet what each man finds pleasurable or disagreeable depends to some extent on the kind of man he is. Pleasure *can* accompany and signal the successful doing of *all* kinds of activities, even, for those people who are sufficiently corrupt, activities which are utterly perverse.[46] Since the experiencing of pleasurable sensations does not necessarily guarantee either that our faculties are sound or that we are using them rightly, merely experiencing pleasure cannot be equated with the experiencing of what is genuinely good. Pleasure alone does not provide us with an objective criterion of what is good, whether we are thinking of activities or characteristics. It is the other way around: good activities and good characteristics are naturally accompanied by pleasure.[47]

Aristotle does have an objective standard, even on the side of subjectivity, for what is both pleasurable and good. That standard is the expert; he provides us with a way of testing discrimination independently of enjoyment, and enjoyment in general independently of enjoyment on any particular occasion.[48] We will briefly return to this appeal in the final section of this chapter, but the elucidation of the qualities of such a man will require a detailed analysis, which will be the burden of Chapter 6. For now we need to stress that, because men can and often do confuse the relationship between what is pleasurable and what is good, Aristotle is careful to ground his discussion of the nature and goodness of pleasure in his discussion of kinds of activities:

> Now, activities differ from one another in goodness and
> badness. Some are desirable, others should be avoided,
> and others again are indifferent. The same is also true of
> pleasures, since each activity determines its own proper
> pleasure. The pleasure proper to morally good activity is
> good, the pleasure proper to bad activity evil.[49]

Just as the discussion of kinds of activities closed with the qualification that what holds in general for practice may not hold in a particular case, so also here it is necessary to qualify the general claims made about pleasure. Even though a particular pleasure may not be good when considered abstractly, still it may be good for a particular person on a particular occasion for a short time. The pleasure accompanying recuperation, for example, is not desirable as good in itself, and the healthy man would be perverse for desiring it; but it clearly is desirable for the man who is ill, if only until he recovers his health.[50]

It may be necessary here to warn against interpreting Aristotle as a relativist. He still holds a very strong doctrine concerning objective criteria for discriminating among pleasures. In effect, he is merely warning us not to confuse objectivity with absolutism.

POIESIS AND PRAXIS: MAKING AND DOING

Before concluding our examination of the surface of kinds of activities and pleasures, we need to see how Aristotle applies the distinction between instrumentally and intrinsically good activities. Since he claims that the division is exhaustive, we can expect that all practicalities will fall into one or the other of the two categories.[51]

Under the first, activities which are by nature only instrumentally good, Aristotle includes all cases of making or producing (poiēseis) In this kind of activity, the agent (the efficient cause) works on malleable things (the material cause) in order to bring into existence something other than the action itself. The end of production can be called an artifact, at least in an extended sense, and it is the final cause of making. Because the goal determines what must be done to reach it, the activity itself is assessed primarily in terms of its effectiveness in attaining its goal; and the cost of the means is relative to the value of its product.[52]

Any action must be considered a case of production if it fits this description, whether it be manual labor, the semi-skilled work of the mechanic, or the skilled movements of the artisan or the artist. There is no significant difference between the fine and the useful arts; they are, by nature, alike because they both strive for something other than the activity itself. Menial and servile work generates products necessary for specifically human living, and so does craft. They all are kinetic processes, with stages which take time. The end of striving is *not* intrinsically good by the mere fact that it is the end of productive activity; it is still a product which needs to be put to some use, and so it can be no more than a necessary condition for or a means in some intrinsically good activity.[53] How a product is to be used is not the direct concern of production but of the other kind of practical activity, which we will now consider.

The second kind of practice consists in those activities of human agents which are worth doing for their own sake; this is *praxis* in the strict and technical sense of activity susceptible to appraisal as either morally right or morally wrong.[54] The area of *praxis* consists in all our dealings as social and political beings with other men as we act on them, with them, or against them and, within this context, how we use things to extend our agency.[55]

Within these boundaries, Aristotle offers this general behavioral description of "right action": we act rightly when we perform the right action, toward and/or with the right (kind of) object(s) or people, in the right manner, in the right circumstances, using the right means, at the right time, for the right length of time, and with the right result.[56]

Since actions are a matrix of particulars, this characterization may seem distressingly vague. But if we were to try to define right practice by introducing more particular descriptions, we would lose the form of generality. Moreover, there is no single way in which a particular instance of right action *must* become definite; the number, variety, and sequences of physical movements which can occur during the course of a particular action are indefinitely large, and the particulars on the outside of action can vary so significantly that there is no way in which we can offer a more precise while still general behavioral description of right action.[57]

But Aristotle does have another, though not finally distinct, way of describing the surface of right practice: all instances of practical activity involve our acting in a certain *manner* which can be described in terms of the emotional characteristics we display when we act. Right practice, therefore, can be described as participating in the right pleasures in the right manner. The man who does the right action but in the wrong way is that man whose overt emotional characteristics before, during, or after an action are somehow either deficient or excessive, while the emotional characteristics of the man who does the right action rightly are somewhere in the middle (*mesotēs*), avoiding the extremes of either too much or too little.[58] If we divide morally significant actions into two types, competitive and cooperative, a man should compete in a courageous manner, while showing just the right amount of pleasure in cooperative activities, whether they concern relations characterized by justice (*dikaiosunē*) or loving concern (*philia*).[59] Likewise a man will avoid the extremes of too little and too much, e.g., acting cowardly or rashly, or performing just acts begrudgingly.

Aristotle admits that, by itself, the notion of the mean is not very helpful.[60] How do we ascertain the mean (*to meson*) in a particular situation? Aristotle believes that what is needed is the moral sensitivity (*aisthēsis*) to take into account and to weigh the importance of the variables in such situations, and that kind of sensitivity is more difficult to attain than the mastery of skills as complex as those of the physician.[61] He writes:

> It is not easy to determine in what manner, with what person, on what occasion, and for how long a time one ought to be angry, and at what point right action ends and wrong action begins. We do not blame a man for straying a little either toward the more or toward the less. Sometimes we praise those who are deficient in anger and call them gentle, and sometimes we praise the angry as manly and regard them as capable of ruling. Therefore it is not easy to give a formula how far and in what manner a man may stray before he deserves blame, for the decision depends on the particular circumstances and on our (moral) sense.[62]

If we seek greater definiteness through maxims which take a middle ground between complete generality and complete specificity, we tend to end up with formulae which are as trite as they are unhelpful, with neither universality nor enough particularity to help us know how and when to apply those maxims to our own situations.[63] It is easy to feel a deep dissatisfaction when we read Aristotle's discussion of the kinds of right conduct in Books 3 to 5 of the *Nicomachean Ethics*, since those books concern what can be said in a middling way about practical matters.

For example, Aristotle writes that "in each particular case [a good man's] behavior will be appropriate to the person" with whom he is dealing, and we have special obligations to friends that we do not have to strangers.[64] A friend is one who, in general, gives pleasure, not pain. But since acting rightly means acting according to "the standard of what is noble and beneficial," when giving pleasure violates that standard we should refuse to give pleasure, even if that means also inflicting pain.[65]

If we are looking for practical advice, such statements do not seem very helpful, nor do listings of terms referring to various right manners of acting, e.g., honestly, justly, considerately, etc.[66] Consequently, Aristotle recommends that, when we do not know how to act, we look for a model. The contingencies which make up individual situations can vary so much that there can be no norm, ready made and impersonal, which can determine how each person ought to act in every circumstance of his life. But the good person characteristically does know how he should act, and that makes him a living norm. Just as, in matters of perception, the standard is the healthy man with the keenest senses, not a sick or maimed person, so the standard for morality and for pleasure is the person who is morally good and experienced in moral matters; he can "see the truth in each particular moral question."[67]

In recommending moral models, Aristotle is not saying that we must live our lives out under the guidance of moral mentors. As we shall see, Aristotle argues that we are not as morally good as we ought to be unless we ourselves become experienced and wise in moral matters (be *phronimoi*), so that we can ourselves judge what is morally right for us in our own circumstances. We cannot, as D. J. Allan puts it, "as we do in the otherwise similar case of medicine, rely on the trained judgement of a few experts. Every man requires *phronēsis* [moral wisdom] for himself."[68] Moral paradigms are essential, however, for the young and the inexperienced, to help them learn how to act in situations with which they are unfamiliar.

There are serious problems with paradigms, though; for one thing, we may, through ignorance, choose the wrong man as a norm, and, for another, we may not be able to find the right model.[69] Aristotle took these problems seriously, and they are at least one reason why he devoted so much space in his *Ethics* to "middle-range" discussions of right action. It is also one reason why he thought it is of immense importance that the state, which has the

function of promoting the common welfare, should have laws
stating as explicitly and exactly as possible which actions are right
and which are not. Aristotle's observations of these matters led him
to place great emphasis on the rule of law; the law, impersonal and
unprejudiced, can best define right action.[70] In a passage of rare
emotion he writes:

> He who bids the law rule may be deemed to bid God and
> Reason alone rule, but he who bids man rule adds an
> element of the beast; for desire is a wild beast, and passion
> perverts the minds of rulers, even when they are the best of
> men. The law is reason unaffected by desire.[71]

In a later chapter we shall investigate the function of the state in the
moral education of its citizenry.

We can conclude this examination of making and doing by
pointing out that, in general, both involve thoughtful action directed to an end and are concerned also with the means for achieving
it; each is an exercise of a power proper only to man as a rational agent.
Although making (*poiēsis*) and its products are under the direction of
doing (*praxis*), the two are such radically distinct kinds of activity
that "one does not include the other."[72] Even the instruments they
use are different in kind. Making does not of itself ever rise to the
level of practice in the strict sense of *energeia;* at best it produces the
conditions and instruments necessary for *praxis.*[73] Only the latter is
worth doing for its own sake, and, as we shall see, the best life is one
in which such *energeiai* predominate.

Notes to Chapter 3

1. See "Third Contrast" in chap. 2.

2. 7. 12. 1152b33; cf. 2. 3. 1104b13; 8. 5. 1157b5-13.

3. See 1. 8. 1099a13; 3. 4. 1113a22-33; 9. 4. 1166a12-18; 9. 9. 1170a11-16; 10. 5. 1176a16-22.

4. See 3. 4. 1113a15-24; 10. 6. 1176b19-27. Aristotle's claim seems in accord both with our ordinary language and with contemporary practice of the law: we need to be clear about the nature of a particular kind of action before we can determine whether or not a man in fact performed it. Since different kinds of activities are accompanied by their own kinds of pleasure, we also can talk meaningfully about kinds of pleasures and not merely about what different people have happened to enjoy. On this see "Pleasure and Kinds of Pleasure," later in this chapter.

5. 5. 7. 1134b18-19; cf. 25-26. Aristotle also calls that which is good "by nature" (*phusei*), good "without qualification" or "considered by itself" (*haplōs agathon*). Because philosophers today commonly criticize arguments which appeal to "nature" as ambiguous, it should be noted that Aristotle is sensitive to the various ways in which we can use the term and its correlates (see, e.g., *Metaph.* 5. 4; *Ph.* 2. 1. 192b7-193a1). Besides the contrast between nature and convention, he proposes several other ways in which we can legitimately use the term "natural". For example,

> [There are] two marks by which we define the natural—it is either
> [1] that which is found with us as soon as we are born, or [2] that
> which comes to us if growth is allowed to proceed regularly, e.g.,
> grey hair, old age, and so on (*Eth. Eud.* 2. 8. 1224b32-34 (Solomon);
> see also *Pol.* 1. 2. 1252b32-33; *Ph.* 2. 8. 199a8-b18).

The first meaning can be subdivided. Since every living creature is an embodied soul, the term "nature" can refer either to its material component (or material cause) or to its essence (*ousia*), its *psuchē*, which, as the form (or formal cause) of what it is to be that kind of creature, determines both its efficient and its final causality, or it can refer to the entire complex of matter and form. See *Part. an.* 1. 1. 641a18-32; *Metaph.* 5. 4; *Ph.* 2. 2. 194a12-18; 2. 8. 199a30-33. Elsewhere Aristotle introduces a third meaning emphasizing the teleological character of nature: "what each thing is when fully developed," i.e., "in [its] most perfect state" (*Pol.* 1. 2. 1252b33 and 1. 5. 1254a38 (Jowett); cf. *Ph.* 2. 8. 198b33-199a33; 7. 3. 246a10ff.). The second and third are not interchangeable, since a senile person fulfills the second definition but obviously not the third. Other uses depend on the notion of power (*dunamis*). In this sense "nature" can mean an animate being's ability to move and change by itself, in contrast to alteration which comes from without. Or it can be valuative by implying that what is more powerful is superior to what is less powerful, e.g., mind, which can comprehend universals, is by its very nature superior to and should be dominant over desires which are limited to particulars (see *Pol.* 1. 5. 1254a34-36).

6. To describe an action as "intrinsically good," for example, is to say that it is valuable in itself and so always in the interest of any human agent, unless reasons can be produced to show why, for him at this time, it is not good. This description is not falsified by the fact that some men may not recognize its truth. See 3. 4; 7. 12. 1152b25-1153a20; 7. 13. 1153b25-37; 10. 5. 1175b2-1176a29; 10. 6. 1176a30-b27; *Pol.* 1. 8. 1256a27ff.; 8. 5. 1339b15-35.

7. See 1. 1. 1094a1-14; 1. 6. 1096b13-15; 1. 7. 1097a16-28; 10. 6. 1176b2-7.

8. See 1. 1. 1094a4-6, 15-16; 1. 6. 1096b13-18; 6. 2. 1139b1-3; 7. 9. 1151a36-b2; *Pol.* 7. 13. 1332a8-16; *Metaph.* 7. 7. 1032b6-10, 18-26; 9. 6. 1048b18-19; 9. 8. 1050a25-b5; *Part. an.* 2. 1. 646b3-5.

9. See 1. 1. 1094a3-4; 1. 6. 1096b17-19; 1. 7. 1097b1-7; 10. 6. 1176b6-7.

10. Although it generally is translated as "means to," the Greek expression "*ta pros to telos*" literally means "things for the sake of the end." The context often shows that Aristotle intends the expression to refer to actions or things merely instrumental in attaining ends which are ontologically and temporally distinct from them. But he also uses the expression when writing about intrinsically good actions which are not instrumentalities but are consummatory and so themselves ends. They are "for the sake of" the good life—but not in the sense that they make possible a life which temporally follows from, is external to and describable apart from those actions; rather the good life is composed of such actions, and that is how they contribute to it. H. H. Joachim suggests we may prevent misinterpretations if we call such actions not "means" but "constituent parts of the end." See his *Aristotle, "The Nicomachean Ethics": A Commentary*, p. 188; cf. p. 102. For further discussion, see "The Unity of Practical Wisdom and Moral Excellence" in chap. 6.

11. See *Pol.* 4. 1. 1288b10-24.

12. See 1. 1. 1094a9-18; 1. 6. 1096b17-19; 1. 7. 1097a30-b5. This claim will create very serious difficulties in the case of morally good activities which, as Aristotle describes them, *must* be done *only* for their own sake. See "Moral Excellence" in chap. 5 and "A Final Problem" in chap. 9.

13. Many philosophers have tried to reconstruct Aristotle's doctrine here in what they hope is a more satisfactory way, for it seems that the same

action can be characterized either as kinetic or nonkinetic, depending on the way it is described. Anthony Kenny, for example, calls kinetic actions "performances" and divides the nonkinetic into "states" and "activities." See chapter 8 in his *Action, Emotion and Will*. Gilbert Ryle, on the other hand, writes of "task verbs" and "achievement verbs"; see his *The Concept of Mind*, pp. 149-153. Against Ryle, Nicholas Rescher argues that only activity verbs represent actions; achievement verbs represent the termination of an activity (see *The Nature of Human Action*, p. 248).

14. See *Part. an.* 2. 1. 646b15-17; *Metaph.* 6. 12. 1019a15-16.

15. See 10. 3. 1173a28-b7; 10. 4. 1174a14-b13; *Metaph.* 9. 6. 1048b18-27; 9. 8. 1050a24-b5. My discussion here generally is in agreement with the excellent analysis of J. L. Ackrill; see his "Aristotle's Distinction between *Energeia* and *Kinesis*," in *New Essays on Plato and Aristotle*, pp. 121-141.

16. See 7. 11. 1152b13-14; 10. 4. 1174a23-28; *Metaph.* 8. 7. 1032b6-26; 9. 6. 1048b18-22; 11. 9. 1065b14-1066a7; *Ph.* 3. 1. 201a10-b15.

17. See 10. 4. 1174a19-b15.

18. See *Metaph.* 9. 6. 1048b28-30; 9. 8. 1050a30-32; *Ph.* 3. 1. 201a15-17. The latter three are not actions even in a wide sense, but they are not completely out of place here, since a *dunamis* can be a capacity for undergoing as well as for initiating change (see 7. 12. 1153a9-12; *Metaph.* 5. 12).

19. See *Pol.* 1. 9. 1257b23-1258a17.

20. See *Metaph.* 9. 6. 1048b22-24; 9. 8. 1050a24ff.; *Eth. Nic.* 10. 6. 1176b6-8.

21. See 10. 4. 1174b8-13.

22. 10. 4. 1174a28; cf. 1174a14-b13; also *Metaph.* 9. 6. 1048b18-35; 9. 8. 1050a24; *Sens.* 446b2.

23. See 7. 14. 1154b24-31; 10. 7. 1177a19-27, b26-31; 10. 8. 1179a23-32; *Metaph.* 12. 7. 1072b14-30, esp. 30; *De an.* 2. 5. 417b3-9; *Top.* 3. 1. 116a28-31.

24. See 1. 6. 1096b16-19; 7. 12. 1153a7-17; 10. 4. 1174a14-15, b13; *Metaph.* 9. 8. 1050a35-b2.

25. See *Rh.* 1. 9. 1366a33-4. Joachim sums up Aristotle's doctrine well, I think, when he writes: "The activity is, whenever it is at all, all that it ever is or can be, whole and complete in any and every instant of itself" (*Aristotle: The Nicomachean Ethics*, p. 276).

26. See 1. 5. 1096a6-9; 3. 4. 1113a21; 10. 6. 1176a3-23, b22-27; *Pol.* 8. 7. 1342a19-26.

27. See 1. 1. 1094a5-6; 10. 6. 1176b2-3.

28. 7. 12. 1152b27-28; cf. 28-32, 1153a18-20; also 1. 3. 1094b15-18; 2. 3. 1104b23-26; 4. 2. 1122a25-34; 5. 1. 1129b2-7; 5. 9. 1137a26-31; 7. 13. 1153b23-24; 8. 2. 1155b22-24; 8. 5. 1157b26-27; *Pol.* 7. 13. 1332a8-25.

See also note 43 in chapter 4. Apparently Aristotle was thinking of this distinction when he wrote that "things which, though naturally just, are nevertheless changeable, as are all things human" (5. 7. 1134b28-29; cf. 30-35).

29. 7. 12. 1153a20 (my translation); cf. 17-19. But some kinds of actions still seem always wrong; see 2. 6. 1107a8-25.

30. See 7. 14. 1154a8-21.

31. See 2. 3. 1104b28-1105a13; 3. 11.

32. I am omitting Aristotle's preliminary stage of inquiry, the inventorying of various views men have held about the nature and value of pleasure (see 7. 11 and 10. 1-3) in order to concentrate on his own position. Mention has been made already of the peculiar fact that *Eth. Nic.* contains two separate discussions of pleasure, one in Book 7 and the other in Book 10. The bibliography in this volume lists several commentaries which discuss the problem of the two separate treatments.

33. See 7. 11. 1152b12-14; 7. 12. 1153a9-17; 10. 3. 1173a28-b7; 10. 4. 1174a14-b13.

34. See 1. 7. 1097b2-5; 7. 13. 1153b8-32; 10. 4. 1175a11-21.

35. See 7. 12. 1152b33-1153a8; 7. 14. 1154a27-b1, 17-19; 10. 3. 1173b11-20.

36. See 3. 9. 1117b14-15; 7. 12. 1153a24-27; 10. 2. 1172b17-35. A. E. Taylor and W. F. R. Hardie point out that the 'replenishment' theory was held by Plato (see his *Philebus* and *Timaeus*) as well as by Aristotle in his earlier career (see his *Rh.* 1. 11. 1369b33-1370a10, 1371a31-b3). J. O. Urmson argues that, in his care to renounce this view, Aristotle fails to appreciate that there still are some pleasures which are produced by, rather than which accompany, some activities, and that men do sometimes act, e.g., eat, for the sake of experiencing the pleasant sensations which are consequences of and *follow from* such activities. "While most philosophers have wrongly assimilated the enjoyment of activity to the enjoyment of feelings, a mistake for which Aristotle duly castigates them, he himself makes the uncommon error of assimilating the enjoyment of feelings to the enjoyment of activity." Aristotle, however, does not make this error. He admits remedial processes such as eating can produce feelings of pleasure, but they are not paradigmatically *human* pleasures; and in intrinsically good activities we do not enjoy a *feeling*, we enjoy the activity, whatever it may be, because we see it is worth doing for its own sake. See J. O. Urmson, "Aristotle on Pleasure," in *Aristotle: A Collection of Critical Essays*, pp. 323-333.

37. See 1. 8. 1099a11-22; 7. 12. 1153a12-15; 7. 14. 1154b17-21.

38. See 9. 9. 1170a18-b15; 10. 2. 1172b20-23; 10. 4. 1174a14-1175a3. Pleasure does wane, of course, as we become tired, or sated, or distracted (see 10. 4. 1175a3-10).

39. See 10. 4. 1174a14-b17, 1175a11-21; 10. 5. 1175b31-36.

40. See 7. 12. 1153a21-23; 10. 4. 1174b14-32, 1175a15-17; 10. 5. 1175a29-b23; 10. 7. 1177b21.

41. See 2. 3. 1104b34-35; 3. 10. 1118a17-b7; 7. 12. 1153a31-36.

42. Pleasurable activities involving the other senses do not share this characteristic nor do pleasurable memories and anticipations (see 3. 10. 1118a23-b1; 10. 3. 1173b8-20). Later we shall see that the necessary pleasures involving touch and taste constitute the subject matter of most moral dispositions, e.g., self-control, moral strength, moral weakness, and self-indulgence. On this see 3. 10; 7. 4. 1147b23-1148a17; 7. 5. 1149a21-23; 7. 6. 1149b25-31; also chaps. 5 and 8. If so many moral dispositions are concerned primarily with processes which, Aristotle argues, are only 'incidentally' pleasurable, how can moral activity be intrinsically good? How can morality be other than a second-rate activity, concerned with second-rate pleasures? Aristotle does not face this problem until the tenth book of *Eth. Nic.*, and there he concludes that morality *is* a part of the good life only in a secondary sense. For further discussion of this problem, see "A Final Problem" in chap. 9.

43. See 3. 4. 1113a35-b2; 7. 4. 1147b23-28, 1148a25-26; 7. 7. 1150a17-24; 7. 13. 1153b33-36.

44. See, e.g., 10. 5. 1176a23-28.

45. See 3. 10. 1117b27-1118a2; 5. 1. 1129b17-18, 26-1130a5; 5. 6. 1134a23-31; 10. 8. 1178a9-13. Besides the pleasurable and the noble, Aristotle also writes of the "beneficial" (*ta sumpheronta*) as contrasted with the harmful (*ta blabera*); sometimes the beneficial is what contributes to or what is coextensive with what is noble; other times the term "beneficial" is used in a derogatory way to refer to mistaken views of what is good, and then it is contrasted with what is genuinely good. The meaning must be ascertained from the context. See, e.g., 1. 3. 1094b17-18; 2. 2. 1104a4-5; 2. 3. 1104b29-1105a1; 3. 1. 1110b30-31; 4. 6. 1126b30, 1127a5; 5. 1. 1130a4-5; 6. 5. 1140a7; 6. 7. 1141b6; 6. 9. 1142b33; 8. 2. 1155b17-27; 9. 8. 1169a4-6; *Eth. Eud.* 1. 1. 1214a32; 1. 4. 1215a32; 7. 2. 1235b32-1236a6; *Rh.* 1. 3. 1358b20-29. See also A. W. H. Adkins, *Merit and Responsibility: A Study in Greek Values* pp. 317-319.

46. See, e.g., 3. 4; 7. 5. 1148b17-30; 7. 13. 1153b24-30; 7. 14. 1154a31-b2; 10. 3. 1173b22-31; 10. 5. 1176a3-29; 10. 9. 1179b32-35. See also "Brutishness" in chap. 8.

47. See 1. 8. 1099a7-25; 10. 3. 1174a8-10; 2. 3. 1104b21-1105a13.

48. See *Pol.* 8. 3. 1338a4-19; also Kenny, *Action, Emotion and Will*, chap. 6.

49. 10. 5. 1175b24-28; see 10. 3. 1174a8-10; 10. 4. 1175a20-21; 10. 5. 1175b2-37. Obviously it is a mistake to take Aristotle to be an ethical hedonist. He does agree that all men pursue pleasure, but he rejects the

claim of Eudoxus that pleasure is the ultimate good, and he argues that men often should be pursuing what is good when they care only for what is pleasurable. See 7. 13. 1153b30; 10. 2. 1172b27-1173a6; 10. 3. 1173b32-1174a10.

50. See 3. 4. 1113a26-28; 7. 12. 1153a3-8; 10. 3. 1173a25-27, b7-20.

51. Aristotle discriminates between sorts of activities on the basis of the difference between *energeia* and *kinēsis*, although this distinction does not correspond exactly to the distinction between *praxis* and *poiēsis*. All cases of *poiēsis* may be cases of *kinēsis*, but not all cases of *kinēsis*, e.g., learning, are cases of *poiēsis* in the usual sense. Moreover, not all cases of *energeia* are *praxeis*; seeing, for example, is an *aisthēsis*, and some thinking is *theōria*.

52. See 6. 4. 1140a11-16; *Metaph*. 7. 7-9; 9. 8. 1050a25-33.

53. See 6. 2. 1139b2-3; 7. 12. 1153a25-26.

54. See 6. 5. 1140b4-11. Aristotle is not always consistent in making this crucial distinction between making and doing. In several passages he describes *all* action as only instrumentally good. See, e.g., 3. 3. 1112b33; 3. 5. 1113b5-6; 10. 7. 1177b6ff. Scholars have long debated this embarrassing contradiction. For further discussion, see "A Final Problem" in chap. 9.

55. See 6. 5. 1140b8-11; 6. 7. 1141b8-22; 6. 8. 1141b29-1142a10.

56. See citations in note 74, chap. 2.

57. See 2. 3. 1104b24-26; 5. 10. 1137b5-32.

58. See 2. 2. 1104a12-26; 2. 6-9; 3. 7. 1116a4-9; 4. 4; 6. 1. 1138b19-21. Aristotle is careful to point out that we need to distinguish between the mean taken abstractly as an objective norm for all men and the mean taken relative to individual agents (see 2. 6. 1106a30-b7). Even in the first sense, the mean usually cannot be stated with mathematical exactness; it admits of exceptions; and it cannot be applied to every kind of action in the same way nor to some actions at all. Consequently, the notion of the mean is not sufficient as a norm for right action. See 1. 7. 1098a26-32; 2. 2. 1103b34-1104a10; 2. 6. 1106a26-1107a27; 2. 7. 1107b4-6; 2. 8. 1109a1-12; 5. 3. 1131a10-19; 5. 4. 1132a17-24; 5. 5. 1133b30-1134a13; 6. 1. 1138b19-34; 9. 10. 1170b29-33. We risk confusion if we translate *meson* as "moderation," as, for example, Hardie and Ostwald occasionally do. Aristotle is not arguing for lukewarm (or "watery") lovers nor for half-hearted warriors. He in fact argues that in one sense the right manner of acting is an extreme, requiring us to withhold no effort in order to act well. See 2. 6. 1107a7-8; 8. 6. 1158a12; 9. 8. 1169a18-33; 9. 10. 1171a10-13; *Pol*. 2. 4. 1262b15-22.

59. See, e.g., 5. 2. 1130b17-25; 8. 1. 1155a23ff. The close relation between the paradigmatically good man and the notion of the mean has been described in detail by Theodore James Tracy in his *Physiological Theory and the Doctrine of the Mean in Plato and Aristotle*. Tracy shows that for both Plato and Aristotle the notion of the mean originated in a physiological view that health for complex organisms like man consists in the constituents being blended and maintained in proper proportion, to a mean, so that the

organism functions naturally and well. The *mesotēs* of moral excellence, then consists in a person's functioning well, i.e. in his ability to judge moral matters correctly and in his disposition (*hexis*) to take pleasure only in acting rightly. See pp. 157-343 of Tracy's book; also *Ph.* 7. 3. 246a10-248a9; also the citations in note 67 below.

60. See 6. 1. 1138b19-34.

61. See 2. 2. 1103b32; 2. 6. 1106b28-1107a1; 2. 9. 1109a24-b23; 5. 9. 1137a9-27; 6. 1. 1138b19-34. For a discussion of moral sensitivity, see chap. 6.

62. 4. 5. 1126a33-b4; cf. 2. 9. 1109b14-26; 3. 1. 1110b7-8; 5. 9. 1137a12-17.

63. See, e.g., 9. 2.

64. 4. 6. 1126b27; cf. 22-28.

65. 4. 6. 1126b29-30; cf. 28-35.

66. Terminological agreement can conceal substantial disagreement over content. For this reason parables have great value, and casuistry is not without merit.

67. 3. 4. 1113a33; cf. 1. 7. 1098a7-15; 1. 8. 1099a22-23; 3. 4. 1113a24-b2; 9. 4. 1166a12-17; 9. 9. 1170a14-16; 10. 4. 1174b14-23; 10. 5. 1176a10-29; 10. 6. 1176b25-27; *Metaph.* 11. 6. 1062b33-1063a11.

68. D. J. Allan, *The Philosophy of Aristotle*, 2d ed., p. 127.

69. See 2. 8. 1108b13-27.

70. See *Rh.* 1. 1. 1354a36-b20; *Pol.* 3. 9. 1280a9-23; 3. 15. 1286a17-31; 3. 16. 1287a20-b30; Plato *Apology* 19a, 34-36. There are other reasons which also led Aristotle to this conclusion. He believed the tactics of lawyers are too often puerile and corrupt. He also believed that the deliberate speed with which cases usually are heard in court is incompatible with the long deliberations necessary for framing good laws (see 5. 1. 1129b19-25). Moreover, the judgments of men can be and frequently are clouded by their passions and personal considerations; "when it come to pleasure we cannot act as unbiased judges" (2. 9. 1109b8-9), for we tend to judge according to our own characteristics, whether we are good men or not (see 2. 8. 1108b15-27). So "a brave man seems reckless in relation to a coward, but in relation to a reckless man he seems cowardly" (2. 8. 1108b18-20; cf. *Pol.* 3. 9. 1280a13-21; 3. 15. 1286a19-20; 3. 16. 1287a42-b3). Aristotle concludes "that well-drawn laws should themselves define all the points they possibly can and leave as few as may be to the decision of the judges" (*Rh.* 1. 1. 1354a32-33; Roberts). What must be left to the courts is the determination of the individual facts and their importance to each case.

71. *Pol.* 3. 16. 1287a28-31; cf. *Eth. Nic.* 5. 6. 1134a35-b6; 10. 9. 1180a21-22; *Rh.* 1. 1. 1354a16-31.

72. 6. 4. 1140a5; cf. 1-23; also 5. 1. 1129a12-14; 5. 9. 1137a12-26; 6. 2. 1139b2-5; 6. 5. 1140b1-7, 20-30; *Pol.* 1. 4. 1254a1-17.

73. See 7. 12. 1153a25-26.

4

On the Inside:
Practical Reasoning—
Deliberation and Choice

In the second chapter we saw the two-ply nature of human action, and we inventoried the items in each dimension. In the third chapter we examined in more detail the outside of action; we saw that Aristotle distinguishes between classes of action on the basis of their objective characteristics. We now need to turn to the inside of action to see how our efficacy as agents should be understood and what, on the inside of action, is of moral significance.

Because men can engage in radically different kinds of activities, Aristotle argues, we have good grounds to construe the human agent as a complex, with several powers or faculties.[1] Man has the power to eat and to grow; he has desires; and he has the ability to reason. Desires form a middle ground between the completely irrational (the 'nutritive' or 'vegetative' soul) and the completely rational (*nous* or *logos*).[2] Because they are not themselves rational, desires can operate contrary to the direction of reason, but they also are susceptible to control by reason.[3]

We have also seen that what distinguishes specifically human actions from other actions is the directing presence of intelligence. Since we can engage in both theoretical and in practical activity, Aristotle suggests that we think of the intellect as having two distinct functions (*erga*) and thus as being two faculties, one the scientific (*to epistēmonikon*), the other the calculative or deliberative (*to logistikon*). The best state or excellence (*aretē*) of each kind of thinking consists in its having those qualities or characteristics (*hexeis*) which make it good and able to perform its own special functions well.[4] When brought to perfection, the scientific faculty attains theoretical wisdom (*sophia*), consisting in mastery of speculative truth.[5] Aristotle calls the perfection of the calculative faculty 'practical wisdom' (*phronēsis*), and this and the following chapters will be devoted to its explication.[6]

Our agency is not explicable only in terms of thinking; we must also be capable of desiring.[7] If we are indifferent to or content with our situation, we have no reason to act; apart from desires, our thinking remains theoretical.[8] Today, as Yves Simon has pointed out, the expression "wishful thinking" suggests that reasoning somehow is contaminated when it is influenced by desires and wishes.[9] But the kind of reasoning which is practical must be affective. This complexity of our agency leads Aristotle to hold that practical excellence requires not only that our reasoning be true but also that our desires be good.[10] Our predominant desires gradually firm into qualities (*hexeis*) of character (*ēthos*), and the ideal, moral excellence (*ethikē aretē*), consists in a man desiring what he should as he should.[11]

Practical wisdom and moral excellence are but aspects of the same ideal moral agent, and one cannot exist without the other. Yet we can more clearly set out the special nature of each by first considering them separately. In this chapter we will be concerned with understanding how reasoning enters into and influences practice through deliberation and choice, and with seeing why reasoning of this kind is distinctively practical, not theoretical. The doctrines in this chapter are not a complete explication of Aristotle's thoughts about the nature and operation of practical reason, but they are a further step in that direction.

DELIBERATION AND CHOICE

We can act carelessly, passionately, impetuously, absentmindedly, and from habit; most situations are so familiar that we do not have to think about how to act, and then we act as we characteristically act in such situations.[12] Aristotle does not argue that every human action requires a special decision, but he does hold that genuinely human action is not merely a mechanical reaction to some stimulus, even when it is habitual action. A human agent normally will have a certain minimal awareness of self, of the situation of which he is a part, of possible courses of action open to him, and of ways of valuing those possibilities. Unless there are some special reasons to the contrary, he always is in a position in which he can say what he is doing if he so wishes.

The best approach to examining the role of reason in action is through an analysis of those actions in which that role is neither obscured by habituation nor marred by defection. These are choices (*proaireseis*) which are immediately preceded by a thoughtful inquiry into the alternatives, an inquiry which, when successful, concludes to our choice, i.e., to our acting as we have decided.[13] Aristotle again emphasizes that actions arise out of a complex of both reason and desire by defining choice as 'desiring thought' (*orektikos nous*) or, alternatively, as 'rational (or deliberate) desire' (*orexis bouleutikē* or *dianoetikē*).[14]

Not every inquiry is practical, for we sometimes seek only to know, and so Aristotle gives practical inquiry a special title, deliberation (*bouleusis*).[15] He also gives the term a technical meaning by restricting it and its conclusion, choice, to the kind of practical inquiry which concerns the means to ends already desired or wished for. The subject matter of both deliberation and choice is not and cannot be the ends of action—the pleasant and painful nor the morally good—but what is possible and effective.[16] Given this restriction, deliberation is possible only when three conditions obtain.

(1) We only deliberate about how to act when we already desire something we see as good in some sense for ourselves and which we think we can attain by acting. Desires or wishes, therefore, are the starting point of deliberation.[17]

(2) It would be irrational to deliberate (but not to daydream) about how to act, if we did not believe there are genuine alternatives open to us. We do not, for example, deliberate about facts; rather, we discover them. If a particular course of action is either impossible or unavoidable, there clearly is no point in deliberating over it; we can deliberate only about what we believe is changeable—"the sphere of coming-to-be," futurities not yet fully determined.[18] Further, not every possibility is a possibility for us, and we only deliberate about what we believe can be done by our own agency or with the help of others.[19] If, during our inquiry, we find our way

completely blocked, there obviously is no point in continuing an inquiry in that direction.[20]

(3) We do not deliberate about predictable matters with which we are familiar, but only about those which present uncertainties.[21] The more our uncertainty, the greater is our need to deliberate; and the more serious the issues, the more we feel the need to seek the advice of others.[22] Sometimes we need to find out what the means are or which is the easiest or best; sometimes we need to learn how a means can be achieved or acquired; and other times we need to learn how a means is to be used.[23]

The aim and conclusion of deliberating is choice, which consists in our immediately acting upon the basis of our deliberation. All reasoning about future possible action is practical, but only the ultimate judgment has the character of an imperative legislating for what should be done and how it should be done. Since it is our own reason commanding us how to achieve what we already want, there is no hiatus between command and execution. Once made, a choice is not merely preliminary to our acting; it is the beginning of our action, even if working it through takes days or weeks or years.[24]

To summarize, thinking becomes practically efficacious when, under the stimulus of desires or wishes, it informs our physical movements; and it is the directing presence of our thinking that makes our movements specifically human actions. Deliberation is not only an ingredient in our actions, it also is prior to them, for we do not begin to act until we conclude our deliberating. When he discusses what it is to have the power (*dunamis*) to act (*poiein*), Aristotle specifically rejects the suggestion that we

> add the proviso that there be no external hindrance; for what has the power has the power of acting, and it has this, not in all circumstances, but in those circumstances in which external hindrances are by definition excluded.[25]

In effect, Aristotle is again saying that the most fundamental notion in agency is that of power, and until power is exercised (the outside of agency), an action has not yet been done.

The Logical Form of Deliberation and Choice

Like all genuine thought, practical thinking involves generalities.[26] Every human action is describable in terms of a generalized rule—a rule which not merely subsumes some particular action under it but which has an efficacious role in the production of the action. Books 3, 4, 5, 8, and 9 of the *Ethics* are full of such rules. More, since actions consist of particulars, practical reasoning must also take them into account.[27] The deliberation preceding a choice, therefore, includes at least one universal and one particular judgment.

All discursive reasoning, whether theoretical or practical, is done correctly only if our inferences have a valid logical form.[28] Aristotle describes correct deliberation, therefore, in terms of a model which has come to be called the 'practical syllogism', in which a universal (a practical rule setting out the end to be attained by acting) is related to particulars (of an actual situation).[29] He writes:

> . . . the one premise or judgment is universal and the other
> deals with the particular (for the first tells us that such and
> such kind of man should do such and such kind of act, and
> the second that *this* is an act of the kind meant, and I a
> person of the type intended).[30]

Again, "one of the premises, the universal, is a current belief, while the other involves particular facts which fall under the domain" of practical perceptiveness (*aisthēsis*).[31]

Although a demonstrative syllogism may contain only universal terms, Aristotle states that the chief difference between theoretical and practical thinking is not to be found in their logical form but in the purpose of each kind of reasoning:

> Apparently the same thing happens [when one reasons
> practically] as when one thinks and forms an inference about
> immovable objects. But in the latter case, the end is
> speculation (for when you have conceived the two premises,
> you immediately conceive and infer the conclusion); but in
> the former case the conclusion drawn from the two premises

> becomes an action. . . . Now when the two premises are combined, just as in theoretic reasoning the mind is compelled to *affirm* the resulting conclusion, so in the case of practical reasoning [*poiētikais*] you are forced at once to *do* it.[32]

The minor, therefore, sets out what is possible and, when joined by the universal setting out some good attainable by action, initiates an action which is the conclusion.[33] As we saw in Chapter 2, we may completely misapprehend the nature of a person's action unless we understand the reasoning which, on the inside, has led to and shaped it, making his action the kind of action it is.[34]

When he elucidates the form of correct deliberation, Aristotle does not argue that every man who deliberates correctly does so linearly, in neat proofs; nor does he maintain that an agent must deliberate about and explicitly formulate a maxim for each of his actions. What he is elucidating here is the awareness involved in rational agency. A rational agent normally is aware of what he is doing, and, if he were to describe his own action completely, he would tell why he acted as he did (the rule under which he acted) and explain which particulars he took into account and why. But a man can be an expert practitioner without being able to articulate his practice in a convincing generalized way.[35]

This brief examination of the logic of practical reasoning tells us two things. First, the logical form of practical reasoning is substantially the same as that of theoretical reasoning.[36] Second, although theoretical reasoning is aimed at knowing and understanding and practical reasoning is aimed at acting, there is this radical similarity between them: just as believing something to be true *means* assenting to it, so also believing something to be good *means* acting upon that belief when it is appropriate to do so and when we are not prevented from doing so.[37] The only difference between the two uses of reason might appear to be their respective uses; although both theoretical and practical reasoning aim at truth, each has its own kind of truth: "What affirmation and negation are in the realm of thought, pursuit and avoidance are in the realm of desire."[38] Today we are accustomed to thinking of theory and practice as two moments within the same sort of activity; one is "pure" and the

other "applied" science. But Aristotle argues that the practical and
theoretical uses of reason have such radically disparate subject
matters that there can be no significant relation between them.[39]
We will now examine that claim, and in doing so see another reason
for the distinctiveness of practical reason, beyond the fact that
deliberation concludes to an action and not a belief.

PRACTICAL REASONING AND THEORETICAL REASONING

Every deliberation is an inquiry, but not every inquiry is a deliberation;[40] for significantly different kinds of objects will entail different
ends to inquiry and important differences in the kinds of knowledge
appropriate to each.[41]

The objects of theoretical inquiry are entities and laws which
are eternal, immutable, and necessary, and they permit us to aim at
knowledge which is exact, necessary and universally true.[42] Deliberation, on the other hand, is concerned with changing what is
mutable, and it obviously makes no sense to deliberate about what is
immutable and eternally and necessarily what it is. Moreover, the
plasticity of the contingencies involved in practice—an indefinite
number of possible combinations of varying particularities—
prevents practical principles from being universal and necessary
laws, no matter how carefully they might be stated. At best,
practical reasoning can give us only a sketch, which holds good
"only as a general rule but not always;" and particular judgments are
often the more accurate for their being particular.[43] The practitioner always needs to take into account the circumstances in
which he finds himself, and there is always a possibility that he may
need to formulate *ad hoc* rules or make an exception to some general
practical rule in order to act as he should.[44]

Aristotle's doctrine is clear: there is and can be no such thing as
'practical theory' in the sense of reason legislating for practice on the
basis of exact and universally true norms of conduct. Theoretical
knowledge is, by its very nature, useless to practice;[45] and practical
knowledge is much more of an art than a science: the neophyte must
practice how to produce an art-object, and the master artisan is a
man who has expertise in how to use his tools on materials which

never quite duplicate themselves. He knows from experience when and where and how to apply the rules of his craft, and he knows, too, when to ignore and break them, since they do not and cannot define his expertise.[46]

Learning how to deal with the particularities involved in action demands the sort of familiarity which comes only with experience; it must "grow to be a part of [a man], and that takes time."[47] So the advice of older men on practical matters has the presumption of truth without further support, simply because of their experience.[48] Writing to this point, Aristotle points out that

> we see experienced men succeeding even better than those who know the reasons [*logoi*], but who lack experience. The reason is that experience, like action or production, deals with things severally as concrete individuals, whereas art deals with them generally. Thus, a physician does not cure 'man' (except incidentally), but he cures Callias, Socrates, or some other individual with a proper name, each of whom happens to be a man. If, then, someone lacking experience, but knowing the general principles [*logoi*] of the art, sizes up a situation as a whole, he will often, because he is ignorant of the individuals within that whole, miss the mark and fail to cure; for it is the individual that must be cured.[49]

We might still want to object that every practical enterprise requires *some* theoretical knowledge (even in the Aristotelian sense), that the practice of politics requires a good deal of information about both the natural and the social sciences, the practice of medicine requires knowledge of physics and the biological sciences, and the practice of engineering requires knowledge of mathematics. Aristotle's own ethical doctrines presuppose fundamental distinctions which belong to his theoretical writings, as the citations in every chapter of this book show.

Aristotle admits that the practitioner cannot get along without some knowledge of the nature of things.[50] But such knowledge is only quasi-theoretical, for it is valuable only as an instrumentality, only insofar as it helps guide practice.

Socrates . . . thought that knowledge of virtue to be the end
. . , for he thought all the virtues to be kinds of knowledge, so
that to know justice and to be just came simultaneously; for
the moment that we have learned geometry or architecture
we are architects and geometers. Therefore, he inquired
what virtue is, not how or from what it arises. This is
correct with regard to theoretical knowledge, for there is no
other part of astronomy or physics or geometry except
knowing and contemplating the nature of the things which
are the subjects of those sciences; though nothing prevents
them from being in an incidental way useful to us for much
that we cannot do without. But the end of the productive [or
practical] sciences is different from science and knowledge,
e.g., health from medical science, law and order (or
something of the sort) from political science. Now to know
anything that is noble is itself noble; but regarding virtue, at
least, not to know what it is, but to know out of what it
arises is most precious. For we do not wish to know what
bravery is but to be brave, nor what justice is but to be just,
just as we wish to be in health rather than to know what
being in health is, and to have our body in good condition
rather than to know what good condition is.[51]

There are other reasons for Aristotle's arguing that the knowledge necessary for good practice is not applied theoretical knowledge. For one, the natural sciences investigate, not individuals, but
the laws and principles governing changes in individuals; consequently, the theoretical sciences do not try to understand or
explain what is good or bad for any individual.[52] Moreover, as we
have seen, practical knowledge simply cannot attain the universality and precision of theoretical knowledge. The analysis of
practice can yield some doctrines which seem to hold without
exception, e.g., the nature of moral character, but practical knowledge cannot give us precise and universally valid rules for how to
act.[53] Moral thinking, as C. J. Rowe writes,

is categorised as non-scientific simply because it cannot lay
down exact prescriptions for individual cases, which must

always involve the consideration of particular circumstances; or, in other words, because what it can lay down must inevitably be too general to be sufficient in itself as a guide for action.[54]

The final reason why moral knowledge is distinct from theoretical knowledge is the former's dependence on affective experience. Aristotle tells us that "a boy can become a mathematician," for mathematical objects are theoretical abstractions which can be mastered with little or no experience with the world, but "a young man is not equipped," because of his inexperience, to profit from discussions about practice.[55] Knowledge is practical only if it has an effect on practice, and we do not get that effect merely by reading, or by listening to lectures, or by arguing; practical knowledge must originate in and be based on practice, on doing.[56] A person with good practical experience is one who has learned how to act rightly from acting rightly. This means that he has developed the right emotional characteristics (*hexeis*) necessary for his understanding and judging moral questions.[57]

In the next chapter we will examine Aristotle's analysis of the nature of moral character, and then, in Chapter 6, we will see how the pervasive influence of character on practical reasoning also prevents that reasoning from being theoretical.

Notes to Chapter 4

1. See 1. 13; 6. 1. 1139a4-15. Aristotle tries to sidestep a problem familiar to Plato and students at his Academy: how the soul can be a principle of unity and still itself be composed of parts. Twice Aristotle states that the student of ethics and politics need not concern himself with whether the various human faculties are distinct ontologically or merely conceptually (see 1. 13. 1102a13-32, b24-25). However, the manner in which we understand the relations between theoretical reason, practical reason, and appetition will have immense consequences for the way in which we understand the relations between their excellences—theoretical and practical wisdom and moral excellence. Aristotle's most mature psychology emphasizes man's organic unity by defining the soul as the 'actuality' (the *energeia* or *entelecheia*) of the body (see *De an.* 1. 1, 4; 2. 1, 4). But this doctrine did not have sufficient impact on *Eth. Nic.*, for Aristotle eventually reverts in the later books to an earlier view in which man is defined finally only or primarily in terms of reason (*nous*). Because Aristotle did not, at least in the notes we have, always admit that emotions are as much a part of man as his reason, he also tends to portray their excellences, moral goodness and practical wisdom, as distinct, although that division cannot finally be maintained. On these problems, see chaps. 6 and 10.

2. By 'soul' (*psuchē*) Aristotle means 'life' or, for human beings, 'conscious and self-conscious life'. The nature of the soul is defined by its special or proper function (*ergon*) and this in turn is defined by its peculiar teleology (see 1. 7. 1097b21-1098a18). The functions of the vegetative soul either are subsumed by appetition or they operate automatically, and so they are irrelevant to specifically human practice. Consequently, Aristotle does not consider this lowest part of the human soul any further in the *Ethics;* see 1. 13. 1102b11-12; 6. 12. 1144a9-11.

3. See 1. 7. 1098a3-4; 1. 13. 1102b12-1103a3; 6. 1. 1139a3-4; *Eth. Eud.* 2. 8. 1224a23-30; *Pol.* 7. 14. 1333a17-18. See also W. W. Fortenbaugh, *Aristotle on Emotion*.

4. See 2. 6. 1106a13-21; 6. 1. 1139a5-17; *Ph.* 7. 3. 246a10-247a4; see also *Eth. Eud.* 2. 1. 1218b37ff., where Aristotle emphasizes that the excellence of a thing *is* its proper function. In 1. 13. 1103a5-6, 6. 3. 1139b14-17, and 6. 6., Aristotle lists not two but six excellences of the intellect: art (*technē*), scientific knowledge (*epistēmē*), understanding (*sunesis*), practical wisdom (*phronēsis*), philosophic wisdom (*sophia*), and intuitive reason (*nous*). Art, understanding, and practical wisdom are excellences of the calculative faculty or practical reason; scientific knowledge and philosophic wisdom, of the scientific faculty or theoretical reason; and intuitive reasoning is exer-

cised by both theoretical and practical reason, its functioning being adaptable to the particular needs of each use of reason.

5. See chap. 9.

6. For now it is sufficient to describe practical wisdom as enabling us to attain what is unconditionally good for us as human agents. See 1. 13. 1103a4-10; 6. 1. 1139a5-17; 6. 2. 1139b11-13; 6. 5. 1140a24-32, b4-5, 20-30; 6. 11. 1143b14-16; *Pol.* 7. 13. 1331b27-38; *Metaph.* 6. 1. 1025b21-24. Excellences (*aretai*) of the *psuchē* are instrinsically good apart from any further good but each in fact does contribute to the good life (*eudaimonia*) (see 6. 12. 1144a1-3; 6. 13. 1145a2-7). *Phronēsis* is sometimes translated as "prudence," but we are too infected today by the Kantian doctrine of the amoral nature of prudence to use this term to refer to a quality which is essentially moral in nature.

7. See 6. 2. 1139a33-b5.

8. There are two ways in which having emotions is a necessary precondition for our being human agents. (1) If we were to find someone always and completely apathetic, we would have to conclude that something must be disastrously wrong with him; he cannot exercise even the agency possible to animals and children, much less that of adult humans (see 3. 2. 1111b12-13; 3. 11. 1119a6-11). (2) There are some things and some situations which ought to be fearful or pleasurable to *any* man, and again, there would be something fundamentally defective about a man who did not feel the appropriate emotions in such cases (see 3. 1. 1111a30-32; 3. 7. 1115b7-9, 24-28; 3. 11. 1119a6-11).

9. Yves R. Simon, "Introduction to the Study of Practical Wisdom," *The New Scholasticism*, 34, pp. 23-24.

10. See 6. 1. 1138b21-34; 6. 2. 1139a23-30; 6. 12. 1144a23-36; 6. 13. 1144b14-25.

11. See 1. 13. 1103a4-10; 2. 3-6; also note 5 in chap. 5.

12. See 3. 2. 1111b7-10, 1112a13-15, b2; 3. 8. 1117a17-22; 5. 8. 1135b19-25; 7. 7. 1150b18-27.

13. See 3. 2-3; 6. 9. In some passages, Aristotle portrays choices as always immediately preceded by deliberation (see e. g., 3. 2. 1112a13-17; 5. 8. 1135b8-11). This cannot be correct, for then habituated actions, which require no deliberation, could not count as chosen actions. As we shall see in the next chapter, a man is responsible for the actions which habituate him and he therefore is also responsible both for his own character and for his characteristic ways of acting (see, e.g., 3. 5. 1114a3-30). This doctrine can hold only if habituated actions were once preceded by deliberation, even though that deliberation is now far removed in time. Moreover, one of the conditions necessary for moral excellence is that a man must choose to act as

he does; yet the morally best man is so habituated to acting rightly that he does so characteristically (see, e.g., 3. 8. 1117a18-22). Aristotle cannot hold these two doctrines without also allowing habituated actions to be considered to be choices. D. J. Allan argues that there is development within Aristotle's analysis of chosen actions, a loosening of what Aristotle first took to be a constant and close connection between choice and deliberation. This seems the best way in which to account for Aristotle's later account of those choices in which deliberation drops out and a man intuitively applies the practical principles he has adopted to the various sets of circumstances in which he finds himself. See Allan's "The Practical Syllogism," in *Autour d'Aristote*, pp. 325-340; also his *The Philosophy of Aristotle*, 2nd ed., p. 132.

14. See 6. 2. 1139b4-5; also 3. 2. 1112a16; 3. 3. 1113a10-11; 6. 2. 1139a23-b6; *De an.* 3. 10. 433a10ff. Choice cannot be analyzed adequately as nonrational appetite (*epithumia*), but sheer appetite can account for the actions of nonrational agents as well as for the lapses of the morally weak. See 3. 2. 1111b11-18.

15. See 3. 3. 1112b23-24, 33; 6. 9. 1142a31-32. "Deliberation" and "calculation" are simply different names for the same sort of activity (see 6. 1. 1139a13). Aristotle makes other contrasts (see 3. 2. 1111b11-1112a13). Choosing is not the same as wishing, for we can wish for things within no man's power or at least not within our own; wishes can be completely inefficacious, and they are directed at ends rather than at means (see 3. 2. 1111b11-30). Neither is choosing the same as conjecturing, which requires little or no reasoning (see 6. 9. 1142b3-6). Nor is choice a kind of opinion or knowledge. Like wishes, opinions and knowledge can be had on matters not susceptible to change (see 6. 9. 1142a35-b1). Also choices and opinions each have their own unique ends: a choice is called "good" or "bad," depending, among other things, on the correctness and effectiveness of the chosen action, while opinions are called "true" or "false," depending on how accurately they set out "what a thing is, whom it will benefit, or how" (3. 2. 1112a4). Finally, there is no necessary correspondence between one's theoretical opinions and his character, while choices do influence and finally determine character (see 2. 4. 1105b9-17; 3. 2. 1111b31-1112a12; 6. 5. 1140b12-17).

16. See 3. 2. 1111b17-18, 25-30; 3. 3. 1112b12-16, 34-35 and 1113a3-14; 3. 4. 1113a15; 3. 5. 1113b3-6; 6. 2. 1139a31-36, b6-12; 6. 7. 1141b8-12; 6. 9. 1142b28-34; *Eth. Eud.* 2. 11; *De an.* 3. 10. 433a13-17. Although deliberation, in Aristotle's technical sense, may be only over means, the functioning of practical reason cannot be limited to deliberation; some of our most serious practical inquiries center on what our ends should be, as chaps. 1 and 10 of Aristotle's *Ethics* claim. On this topic, see chap. 6.

17. See 3. 3. 1112a21-30, b12-16; 6. 2. 1139b33; 6. 7. 1141b10-12; *Motu an.* 6. 700b22-28; 7. 701a7-25.

18. 6. 12. 1143b20; see also 3. 2. 1111b20-22, 29-32; 3. 3. 1112a18-30, b1-3, 34-1113a2; 6. 1. 1139a6-14; 6. 2. 1139b6-11; 6. 4. 1140a1-2, 12-13; 6. 5. 1140a32-b1; 6. 7. 1141b10-11; 6. 9. 1142b11-15; *Ph.* 1. 7. 190b5-16; 3. 3. 202a17-18; *Rh.* 1. 2. 1357a4-7.

19. See 3. 2. 1111b25-26; 3. 3. 1112a30-35, b26-28, 33-34 and 1113a9-12.

20. See 3. 3. 1112b24-26; 6. 5. 1140a33-34.

21. See 3. 3. 1112b1-9; 6. 9. 1142b1-3. Most situations we face are a normal part of our everyday life; since there is little or no need to deliberate about them, we spontaneously act as we are accustomed. Deliberation, therefore is episodic, occurring only in situations of sufficient novelty that we cannot wholly rely on our habits to carry us through. See 3. 3. 1112b4-9; 3. 8. 1117a17-23; *Motu an.* 7. 701a25-30.

22. See 3. 3. 1112b9-11; 6. 9. 1142b3-7, 26-28.

23. See 3. 3. 1112b15-32.

24. See 3. 3. 1112b24-27, 1113a3-12; 6. 2. 1139a31, b3-5; 6. 8. 1141b27-28; 6. 9. 1143a7-8; 7. 3. 1147a24-32, b9-10; *Motu an.* 7. 701a20-34. This is necessarily the case, but not a case of compulsion; see "Third Contrast" in chap. 2.

25. *Metaph.* 9. 5. 1048a17-20 (Hope). It is surprising to find W. F. R. Hardie interpreting Aristotle as holding that, because an agent may find his chosen action frustrated by some unforeseen circumstance, physical activities of an agent should be regarded as the *result* of his action, and the action itself is "not the causing of a change but the willing of a change" (*Aristotle's Ethical Theory*, p. 170). R.-A. Gauthier errs in the other direction, I think, when he writes that Aristotle "has no conception of an intention which is not expressed in action. . . . Only the desire for the end which expresses itself in action is moral intention, and this is why virtue necessarily implies the decisive intention which is *probairesis* and the exterior act which is *praxis* (*E. N.* X, 8, 1178a34-b1). The first does not occur without the second" ("On the Nature of Aristotle's Ethics," in *Aristotle's Ethics: Issues and Interpretation*, pp. 17-18). Although Aristotle holds that effectiveness is a criterion for *good* deliberation, he does not deny that frustrated choices are choices, albeit frustrated ones (see, e.g., 7. 3. 1147a28-31).

26. See chap. 2, "Third Contrast."

27. See 6. 7. 1141b14-22.

28. Aristotle himself does not explicitly make this claim for practical thinking, and his remarks about the logical form of deliberation are few and scattered; consequently not all commentators agree with my interpretation

in this section. D. J. Allan, for example, holds that the practical syllogism should be understood as "a psychological account of action in accordance with principles . . . [it is] an erroneous view, that the syllogism is meant to be a kind of reasoning which precedes actions and informs us what we have to do" ("The Practical Syllogism," pp. 325n, 336n). For a similar view that the practical syllogism "ought not to be regarded as part of practical reasoning at all," see John M. Cooper, *Reason and Human Good in Aristotle*, p. 51; cf. 23-5. I find it difficult to agree with such views, for, as Hardie points out, Aristotle does explicitly connect the practical syllogism with delibera- tion, e.g., in 6. 8. 1143a20-23 and 6. 9. 1142b22-25 (see Hardie, *Aristotle's Ethical Theory*, p. 249). Aristotle characteristically explains practical error in terms of defective deliberation, schematizable syllogistically, and he argues that when a man reasons incorrectly but still concludes to the right action, he is only lucky. Allan also holds that because deliberation is concerned not with what is good but what is possible, it is "not a distinctive operation of the practical reason"; practical reasoning is "the thought displayed in action, not that which precedes action" (p. 328, 340). Yet Aristotle specifically says that calculation is neither a kind of opinion nor theoretical thinking, and in the next section of this chapter we shall see why he takes this position (see also 6. 9. 1142b7-23; 6. 12. 1144a23-37). In the next chapter we shall see how character influences deliberation, making it practical (see also 1. 3. 1095a1- 11; 2. 4. 1105b9-17; 3. 2. 1111b31-1112a13; 3. 5. 1114a14-18). The fact that habituated choices do not require deliberation does not rule out the fact that there are still choices requiring prior deliberation. Consequently, practical reasoning needs to be understood both as the reasoning which sometimes immediately precedes and determines action *and* as thought expressed in and controlling action, whether actions follow from deliberation or from settled dispositions. Ando accurately reflects Aristotle's doctrine when he takes the practical syllogism to be, not an account of the psychology of deliberation, but as a reflective reconstruction and justification after the fact; see Takatura Ando, *Aristotle's Theory of Practical Cognition*, 3rd rev. ed., p. 230.

29. One of the most critical portions of Aristotle's elucidation of practical reasoning concerns the nature and genesis of what is here called 'the universal premise'. Here we are examining it only as a truth-functional enunciation of right reason, but it generally is also the expression of more or less settled dispositions, and it generally is not enunciated because the experienced agent's judgment is more accurately described as an act of intuition than as inferential reasoning. On this, see chap. 6; also 6. 12. 1144a29-36; *De an.* 3. 11. 434a19-22.

30. *De an.* 3. 11. 434a16-19 (Smith); cf. *Eth. Nic.* 5. 7. 1135a6-13; 7. 3. 1146b36-1147a7. Although Aristotle discusses the form of practical reason- ing in terms of a single major and a single minor, deliberation, if

schematized, may involve several minors or even a chain of syllogisms until the means to an end is made sufficiently plain. See 3. 3. 1112b16-19.

31. 7. 3. 1147a26-27; cf. 6. 8. 1142a23-30; 6. 11. 1143a33-b5; *Metaph*. 4. 4. 1006a5-8. It is misleading, I think, to translate *aisthēsis* here as "sense perception." See "Practical Wisdom and Moral Philosophy" in chap. 6.

32. *Motu an*. 7. 701a8-12 (Forster) and *Eth. Nic*. 7. 3. 1147a27-28 (Rackham); see also 7. 3. 1147b9-10; *Motu an*. 7. 701a13-37; 8. 702a16-20.

33. See 3. 3. 1112b24-27; 7. 3. 1147b9-10; *De an*. 3. 11. 434a16-22; *Motu an*. 7. 701a23-25. As support for the view that practical reason must not be limited to determining means but also consider the ends of action (see note 16 above), D. J. Allan interprets the sentence, "The premisses which lead to the doing of something are of two kinds, through the good and through the possible" (*Motu an*. 7. 701a24-25; Forster), to apply only to the major premise of the practical syllogism. He then argues that Aristotle offers us two kinds of practical syllogisms: when the major is "of the possible" and expresses "the desirability of some End," then practical reasoning calculates about the means of achieving the end; and when the major is "of the good" and expresses a general rule to be realized in action, then practical reason subsumes particular actions under that rule, realizing and exemplifying it. See his "The Practical Syllogism," pp. 330-331, 336. Briefly, I believe Allan strains the meaning of the passage cited; the most obvious interpretation is that Aristotle is discussing kinds of premises, not kinds of syllogisms, and saying that the major enunciates the good and the minor(s) the possible.

34. It is, of course, always possible for a spectator to misinterpret what an agent is trying to do and why he is trying to do it.

35. See 10. 9. 1180b28ff. Plato's *Laches* gives an excellent example of such a man. Laches obviously is a brave man and he knows well how brave men act in situations calling for courage; yet when he is asked for a generalized description of courageous action, he becomes virtually incoherent (see 194A-B). There can be morally good men like Laches because (1) not everyone is equally adept at explaining what he knows; a good practitioner must have other skills before he is also a good teacher; (2) the ultimate recourse in explaining and defending practical rules (and their exceptions) is to experience, and to a great degree such appeals do not lend themselves to elaborate defenses; (3) matters of practice present such great variations that practical rules do not always hold, and it is always possible to think of exceptions to them, which are not genuine counter-examples since, Aristotle argues, the rules cannot hold with genuine universality.

36. This may be one reason why Aristotle does not offer a systematic examination of the logic of practical deliberation. His insistence on practical reason as a distinct faculty should signal us that an analysis of its logical form

78 MORALITY AND THE GOOD LIFE

cannot account for the fact that deliberation terminates in an action, not a belief, any more than our agency can be explained only in terms of our ability to reason.

37. There is no doctrine more crucial than this to Aristotle's analysis of the relation between practical reason and action.

38. 6. 2. 1139a21-22; see also 23-30, b12-14; 3. 3. 1112b23-24.

39. This was not always Aristotle's view. In his monograph, *The Eudemian and Nicomachean Ethics: A Study in the Development of Aristotle's Thought*, C. J. Rowe points out that in the earlier *Eudemian Ethics*, Aristotle followed Plato in using the single term *phronēsis* to refer to both speculative and practical wisdom; "the only difference is one of end; practical thinking aims at something outside itself, speculative thinking does not" (p. 67). In the *Nicomachean Ethics* Aristotle swung to the opposite extreme: theoretical and practical thinking must be radically distinct faculties. On this, see also Plato *Philebus* 57e-66b; also Emmanuel M. Michelakis, *Aristotle's Theory of Practical Principles*, pp. 1-6.

40. See 3. 3. 1112b23-24; 6. 9. 1142a31-b15.

41. See 6. 1. 1139a3-17; 6. 7. 1141a22-b22; 6. 8. 1142a12-23; 6. 12. 1143b17-1144a7.

42. See 6. 3. 1139b18-23; 6. 6. 1140b31-1141a3; 6. 7. 1141a9-b3.

43. See 1. 3. 1094b13-27; 1. 7. 1098a26-32; 2. 2. 1103b34-1104a11; 2. 7. 1107a29-32; 3. 3. 1112b1-9; 5. 7. 1134b23-1135a5; 5. 10. 1137b6-33; 6. 5. 1140a32-b3; *Pol.* 2. 8. 1269a10-12; *Metaph.* 11. 8. 1064b30-1065a6. Under some circumstances, actions we consider good in the abstract may turn out to be not good for an individual but harmful. For example, in one case the pursuit of a particular pleasure may be instrumental in a man's generating and developing a desirable character trait; in another case, the pursuit of the same pleasure may be the exercise of a trait a man already has, and in a third case, it may be destructive of that same character trait. See 2. 2. 1104a1-11, 27-b2; 7. 12. 1152b27-32, 1153b17-20; Plato *Statesman* 294a-c; also chap. 3 above.

44. See 1. 3. 1094b13-27; 2. 2. 1104a5-10; 5. 10; 9. 2. 1164b23-1165a13; 10. 9. 1180b7-16; *Metaph.* 6. 2; *Rh.* 1. 13. 1374a18-b23; 1. 15. 1357b3-5. The term Aristotle uses here is *epieikeia*, which literally means "equity"; this doctrine provides a rationale to prevent morality from degenerating into legalistic rigidity, for there are situations in which, if a man is to act rightly, he must *violate* rules. "With the problem of epieikeia . . . we enter upon a section of Aristotle's moral and legal theory for which he can claim sole and first authority. . . . [His] great achievement lies in the fact that he was the first to explain that epieikeia constitutes only the corrective function of law and is not something different from law! . . . Ultimately [*epieikeia*] serves but one purpose: to achieve a true justice that will be both

reasonable and humane." From Max Hamburger, *Morals and Law: The Growth of Aristotle's Legal Theory*, pp. 89, 96, 103; cf. pp. 89-110. Exceptional cases still fall under the intent of the law so that we are not entitled to act as we please.

45. See 6. 7. 1141b3-8; 6. 12. 1143b18-22.

46. See 2. 2. 1104a5-10; *Metaph.* 1. 1. 981a1-25.

47. 7. 3. 1147a22; cf. 6. 12. 1143b23-28; 10. 9. 1080b13-19, 1181a1-3, 9-12.

48. See 6. 8. 1142a12-20; 6. 11. 1143b6-13; 7. 3. 1147a19-22.

49. *Metaph.* 1. 1. 981a14-25 (Hope). Cf. *Eth. Nic.* 1. 6. 1097a11-13; 6. 7. 1141b14-23. Because he is a man whose expertise lies in matters of great abstractness and generality, the theoretician has a tendency to overlook some of the variable particular facts in concrete situations, and so he tends to gain a reputation as a bungler in practical matters, a man who is "absent-minded."

50. See, e. g., 1. 13. 1102a5-25; *Metaph.* 2. 1. 993b21-23; *An. post.* 1. 13. 78b32-79a16. He also seems to admit that matters of practice can be studied philosophically, merely for the sake of knowledge; see *Pol.* 3. 8. 1279b12-16.

51. *Eth. Eud.* 1. 5. 1216b3-26 (Solomon); cf. *Eth. Nic.* 2. 2. 1103b26-31; 6. 13. 1144b17-30.

52. See 6. 12. 1143b18-21; *Metaph.* 3. 2. 996a20-35; 11. 1. 1059a35-40 (but see 13.3 1078a32-b5); *De an.* 3. 9. 432b23-433a8; 3. 10. 433a20-31.

53. Perhaps even this claim is susceptible to some exceptions; see 2. 6. 1106b28-32, 1107a9-15.

54. C. J. Rowe, *The Eudemian and Nicomachean Ethics*, p. 71n1.

55. 6. 8. 1142a17 and 1. 3. 1095a3; cf. 6. 8. 1142a12-20; *Rh.* 2. 12. 1389a2-b11. All intellectual excellences require instruction, and the development of some theoretical knowledge (such as knowledge of natural science) requires also experience (see 2. 1. 1103a15-16), but a different sort of experience than that required for the development of practical knowledge.

56. See 1. 3. 1094b27-1095a11; 1. 4. 1095b2-12; 2. 4. 1105b9-17; 6. 7. 1141b14-20.

57. Note Aristotle's distinction between understanding (*sunesis*) in practical matters and practical wisdom; see 6. 10; also chap. 6 below. The distinction permits Aristotle to hold that we do not ourselves have to be morally excellent persons in order to recognize moral excellence in others.

5

On the Inside:
Skillfulness, Practical Wisdom,
and Moral Excellence

So far we have seen that reason functions in a practical way when it makes definite what must be done to attain a desired goal, and that goal is determined by what we want, so that deliberation and choice concern the means to it. The logic of practical reasoning is not substantially different from the logic of theoretical reasoning, but each sort of reasoning has its own appropriate end, acting or knowing. Yet practical reasoning is not an application of theoretical reasoning because the proper objects of theoretical knowing are not susceptible to change, and deliberation always concerns how we can act on and alter the changeable so as to achieve our ends.

The contrast with theoretical reason has shown the reasons why Aristotle argues that practical reason has its own distinctiveness, but we have not yet seen any justification for thinking that practical reason is, in any common usage of the term, a *moral* faculty. So far our reason has been depicted only as an instrument for guiding and enhancing the power we have as agents. But further analysis of the nature of practical reason leads Aristotle to argue that practical reasoning has two functions, one nonmoral and the other moral. Not surprisingly, these two functions are directly related to the two kinds of practical goods (in the outside dimension of action discussed in Chapter 3) and to the types of activity appropriate to each.

Some kinds of actions are only conditionally or hypothetically good (*ex hupotheseōs*); these are processes which fall under the title of *poiēseis*, makings, and the norm by which they are judged is that of effectiveness. Other kinds of actions are good in an unqualified way (*haplōs*), for their value lies in their doing, not in a product or end state beyond them. These are *praxeis*, actions in the strict sense of morally assessable activities, and the norm for doing such actions rightly has been described in Chapter 3 as 'the mean'. In turn the norm is determined by 'right reason'—the kind of practical reasoning done by the experienced man of high standards (*ho spoudaios*). But the nature of his special excellence has not yet been sufficiently analyzed, and a full account of moral agency has not yet been given.

In this chapter we will develop but not yet complete that analysis. After distinguishing moral from nonmoral practical reasoning, we will consider each of its aspects—the rational and the appetitive—in its ideal form, the rational being practical wisdom and the appetitive being moral excellence. In the chapter following we will consider their relation to each other and also set out the connection between the inside and the outside of morally excellent practice, between good practical characteristics of agents and morally good actions.

PRODUCTIVE SKILL

It is often helpful to elucidate all practical reasoning as an art; in the last chapter we saw that doing so shows why practical reasoning is so radically different from theoretical reasoning. All skills involve the exercise of our calculative faculty, that is, our ability to deliberately act upon and alter what can be other than it is. Skills are developed only through experience, and that experience cannot be caught in absolute and universal rules. Because technical competency is a rational characteristic (*hexis meta logou*), we sometimes speak of a man as wise in his particular area. We also sometimes call a man wise who can deliberate effectively so as to get whatever it is he wants.[1]

Aristotle stresses the importance of knowledge in technical expertise by calling it both the efficient and the formal cause of the product, whatever the product may be:

> In the statuary's art, for example, . . . there must be, to begin with, an efficient cause which is similar in character to the future product. This cause is the art [*technē*] itself, which is just the *logos* (or essential plan), not yet embodied in

matter, of the product. . . . The art is both the principle
[*archē*] and form [*eidos*] of the thing which is produced.[2]

He also points out that, when we judge a man on his ability to
produce something, whether a product or some state of affairs, we
judge him by the norm of effectiveness. His knowledge is the only
item on the inside of his action which is immediately relevant to his
possessing particular capabilities. The exercise of skill requires
appetition as well as know-how, because appetition is necessary for
any sort of action; but the quality of a man's desires is not immediately relevant to his being adept at making things or at getting
what he wants.[3]

Because other considerations are irrelevant to having expertise,
skill is a capacity for opposites: it can be used both to promote and to
defeat the usual aims of the activity in which a man has skill. For
example, a bookkeeper can display his skill either by keeping
accurate records or by juggling his figures; and from the point of
view of technical ability, a clever embezzler is more knowledgeable
than the man who makes mistakes with his arithmetic because he is
incompetent.[4]

This characteristic of skill justifies saying that a description of a
man in terms of his skills is always an incomplete description. It is
always incomplete because we always can ask about the manner in
which a man uses his skills—his purposes and motives in using them
as he does; and questions about purpose and motive concern another
and distinctive way of describing and assessing men as agents, in
terms of the quality of their character. Unlike skills, moral character
is not a capacity for opposites, for it disposes a man to act typically
only in certain ways.[5]

The same point can be made in another way. The ends of skills
always have limited value. Artists produce works of art, architects
and engineers design and build things, writers produce articles and
books, and the list can be extended indefinitely. All these products
are good for something but always for something else, something
beyond themselves. They are only instrumentally good and, because they are, they have only limited value.

Because skills and their products have limits, listing a man's
competencies does not tell us in a comprehensive way what kind of a

person he is. As we will see in the last section of this chapter, a man's character concerns the ultimate goals he seeks and his motives for doing so. A man's ultimate ends condition all his other more limited goals, and that is why they determine the ways in which a man uses his skills and abilities, and why description of a man's character deals with him in the most fundamental way possible as a man.[6]

PRACTICAL WISDOM

Like most other philosophers, Aristotle is convinced that every rational person necessarily wishes for what is good for himself or at least what appears good to him; and every man wishes for his own best welfare more than he wishes for anything else.[7] It is also a fact of life that not all men know what is truly good and in their best interest, and, as difficult as it is to explain, not all those who know what is truly good for themselves pursue it as they ought.

'Practical wisdom' (*phronēsis*) is the name Aristotle gives to that excellence of the deliberative faculty which enables us to live the best life possible to us. The man of practical wisdom (*ho phronimos*) is that man who knows what is genuinely good for himself, who loves it, and who pursues it effectively by performing actions which are intrinsically good and advantageous (*agatha kai sumpheronta*), just and noble (*dikaia kai kala*). Consequently, Aristotle defines practical wisdom as a characteristic disposition (a *hexis*) to deliberate well in an unqualified sense, that is, so as to attain the best, ultimate, and most comprehensive ends open to man.[8]

In his discussion of deliberation, Aristotle makes it clear that effectiveness is a necessary but insufficient condition for deliberation to be good in an unqualified sense. It is insufficient because, for deliberation to be wholly good, the end of the action must also be what is wholly good—the good life for man.[9]

An artisan knows how to deliberate effectively about how to produce things, and financiers often deliberate effectively about how to make money, but the ends of their deliberations have only limited value. Consequently, that kind of effectiveness is a limited wisdom which Aristotle calls "cleverness" (*deinotēs*) or, if a person's desires are morally bad, "slyness" or "wiliness" (*panourgia*).[10]

The contrast Aristotle is drawing here is crucial to his elucidation of the nature of moral reasoning. If the Socratic paradigm and at least the early Platonic model of the morally adept man was the man of artistic expertise, Aristotle clearly wants to offer another, radically different analysis. Practical reason has two distinct functions and, in a sense, two distinct excellences: technical competence and moral wisdom. They are generically distinct so that one cannot be collapsed into the other.[11] Moral wisdom is not to be subsumed under *technē* as a special kind of artistic expertise, but similarities between the two can mislead us into confusing the two, and that is an enormous blunder.[12] In moral matters it is not sufficient, as it is in matters of skill, that a man know how to perform actions of a certain kind. For a person can show his technical ability just as well in either a morally acceptable or unacceptable way, while a person could hardly be considered a man of practical wisdom if he acted immorally.[13]

The mark of practical wisdom is unqualifiedly correct deliberation, and that requires a man both to know how to attain the best life for himself as a man and also to actively pursue that life. It is both a wisdom and a practical excellence. "Practical wisdom issues commands: its end is to tell us what we ought to do and what we ought not to do."[14]

The fact that it is a wisdom shows that it, like art and cleverness, is a rational characteristic (a *hexis*), a knowing how. So, Aristotle writes, although cleverness is not practical wisdom, "practical wisdom does not exist without it."[15] But practical wisdom is not a rational characteristic alone, for it is possible for a person to know how to live rightly without doing so. Aristotle calls this kind of knowledge 'understanding' (*sunesis*).[16] It is neither theoretical knowledge, for it is about practice, nor practical wisdom, for it does not conclude to action. It is the ability to judge "statements made by *another* person about matters which belong to the realm of practical wisdom."[17] So even the fact that a man knows how to act rightly does not, of itself, make him a morally good person.

What transforms both cleverness and understanding into practical wisdom and what ensures that that wisdom will efficaciously guide a person to live as he ought, making that wisdom unconditionally good, is the presence of morally good character. The man of practical wisdom not only deliberates effectively, he also desires rightly, wishing only to act morally well, and what causes him to desire rightly is his character. "It is virtue which makes our choice right."[18] Consequently, "a man cannot have practical wisdom unless he is good."[19] Aristotle sums up his doctrine in this way:

> Since choice is a deliberate desire, it follows that, if the choice is to be good, the reasoning must be true and the desire correct. . . . A man fulfills his proper function only by way of practical wisdom and moral excellence or virtue: virtue makes us aim at the right target, and practical wisdom makes us use the right means.[20]

We need now to turn our attention to the nature and role of character. There are other kinds of character than the best, but there is merit in postponing examination of them until we are clear on how the inside of moral practice ideally should be structured. It will be easier to understand how other kinds of character are defective and why, if we first understand what practice is like without defect or blemish.

Moral Excellence

In a brief but crucially important passage in the *Nicomachean Ethics*, Aristotle lists four conditions which, together, are necessary and sufficient for an agent to act morally well (*eupraxia*).[21] The first two are conditions necessary for a man's doings to be his action: he must know what he is doing, and he must act willingly; in a word, he must choose to act as he does.[22] Besides these, Aristotle says that the agent must choose his action for its own sake, because it is the right way to act, and that his decision must spring from a firm and stable character so that he acts as he does because he is the kind of man he is.

According to the third condition, a man must not only act rightly; it must be the efficacious presence of the right motivation which leads him to act rightly. On the outer side of action, we have to allow some leeway to an agent; he can stray a little from the norm of right action without our thinking he is a morally defective man.[23] But on the inner side, in the matter of his motivation, there is no leeway: if a man does not act from the right motive, he is not a good man.[24] When a man acts in a morally excellent way, the final and formal elements of his action coalesce and he chooses the right action for its own sake, because it is the right and noble thing to do and never as an instrumental means to something else.[25] "Action [*praxis*] does not . . . [have] an end other than itself: good action [*eupraxia*] is itself an end. . . . the doing of an action is its own end [*eschaton*]."[26] Consequently, if a man performs the right action but does so for the sake of something else, he does *not* act in a morally excellent fashion.[27]

We now can turn our attention to the final condition for moral excellence: when a man acts well, his decision about how to act must spring from a firm and stable character (*ēthos*).[28] Moral character concerns both a man's emotions and his actions; it concerns his actions both because it is formed by them and because, once formed, it helps determine them, and it concerns his emotions because character shows itself in a man's loves and hates.[29] "By emotions," Aristotle writes, "I mean desire, anger, fear, confidence, envy, joy, friendship, hatred, longing, jealousy, pity, and generally those states of consciousness accompanied by pleasure or pain."[30] Although it is concerned with pleasures and pains, moral excellence is not merely a matter of experiencing certain feelings.[31] For example, we can be affected emotionally, independently of our choices, and in such cases we are patients, not agents.[32] Feelings also are in a sense somatic, that is, they tend to manifest themselves in physical ways such as blushing and turning pale, while moral character manifests itself in a man's interests and concerns as well as in the kinds of actions he performs.[33] Most importantly, feelings are transitory; they come and go. But once formed, traits of character (*hexeis*) are stable and self-perpetuating, and that is why they make a man the kind of man he is: he spontaneously acts "in character" in matters involving pleasure and pain, and his doing so reinforces his characteristics.[34]

Just as "one swallow does not make a spring, nor does one sunny day,"[35] so also desiring as one should on one or several occasions does not make a man morally excellent. For that he must *consistently* act well until he does so, finally, "because he is the kind of man he is."[36] He has a settled and efficacious disposition (*hexis proairetikē*) toward acting rightly, a disposition displayed in his choices, in the kinds of activities which give him pleasure and cause him pain, and in the manner in which he does them.[37] Because "each man exercises his favorite faculties upon the objects he loves most," a reasonably accurate "index to our characteristics is provided by the pleasure or pain which follows upon the tasks we have achieved."[38] Something is clearly amiss with a man's character if he takes pleasure in the wrong kind of actions or when he acts rightly but in a pained and begrudging manner.[39]

The stability of character and its pervasive influence on practice lead Aristotle to say that a man of excellent character (*ho spoudaios*) is, "as it were, *a law unto himself;*" he is a living norm or paradigm of practical excellence.[40] He has so habituated himself to desiring and acting well that he seldom has to reflect, except marginally, about the possibilities open to him. This does not mean that his actions are done mechanically; rather, he has reached a level of moral accomplishment which enables him to act as he should, effortlessly, characteristically, and spontaneously.[41] We do not blame a man if he is overcome by pleasures or pains of such extraordinary strength that "no one could endure" them.[42] But in matters of pleasure and pain, especially the necessary pleasures, it is the mark of the morally excellent man that he has so mastered himself (is *sōphrōn*) that he normally does not experience desires or aversions which are excessive or deficient.[43]

The same qualification made in the discussion of practical wisdom applies here: moral excellence (*sōphrosunē*) should not be confused with what, in Chapter 3, was called "acting in the right manner;" there we were concerned only with behavioral characteristics, and for reasons already mentioned there is no necessary connection between that and what, on the inside, we have called a man's character.[44] But the notion of the 'mean' does apply here with equal force, for Aristotle describes moral excellence as the kind of character which observes "the mean relative to us . . . in respect of its essence and the definition of its essential nature virtue is a mean."[45] Men who are morally excellent as well as those who are not face the same kinds of situations, but their typical responses are different.[46] The emotional characteristics of the self-controlled man (*ho sōphrōn*) are somewhere in the middle so that he avoids the extremes of too much and too little; that is why he is morally the best man. He has perfect control over his emotional responses, and he has just the right emotional reactions. He enjoys what he should as he should—that which is "by nature good . . . and pleasant in itself"—and that is why he is a law unto himself for what is both pleasurable and noble.[47]

The life of the morally excellent man is also normally a life of intense pleasure. As we have seen, we usually find pleasure in the unimpeded exercise of our natural powers (their *energeia*); right actions are intrinsically good and so normally pleasurable to do; and the morally excellent man performs them because he values them as intrinsically good.[48] But there can be occasions when the performance of the right action may demand foregoing pleasure and enduring even great pain.[49] If we are morally excellent men "it makes no difference whether pleasures necessarily accompany these things, for we would choose them even if we were to get no pleasure from them."[50]

Moral excellence is an unconditional good and must be so since, insofar as a man is morally excellent, he always desires what he should and he acts as he should.[51] Any other analysis would be self-contradictory, permitting the immoral use of a quality which is of its very nature always and intrinsically moral. We can see now why Aristotle concludes that, just as "a man cannot have practical wisdom unless he is good," so also moral excellence "cannot be attained without practical wisdom."[52] A man cannot have excellent character without knowing how to perform the kind of actions by which his kind of character was formed, and a man will not perform the right kind of actions consistently and for the right reason if he does not have the kind of character which leads him to cherish acting rightly. This analysis creates a problem for moral education, for if one characteristic demands the other, there seems no way in which to generate either.[53]

There is another problem to which we must attend before concluding this chapter. Aristotle has defined the man of practical wisdom as a man who seeks what is the best for himself above all else; this doctrine, as he is aware, lays him open to the charge of fostering egotism, and in ordinary language, that term is almost always used pejoratively. People think of an egotist as a morally corrupt man, not as morally excellent. If a man is to be morally good he must, people say, be an altruist; and an altruist is a man who acts on noble motives precisely because he wishes for and promotes the best welfare of others, even when no one else knows of his actions nor ever will and even when he must neglect his own interests to do so.

In the fourth and eighth chapters of Book 9, Aristotle argues that it is misleading and inaccurate to try to make the distinction between morally good and evil men by using the catagories "unselfish" and "selfish." He argues that it simply is not possible for a rational person not to love and care about himself, and that this is the way it should be, since friendship with and concern for others are best understood as extensions of love of and concern for one's self. A man who detests himself is not in the best position from which to know what it is to care about others. The problem is to be a morally good egoist, to love ourselves as we should, and that is a matter of recognizing and properly valuing what in our own nature is of the greatest worth as well as valuing external goods as we should.

People rightly criticize a person who treasures most highly the sensual part of his nature and material possessions (the "gifts of fortune"); such a man is unjust to others because he tries to get more than his share of these, and he destroys the common good by causing strife and anger.[54] But, Aristotle continues, it is insensitive to criticize that kind of person for being too selfish. He is morally reprehensible because he does *not* love himself sufficiently and well, for if he did he would treasure his rationality and his ability to perform noble actions more than material goods. This is just what the true egoist does: he follows his reason while controlling his emotions. Who would find fault with such a man?

But it still does not seem that a man is morally good if he helps others only in the hope of using them, of gaining some advantage through them. Aristotle agrees; but, he argues, this is not the right way in which to view the actions of the morally good egoist. We are, by nature, social and political beings. Although the *Ethics* concentrates on the moral life of the individual and the *Politics* on the social aspects of morality, Aristotle insists that one cannot exist without the other.[55] Genuine community and personal development and life are inseparable.[56] In the opening pages of Book 5, Aristotle takes justice to be, in its most comprehensive sense, that moral quality which should characterize all of a man's dealings with his fellow men, and describes it as "perfect and most complete moral excellence in the highest degree, because it involves the exercise of complete moral goodness."[57]

Since all men have the same ultimate goal of living the good life, the morally excellent man wishes for others and helps them attain just what he seeks for himself and for the same reason. In acting rightly toward them he is in fact promoting what is in his own genuine best interest.[58] "If all men were to compete for what is noble . . . , all the needs of the community will have been met, and each individual will have the greatest of goods," namely, the best moral life.[59] Understood this way, true egoism is the source of peace and concord, fostering what is in every man's common and best interest.

Notes to Chapter 5

1. See 6. 2. 1139a31-b2; 6. 4. 1140a6-10, 20-22; 6. 5. 1140a28-32, b28; 6. 7. 1141a9-12; 6. 9. 1142b17-20, 28-33; 6. 13. 1144b14-15.

2. *Part an.* 1. 1. 640a30-33 (Peck) and *Gen. an.* 2. 1. 735a3-4 (Peck).

3. See 2. 4. 1105a22-b1; 6. 4. 1140a6-10; 6. 5. 1140a28-32; *Ph.* 2. 2. 194a37-b8. Aristotle admits that a man can fail to develop skill or to use well the skills he has through lack of character, but he does not develop this point.

4. See 5. 1. 1129a12-17; 6. 5. 1140b23-24; 7. 10. 1152a9-13; *Metaph.* 9. 2; 9. 5. 1048a8-16; 9. 8. 1050b31-35; 9. 9. 1051a5-16. This is why, on one occasion, Aristotle refuses to call art an excellence; see 6. 5. 1140b24-25.

5. See 4. 7. 1127b14-16; 5. 1. 1129a12-15. "To have a quality is to have, or to lack, a capacity or liability or tendency, whether natural or acquired, to respond in certain ways, whether actively or passively, to environmental conditions" (W. F. R. Hardie, *Aristotle's Ethical Theory*, p. 98). In the *Categories* Aristotle lists four kinds of qualities: figure, capacities (*dunameis*), sufferings (*pathēseis*), and dispositions (*hexeis*) (see 8b25ff.). The first is irrelevant to character, and Aristotle does not consider it in *Eth. Nic.* There he does argue that character cannot be a matter of what one merely endures, of what merely happens to us, nor of what can affect us emotionally apart from our own wishes; such are not part of our agency and so are not subject to moral appraisal. Character, therefore, must consist in *hexeis*— intelligent dispositions developed from our capabilities to the point where they determine how we typically act and are disposed to act. See 2. 5; 3. 5. 1114b26-28; 5. 1. 1129a7-17; 6. 5. 1140b12-30; 6. 12. 1143b23; *Metaph.* 5. 20; *Cat.* 8. Skills are also *hexeis*, but rational and not emotional characteristics, and these, Aristotle writes, "deal with a pair of opposites" (5. 1. 1129a13).

6. See 2. 6. 1106a21-23; 6. 5. 1140a25-32.

7. See 3. 5. 1113b15-17; 5. 9. 1136b3-7; 8. 7. 1159a13; 9. 4. 1166a18-22.

8. See 1. 13. 1102a5-17, 23-25; 6. 2. 1139b2-3; 6. 5. 1140a24-32, b4-21; 6. 7. 1141a23-28, b4-13; 6. 8. 1141b29-1142a10; 6. 9. 1142b1-34; 6. 12. 1143b22-23, 1144a23-36; 9. 4. 1166a13-23.

9. See 6. 9. 1142b16-34.

10. See 6. 12. 1144a23-27.

11. See chap. 3 above; also 6. 3; 6. 5. 1140b1-7, 23-25.

12. See 5. 9. 1137a6-26; 6. 2. 1139a31-b5; 6. 3.

13. See 2. 4. 1105a27-b1, 5-8; 5. 9. 1137a6-27; 6. 12. 1144a13-17.

14. 6. 10. 1143a7-8.

15. 6. 12. 1144a28-29.

16. See 1. 3. 1095a8-11; 6. 5. 1140b24-27; 6. 10. Presumably this is the kind of knowledge possessed by persons yielding to moral weakness; see chap. 8.

17. 6. 10. 1143a13-14 (italics mine).

18. 6. 12. 1144a20; cf. 6. 2. 1139a22-b5; 6. 13. 1144b31-1145a6.

19. 6. 12. 1144a37.

20. 6. 2. 1139a23-25 and 6. 12. 1144a7-8; cf. 1144a20-22, 35-37; 6. 13. 1145a2-7; *De an.* 3. 10. 433a8-21.

21. See 2. 4. 1105a28-32; cf. 6. 12. 1144a13-19.

22. See 5. 8. 1135a15-b11, 19-1136a4; 6. 12. 1144a13-15; also chap. 4, note 13.

23. See 2. 9. 1109b14-26; 4. 5. 1126a33-b4.

24. See 2. 4. 1105a17-b12; 3. 7. 1115b11-13; 3. 9. 1117b7-9; 4. 1. 1120a11-4. 2. 1122b7; 5. 9. 1137a14-26; 6. 12. 1144a13-37; 8. 13. 1163a22-23; 9. 1. 1164b1-3; 10. 9. 1179b10-16, 1180a4-18; *Pol.* 7. 14. 1333a9-11.

25. See 2. 4. 1105a33; 1. 8. 1098b17-19; 3. 7. 1115b12-21, 1116a12-13; 4. 1. 1120a13, 23-26; 4. 2. 1122b6-7; 6. 5. 1140b4-18; 6. 12. 1144a17-19; 9. 8. 1168a33-34, b24-28; 10. 6. 1176b6-8.

26. 6. 5. 1140b6-7 and *Metaph.* 9. 8. 1050a25 (Hope); cf. 1050b1-2.

27. See 3. 7. 1116a10-15; 3. 8; 4. 1. 1120a27-31, 1121b1-11; 4. 2. 1123a24-25; 4. 7. 1127b9-17; 5. 8. 1135b3-8, 1136a3-4; 6. 12. 1144a13-19; *Eth. Eud.* 1. 5. 1216a23-27.

28. See 2. 4. 1105a33-35.

29. See 1. 8. 1099a8-10; 2. 1. 1103b7-23; 2. 3. 1104b3-11; 2. 6. 1106b16ff.; 3. 5. 1114a11-30, b26-1115a3; 7. 11. 1152b3-7; 10. 8. 1178a14-15, 19-21.

30. 2. 5. 1105b21-23 (Rackham); cf. 2. 3. 1104b3-1105a14; 7. 11. 1152b1-7; 10. 8. 1178a14-21.

31. See 2. 5. 1105b29-1106a10.

32. If, for example, a man performs an unjust act because he is provoked to anger by another, he has not acted either from choice or from character; the initiative and responsibility rest with the provoker (see 5.8. 1135b19-37).

33. See 4. 9. 1128b10-15.

34. See 3. 5. 1114b26-1115a3; 5. 9. 1137a21-29; 10. 4. 1175a11-17. A man's character becomes so much a part of him—his "second nature"—that Aristotle believes a person generally cannot alter it substantially, once it has been set (see 3. 5. 1114b30-1115a4; 7. 10. 1152a28-33). Even if a person were to wish to change, his present character would only reassert itself in his very efforts to acquire new traits. Aristotle does not rule out all possibility of change; he seems to think it can happen if some great mental trauma occurs,

but he implies this is the exception, not the rule (*Cat*. 8. 8b31). Change is also possible before character is set (see 3. 5. 1114a7-11; 10. 9. 1180a1-17).

35. 1. 7. 1098a17-18.

36. 4. 6. 1126b24; cf. 2. 1. 1103b14-23; 4. 7. 1127a33-b7.

37. See 4. 1. 1120b27-1121a9; 4. 7. 1127a33-b7, 14-17; 5. 9. 1137a21-27; *Metaph*. 5. 20; *Cat*. 8.8b25-9a13. See also chap. 4, note 29.

38. 10. 4. 1175a13 and 2. 3. 1104b4-5; cf. 1. 8. 1099a7-16.

39. See 1. 8. 1099a7-20; 2. 3. 1104b5-1105a12; 3. 12; 4. 1. 1120a26-31, 1121a8-9; 9. 9. 1170a8-10.

40. 4. 8. 1128a33 (emphasis mine); cf. 3. 4; 9. 4. 1166a12-14; 9. 9. 1170a14-16; 10. 5. 1176a16-23.

41. See 3. 5. 1114b26-29; 9. 4. 1166a13-29; *Motu an*. 7. 701a26-b1; *Ph*. 2. 8. 199b27-30. Situations in which we have little or no time to think actually tend to show a person's character better than those in which a person can think things over; see 3. 8. 1117a18-22. Aristotle spends much more time on actions preceded by deliberation, perhaps because the paradigm of activity done from settled dispositions turns out to be activity too much like animal activity, done with little or no conscious thought (see *Motu an*. 7. 701a25-36).

42. 3. 1. 1110a26; cf. 3. 7. 1115b7-8; 7. 7. 1150a7-12.

43. See 7. 2. 1146a9-12; 7. 9. 1152a1-3.

44. But there generally is a correlation between character and activity; see e.g., 2. 1-2.

45. 2. 6. 1106b37-1107a7; cf. 1106b16-24; also 2. 2. 1104a 12-27; 2. 9. 1109a19-29; 3. 5. 1114b28; 3. 7. 1116a4-11; 3. 8. 1117b23-25; 3. 10. 1117b24-27; 4. 7. 1127a16-17; also chap. 3 "*Poïesis* and *Praxis:* Making and Doing," esp. note 58.

46. See 2. 3. 1104b3-9; 3. 7. 1116a4-6.

47. 9. 9. 1170a15-16; cf. 1. 8. 1099a7-30; 2. 6-9; 3. 4; 3. 11. 1119a12-20; 7. 7. 1150a17-24; 7. 12. 1153a27-35; 9. 4. 1166a10-17; 10. 3. 1173b28-30. If Aristotle's morally excellent man seems almost too good to be true, we may need to remind ourselves that Aristotle himself grants he is an extreme; for most men, he is the ideal and not the reality (see 2. 6. 1107a1-8; 4. 3. 1123b13-14; 6. 5. 1140b22-23; 10. 9. 1179b13-19).

48. See 1. 8. 1099a7-22; 3. 9. 1117b13-15; 4. 1. 1120a23-28, 1121a1-3; 9. 9. 1169b28-1170b10; 10. 5. 1176a16-18, 23-28.

49. See 3. 6. 1115a32-b6; 3. 9.

50. 10. 3. 1174a6-8.

51. See 1. 10. 1101a1-6; 2. 3. 1104b27-28; 2. 6. 1106a15-24; 4. 9. 1128b31; 5. 1. 1129a12-17; 6. 9. 1142b28-33; 7. 2. 1146a5-8. Shame (*aidōs* or *aischunē*), which is more of a feeling (*pathos*) than a moral characteristic, has only mixed moral value. It is one of the things a good man should fear; if he is

good at all he would feel ashamed if he were to act badly; and shamelessness is clearly not a moral virtue. In this sense, a feeling of shame is the negative side of respect and love for what is morally good. However, it does not follow that a man shows his moral goodness by first acting badly and then feeling ashamed. Insofar as a person is morally good, he will not act badly and therefore not feel shame. The morally weak man feels shame after instances of his moral weakness, but he is by that very fact morally inferior to the man of moral excellence. See 2. 7. 1108a32; 3. 6. 1115a10-23; 3. 8. 1116a16-29, b19-23; 4. 9. 1128b10-35; also chap. 8 below.

52. 6. 12. 1144a37 and 6. 13. 1144b17.

53. For further discussion of the relation between practical wisdom and moral excellence, see the next chapter; for Aristotle's solution to this problem, see chap. 7.

54. See 5. 1. 1129b1-11; 9. 6. 1167b9-16; *Pol.* 2. 5. 1263a 40-b7; also the discussion of injustice in book 5 of *Eth. Nic.*

55. See, e.g., 5. 11. 1138a5-13; 6. 8. 1142a8-10.

56. See chap. 7.

57. 5. 1. 1129b31-32 (my translation); cf. 5. 1. 1130a7-11; 5. 2. 1130b1-3, 17-20; 5. 6. 1134a26-27, b1-6.

58. See 9. 4. 1166a30-32.

59. 9. 8. 1169a8-10; cf. 9. 6. 1167b5-9.

6

The Integrity of Moral Personality

The analysis Aristotle has offered so far of the nature of practical wisdom and of moral excellence leaves us with very serious problems. He has said that they cannot exist without each other.[1] But he has depicted them as radically distinct, each having its own proper domain and functions. The nature of a thing is defined by its function, the function of a thing is its excellence, and Aristotle describes practical wisdom and moral excellence as the excellences of practical reason and desires respectively. He therefore depicts these parts of the soul as functionally and perhaps ontologically separate. Desires and wishes determine the ends of actions and practical reason apparently is restricted to deliberating about and choosing the means to those ends.[2] Reflection on these divisions shows they are incompatible with other parts of Aristotle's analysis.[3] In fact they can be kept only at the cost of personal responsibility and of morality itself.

If desires alone determined the ends of practice and if reason could become practical only as the servant of desires, their affiliation would lack all moral significance. The goodness of practical reason would be reduced to the norm of efficiency, for deliberation then would only be a quasi-theoretical inquiry into and choice of causal availabilities; and insofar as it would be an intellectual excellence, practical wisdom would be indistinguishable from cleverness and craftsmanship. Its distinctively moral nature would be destroyed, for, to use a Kantian construction, just as reason without desires is empty of practical efficacy, so also desires without intellectual insight are morally blind. An action can be understood as morally good only by reason, not by desires.[4]

Moreover, if practical reason were concerned only with means and if moral excellence were merely a matter of habituation (*ethos*), then human agents would be too much like inanimate objects, producing "effects, as fire burns, without knowing what they are doing."[5] Men who act rightly only because they have been trained to do so, lack the reflective appreciation of what they are doing that is required for them to be moral agents.

Aristotle's account cannot be right. Even when an action is only an instrumentality, we cannot eschew all judgments about the desired end. We are willing to use instrumentalities at some cost to us only if we think an end is worth that cost. Because the evaluation of a means necessarily includes some evaluation of the end to which it conduces, practical reasoning cannot be restricted to questions of possibility and efficiency, but also must determine which practical ends are worth pursuing and to be desired.[6]

Moreover, morally good actions are, Aristotle has insisted, intrinsically good so that, even if we think of them as both means and ends, we cannot consider one aspect (those actions as constitutive means) without also considering the other as well (they are consummatory).

The deep divisions Aristotle sometimes sets out cannot be kept, and it is clear that their amendment is necessary if we are going to be able to make sense out of the rest of his analysis of morality. What we need to do now is to try to understand why he got himself in these difficulties at all.

During the nineteenth and the first part of the twentieth centuries, scholars believed that Aristotle's thought as found in the writings we have comprised a final organic whole. But in 1923 Werner Jaeger published (in German) a book entitled, *Aristotle: Fundamentals of the History of his Development*. In it Jaeger argued that the internal evidence shows that Aristotle's writings do reflect stages of philosophic development. Scholars today reject many of Jaeger's more specific claims, and there is some argument about the exact chronology and even the doctrines involved, but Jaeger's main thesis is now generally accepted: the writings we have were composed at various times during Aristotle's life, were modified by him here and there as his ideas changed, and were *not* brought into a final, internally consistent form before he died.

There are three ways in which Aristotle's views changed, relevant to our concerns. (1) Whereas in his early career he had held ᵗhat theoretical and practical reason are essentially the same, he ' ᷄᷄ᵃme convinced that the differences between them are large enough that they must be distinct in some sense.[7] (2) This first change raised a new question: if practical wisdom (*phronēsis*) is somehow distinct from theoretical wisdom (*sophia*), what is the nature of practical wisdom? As Aristotle grew to appreciate the intrinsic role of emotions in moral reasoning,[8] he also grew further away from Socratic intellectualism which equated virtue with knowledge and identified moral goodness with wisdom.[9] Finally, (3) his view of the constitution of the human psyche changed from a kind of dualism in which the soul inhabits an alien body which it uses, to a view in which man is seen as a single complex being—a besouled body or an embodied soul—whose 'parts' are neither separate nor separable entities.[10]

The latter two changes tend to fight each other: emphasizing the importance of the emotions implies a dualistic picture of man, contrary to the development of a nondualistic psychology. So, for example, the description of self-control (*sōphrosunē*) and courage as "excellences of our irrational part" reflects both Aristotle's old psychology and his appreciation of the importance of the emotions.[11]

It is plausible, then, to argue that the divisions which have caused so much difficulty belong to a transitional stage in which Aristotle was in the process of integrating new insights into views he had not yet changed. The main internal evidence for this interpretation is to be found in the ways in which Aristotle treats the emotions. He is clearly unsettled about what to do with them. Sometimes he portrays them as a part of reason, other times as part of man but distinct from reason, and other times as something alien to man who is really only his reason.[12] In two passages he explicitly avoids taking a clear and definite stand on their ontological status.[13] What is lacking throughout the *Ethics* is the consistent influence of his later psychology, and this creates difficulties and systematic ambiguities throughout. But there is enough of that psychology in critical places to indicate how his mature doctrine of the nature of moral personality should be understood, and it is to that that we shall now turn.

THE UNITY OF PRACTICAL WISDOM AND MORAL EXCELLENCE

We can legitimately interpret the divisions Aristotle has drawn to be logical rather than ontological by attending to two crucial doctrines, found particularly in the sixth book of the *Ethics:* practical reason is not merely reason but is an amalgam of thought and desire, and character is never merely a matter of blindly conditioned desires but is the locus for the relationship between desires and reason, however that relationship is shaped in individual cases. Because each is a synthesis of reason and emotions, character and moral reasoning are but aspects of the same phenomenon, so that their excellences, practical wisdom and moral excellence, also constitute a functional unity; and that is why it is impossible to have one without the other.[14] Since that is the case, their operations—deliberation, choice, and wish—also cannot be radically distinct from another.

Whether we describe a person in terms of his character or in terms of his practical reason, there is only the difference that each way provides its own focus, one emphasizing the importance of appetition (without denying the importance of reason) and the other emphasizing the importance of reason (without denying the importance of the emotions).

Although Aristotle restricts the meaning of deliberation to consideration of means, this does not mean that practical reason does not have a second role of examining and determining the ends of practice. He holds that the ends of our actions are determined either by desires or wishes.[15] His treatment of wishes in the *Nicomachean Ethics* is very brief compared with his elaborate descriptions of deliberation, and it consists mainly in setting out reasons for holding wishes and choices to be distinct. This negative approach tends to obscure his doctrine that wishes are not sheer appetites at all. Like choices, wishes are a synthesis of desire and reason, and for that reason they are not something we share with nonrational agents.[16]

Desires (*orexeis*), Aristotle writes, are not all alike; they can be divided into three different kinds: desires which lack rational insight—sensual appetites (*epithumiai*); one special kind which partakes of reason to some degree—anger (*thumos*); and rational desires or wishes (*bouleseis*).[17] Rational desiring or wishing "is a desire for what is good."[18] It is "close to" choosing, because a person only deliberates about how to act when he desires something he sees as good in some sense.[19] Yet, Aristotle argues, wishing is not identical with choosing, for

Wish is directed at the end rather than the means, but choice at the means which are conducive to a given end. For example, we *wish* to be healthy and *choose* the things that will give us health. Similarly, we say that we *wish* to be happy [*eudaimonein*] and describe this as our wish, but it would not be fitting to say that we *choose* to be happy. In general, choice seems to be concerned with the things that lie within our power.[20]

Wishes, then are right in a different way than choices are right.[21] Our choices are right when we effectively select actions, not already predetermined, which are either instrumental means to or constituents of our desired ends. But our wishes are right when they are for ends which, in an abstract and general form, are ultimately predetermined by the nature of reality, that is, by the nature of kinds of actions and kinds of practical goods, and by our own psychological constitution as human beings.[22]

But once again Aristotle's distinction cannot remain sharp and clear, for in morally good practice, in which the distinction between means and ends is radically altered, the difference between choices and wishes tends to come down to the difference between aiming at an abstract ideal or good and selecting ways in which to instantiate it.[23]

Because wishes are an exercise of practical reason, practical reason does have the function of examining and determining the ends of practice. Aristotle clearly believed this to be a proper role for practical reason, for in several places he defines his ethical and political writings in just such terms.

The end of politics is the good for man. . . . we must try to comprehend in outline at least what this good is. . . . [The political philosopher] is the supreme craftsman of the end [*telos*] to which we look when we call one particular thing bad and another good in the unqualified sense. . . . Those who regulate their desires and actions by a rational principle [*logos*] will greatly benefit from a knowledge of this subject [politics].[24]

Because practical reason has this second function, the major premises in practical deliberations have truth values and are not merely sophisticated grunts.[25]

There is no special difficulty in understanding why the man of practical wisdom is the one best able to discern the right moral principles and assign practical truth-values consistently and correctly; any other analysis would be surprising. Just as in theoretical matters the expert is the one who can best judge the truth of theoretical statements, so also in practical matters the ultimate appeal is to the man of genuine moral expertise. "Whatever the true end may be, only a good man can judge it correctly."[26]

Besides saving the moral significance of our agency, extending practical reasoning to the ends of action also prevents the destruction of personal responsibility. Aristotle argues that, since children have desires long before they can reason, their emotions must be trained before moral instruction can be given. Moreover, he writes, we learn how to act rightly by being habituated to do so. But the genesis of moral personality should not be confused with its later development. Once a person begins to develop the self-awareness which characterizes rationality and genuine human agency, character development can no longer be described merely as training at the hands of others. "Only a man who is utterly insensitive can be ignorant of the fact that moral characteristics are formed by actively engaging in particular actions."[27] Aristotle thinks we are too dependent on others to be totally responsible for what we become, but he also argues that we cannot avoid assuming more and more responsibility for ourselves as we begin to realize that our actions are determining our future self. He does not think a rational person can totally lack the self-awareness fundamental to self-determination and so to moral responsibility as it is commonly understood.[28]

Moral character is impossible without appetition, but brute animals have appetition with no possibility of moral character. What makes the difference is the interpenetration, in man, of appetition and reason, and the difference between morally good and morally evil men is located precisely at this juncture, in the manner in which reason and desire are related to each other.[29] Aristotle repeatedly states that the moral quality of a person's character depends on whether rationality or appetition has the final say in determining wishes and choices. The morally best man regulates his desires by his reason; he "follows right reason."[30] One of Aristotle's strongest statements on the subject occurs at the end of Book 3:

> What desires the base and what grows wild needs to be "checked" or "pruned," and that is, above all, appetite [*epithumia*]. . . . if appetite and desire do not obey and do not subject themselves to the ruling element, they will go far astray. . . . They should, therefore, . . . never oppose the guidance of reason. . . . the appetitive element of a self-controlled man [*ho sōphrōn*] must be in harmony with the guidance of reason.[31]

The really good man, then, like Plato's just man in the *Republic*, enjoys complete internal harmony, an integrity established by reason, and that is why he is morally good; he "finds no pleasure in anything that violates the dictates of reason."[32] Practical wisdom cannot be defined adequately as effective reasoning led by good desires, for a person's emotional characteristics can be morally good only when they are informed and directed by reason. Morally good character consists of emotions docile to and supportive of the ends and rules set by reason.[33]

When reason does not lead appetition, men fall into an ignorance of what is truly good. As we will see in Chapter 8, this is not a kind of theoretical ignorance; moral ignorance consists essentially in wayward wishes. What causes the ignorance is the reversal of the proper order of reason over desire. When this happens, men "gratify their appetites, their emotions in general, and the irrational part of their souls"; by contrast, the morally good man is as different from the morally evil man

> as living by the guidance of reason is from living by the dictates of emotion, and as different as desiring what is noble is from desiring what seems to be advantageous. . . . A good man . . . who orients his life by what is noble will accept the guidance of reason, while a bad man, whose desire is for pleasure, is corrected by pain like a beast of burden.[34]

The same point can be made another way: although our wishes always involve rational consciousness, they are not always for what is morally good. The morally evil person wishes for what is not really good, but it still seems good to him, not because his appetites are so powerful they overwhelm his reason but because he does not adequately subject them to rational examination and control. When desires lack the direction of reason necessary for good practice, they become corrupt.[35]

The adjustments of desires to reason may not be made perfectly, and then we experience internal conflict. This common experience is possible only because we have some desires united with and under the direction of reason and other desires coexisting temporally with them and sometimes opposing them. Aristotle discerns two kinds of moral personalities which experience such internal conflict—the morally strong person and the morally weak person. Neither is completely evil, for both wish for what is genuinely morally good, but both also experience surges of sensual appetite (*epithumia*)

> different from the rational, which fights and resists the guidance of reason. . . . In morally strong and morally weak men we praise the reason that guides them and the rational element of the soul, because it exhorts them to follow the right path and to do what is best.[36]

What distinguishes mere appetites from wishes in both kinds of persons is the way in which each kind of desire is related to reason. Their objects are also apprehended under radically different descriptions, as morally good for wishes, and as merely pleasurable for sensual appetites, even when their objects do not differ ontologically.

The morally strong person is the better of the two, because, in him, "the leadership of reason" prevails. But he is still inferior to the morally excellent person, for the emotions of the latter are "more obedient still. . . . in him everything is in harmony with the voice of reason."[37]

Practical Wisdom and Moral Philosophy

So far we have seen that, stated in general terms, practical reason is our ability to act effectively and appropriately to reach our practical goals. Because the exercise of this ability is complex, practical reason actually has three functions or roles. It is a critical faculty, a creative faculty, and an imperative faculty.

It is a critical faculty in the sense of empowering us to reflect on our goals, to formulate them in generic terms, and to construct policies and rules for attaining them. Some of these goals, such as those attained by production, have limited value; others are of unconditional or absolute value because they are, in the most comprehensive way possible, in our best interest as human beings. Morally good goals condition the lesser, limited goals, not in the sense of dictating standards of craftsmanship and artistry (for practical wisdom is not a kind of super skill) but in the sense of providing a context within which we can decide how the products of making should be used.

When we critically examine alternative proposals for our ultimate goals, we are not free to decide arbitrarily what is good and right. We must, for example, have a clear and adequate notion about what it is to be a human being, for without that we are not in position to discuss what the good life for a human being might or might not be.[38] We also must be acquainted with the various kinds of activities in which people can engage, for we must understand the nature of different kinds of activities before we can discuss their relative worth. This critical use of reason is not theoretical, however, even though it is about what is the case, for it involves and is an enunciation of our moral character.

Practical reason is also a creative faculty, for the changing circumstances of life do not allow practical rules to hold equally and alike in every situation. There are no logical rules of relevancy, determining for each case what facts should be taken into account or what weight should be given them, nor for deciding which rule applies to them or how. Judgments about what is right, about what is the best way to act here and now, are more of a sensitive feel for things rather than a formal process.

Finally practical reason is an imperative faculty, making our wishes efficacious so that we act so as to achieve the ends we have set for ourselves.

It is now apparent that Aristotle's inquiry into morality is itself a paramount exercise of practical reason in its critical function. Despite the fact that he holds that the final purpose in doing moral philosophy is practical, to guide action,[39] he also makes it clear that moral philosophy is not an exercise of practical reason in either its creative or its imperative functions. Because ethics is not an exact science with universally valid laws of conduct, it will not be able to tell us just how we should act within the various particular situations of our lives.[40] Nor can ethics by itself guarantee to make us better people, for discussions, arguments, and lectures cannot substitute for the one way in which good dispositions can be generated—by the doing of right actions again and again until a person becomes habituated to acting rightly.[41]

According to Aristotle, then, moral philosophy is a critical examination of the life of practice. But what exactly should be examined? And how does one go about doing it?

The ultimate data for moral philosophy, Aristotle thinks, are 'moral facts' which can be encountered only in experience.[42] The practical life concerns particulars (*ta kath' hekasta* and *ta eschata*)—this situation with its particular constituents, this agent, this action. Generalities about practice are all drawn from our knowledge of particulars, and "knowledge of particulars comes from experience."[43] Early in the *Ethics* he writes:

> Reasons which are based on fundamental principles are different from reasons that lead up to them. . . . We must start with. . . . what is known to us. . . . The acceptance of a fact as a fact [*to hoti*] is the starting point [*archē*], and when the facts are made sufficiently clear, there is no need to ask for further justification. A person brought up rightly either already knows these facts or can easily learn them.[44]

Moral philosophy, therefore, must be based on experience with what Aristotle calls the plain, observed, actual facts of moral living (*ta phainomena* and *ta erga*).[45]

The facts of the world of practice and our experience with them are never, for Aristotle, radically individual; moral activity occurs only within the context of social and political life. Consequently he recommends we should not ignore generally accepted opinions (*endoxa*) about morality—those which are accepted by everyone or by the majority or proposed by the wise, or those views which have best endured the test of time. It is unlikely that they all can be completely wrong.[46] They must contain some genuine knowledge gained by men living day by day with moral concerns. Because they enunciate lived experience with morality and so can serve as a guide to moral reality, "such articulations have the status of 'facts' of the moral life."[47]

Consequently Aristotle frequently appeals to common and shared moral experience as mediated through moral language, both what is commonly said and how that language commonly operates.[48] Such appeals, for example, are used to support his philosophic psychology in 1. 13. He elicits his definition of practical wisdom "by studying the *persons* to whom we *attribute* it."[49] Again and again he supports his definitions and claims by appealing to common value judgments which will corroborate and illustrate his claims. Some commentators, therefore, have interpreted his ethics merely as a rationalization of Greek culture, but that criticism does not do justice to the rationale for such support: moral language can be a primary font for the moral experiences it enunciates.

Linguistic moral facts, however, are not unproblematic and cannot be relied on uncritically; for they present an embarrassment of ambiguities and contradictory claims.[50] The judgments of people often vary widely from person to person, between different moments in the same person's life, and between cultures.[51] Because moral language is not immune to general requirements of reason such as consistency and coherence,[52] Aristotle concludes that many common moral opinions must be incomplete, or confused, or simply mistaken.[53] One reason for this can be found in the fact that so many people "do not even have a notion of what is noble and truly pleasant," and their judgments are suspect because the quality of their moral experience is in doubt.[54] Even so, Aristotle believes that "ordinary moral language" has embedded in it the accumulated wisdom of many good men, codified in the laws of the state, and transmitted from generation to generation by the state in its function of moral educator. "Some of the conflicting opinions must be removed and others must be left intact. For the resolution of a problem is the discovery of the (truth)."[55]

The proper method, he writes, is to survey the data, examine it dialectically, and then decide where the truth lies.[56] In this process, we should pay particular attention to the reflections of those whose lives indicate sensitivity, lucidity, and high moral quality, for correctness in moral matters depends on a person's having morally good character.[57] But even then, although the opinions of those with good reputations

> carry some conviction, in the field of moral action truth is judged by the actual facts of life [*ta erga kai ton bion*], for it is in them that the decisive element lies. So we must examine the conclusions we have reached so far by applying them to the actual facts of life: if they are in harmony with the facts we must accept them, and if they clash we must assume that they are mere words.[58]

So, for example, Socrates' analysis of morality must be at least partly incorrect, for he ended up denying the reality of moral weakness, and that "is plainly at variance with the observed facts."[59]

The dialectical method of examination, therefore, begins with four presumptive sources of truth: common opinions (*endoxa*) and opinions of the wise; theories (*logoi*) about morality together with arguments supporting them; the "actual facts" of moral life (*ta phainomena*, *ta erga*, and *ho bios*), that is, morally significant ways in which people live, feel, and act; and requirements of reason for clarity and consistency. The dialectical method consists in a reflective analysis of the data and the use of quasi-theoretical notions to help organize relations among explanatory concepts and principles. But the primary data, legislating for both opinions and theories, are the objective facts of the world of practice—the actions, the characters, and the situations of human moral agents.[60]

How is this experience of the facts of morality generated? To answer this question we must examine what Aristotle says about the moral sense (*aisthēsis*) or judgment (*gnōmē*) of the man of practical wisdom (*ho phronimos*). In the *Nicomachean Ethics* Aristotle devotes long discussions to deliberation, and his explicit discussion of moral sensitivity is brief.[61] Yet the most fundamental and the most distinctive operation of practical thought is still what can be called practical perceptiveness, that is, the direct felt encounter of a person with moral value, an encounter involving an affective-intuitive exercise of reason (*nous*). Once we understand its nature, we can see that it is used by Aristotle throughout the *Ethics*, as the ultimate support for his moral analyses and claims.

We can begin to understand its nature by thinking about a larger problem: how do we learn anything at all? Our knowledge must begin somewhere. It cannot begin with arguments, for discursive thinking always presupposes prior knowledge; trying to base everything on that kind of thought would lead to infinite regression and the impossibility of knowing anything. Therefore, Aristotle concludes, all knowledge must begin with intuitions. Some intuitions have as their objects necessary truths which reason can grasp simply by thought alone.[62] The principle of noncontradiction exemplifies this kind of truth: it cannot be denied, because it must be affirmed even in the attempt to deny it. Not all knowledge, however, can be of this sort. Empirical knowledge, whether theoretical or moral, must begin with an immediate intuitive encounter with particularities (*ta eschata*) and proceed inductively, that is, by inducing or abstracting generalities from the particulars which instantiate them.[63] We learn about kinds of character, for example, by seeing particular men, and we learn to formulate practical principles by reflecting on the ways in which we and others have acted. We also gradually learn to select intuitively which particulars and which rules are relevant in various kinds of situations.[64]

Every person who is "well endowed" by nature, Aristotle writes, is born with the potentiality for good practical judgment.[65] Since judgment or moral sense is partly a rational characteristic and since we acquire the ability to reason only gradually, it follows that only "at a given stage of life a person acquires intelligence [*nous*] and good sense [*gnōmē*]."[66] Since a person's intelligence depends on native endowment, good moral judgment cannot be learned from anyone else; but it can and needs to be developed with the help of others and through its exercise. Aristotle calls it "an eye" and "a vision" given by experience.[67] It is an eye or a vision because it involves intuition, and it depends on experience for its development.

Aristotle did not equate this kind of perception with the perception of our individual senses, such as sight and hearing.[68] Nor did he hold that we can immediately discover moral truth by a direct inspection of the world.[69] It is clear from his discussions, not only in the *Ethics* but also in the *Topics* and both *Analytics*, that moral knowledge also requires induction (*epagōgē*) and careful reflection (*dialektikē*). But neither induction nor dialectical reflection occurs without practical intuition, for they always begin with it.[70]

Aristotle's doctrine of the practical syllogism schematizes deductively the deliberations which occur in unfamiliar or difficult situations, but most of our actions do not require prior deliberation, and then the practical syllogism is an "after the fact" reconstruction of a process which did not occur in stages but in a single intuitive grasp.[71] Even when deliberation does occur, there are no logical rules of relevancy, determining what facts should be taken into account or what weight should be given them, nor for deciding what rule applies to them, or how. The creative element in decision-making is more of a sensitive feeling for what is right than a formal process.

Right judgment in moral matters is an exercise of reason, but it is also affective and valuative, and for that reason, practical truth is generated not just from experiences of any kind, but from the right kinds of affective experiences.[72] Likewise, later experiences will be influenced by earlier ones, and when character begins to take form, it begins profoundly to influence a person's felt experiences with moral value.[73]

The good man can justify his actions and support his judgments only by appealing to moral experience and to explanations and principles learned from those experiences. His claims are based on his own moral intuitions, and their validity depends on his own moral character.[74] Although such appeals do not and cannot act like scientific proofs, empirical demonstrations, or logically compelling arguments, they are the only support that finally can be offered.

We should not expect a proof, a causal explanation for why everything is as it is. In some cases, for example, with foundations [archai], it is enough to show satisfactorily that they are what they are. The fact is both the beginning and the foundation [to d' hoti prōton kai archē].[75]

Again,

It is a lack of education not to know that it is necessary to seek demonstrations of some propositions and not of others. For there cannot be a demonstration of everything altogether; there would then be an infinite regress, and hence there would still be no final demonstration.[76]

Unless others have shared similar experiences, at least vicariously, they cannot feel the force of such appeals. If they have had similar experiences, their own moral intuitions will help them sense what is and what is not morally correct. The inference is clear: although arguments can be given for moral claims, argumentation about moral matters is often futile.[77] Different sides can only appeal to their own experience of value; no more ultimate arbiter is available.

Virtually every page of the *Ethics* has some inductive appeals to support or illustrate what Aristotle is claiming. Sometimes the appeal is to the facts of human psychology; other times it is to the practical wisdom embedded in the laws and customs of the state and enunciated in "ordinary" moral language; and, occasionally, Aristotle quotes a man whose judgment he respects. But he always tries to support his conclusions by evidence obtained directly or indirectly from experience.

This, then, is the methodology for moral thought and inquiry as Aristotle sees it. The ultimate appeal is to experience, or alternatively, to moral sensitivity about human life, the good moral judgment which comes only from the right experiences, experienced rightly. Practical excellence comes only through excellent practice (*eupraxia*).

Aristotle is sometimes criticized for not adequately clarifying the nature of the morally good, or in his terminology, the noble.[78] These criticisms are aimed at his "failure" to offer a more adequate characterization of what makes some actions right and others wrong, or alternatively, what it means to say that some actions are morally right and others morally wrong. Several times we have seen that he defines right action in terms of the mean (*meson*), then says that the norm for determining the mean is right reason (*orthos logos*), and then says that the norm of right reason is the "man of high moral standards," namely, the man of practical wisdom. He concludes by saying that an action is morally right when it is done as such a person would do it.[79]

We are now able to understand why he came to this conclusion. Since right practice can only be determined by affective thinking when desiring is good and thinking true, it is impossible to enunciate some ultimate norm—completely impersonal and universally applicable—from which particular moral rules might be derived or by means of which we might recognize whether an individual action is or is not morally acceptable. As C. J. Rowe points out, Aristotle holds that in matters of practice, "the decision must always rest with the particular case"; while it is understandable why people ask for such a norm, "in the end, the request turns out to be mistaken. . . . there is no such thing."[80]

The man of practical wisdom can, of course, offer a very abstract norm, such as "we should always do what is noble"; but this is not very helpful. He also can formulate right rules of conduct and these can be, and often are, incorporated into the laws of the state. But morality cannot be completely "caught" in those laws, so that their memorization and blind acceptance would lead to much foolishness and even greater immorality. We cannot avoid using expressions like "the mean relative to me," and "what is appropriate in this situation," and "what is good for us at this time."[81] This does not mean, as we have seen before, that Aristotle is a moral relativist. He still holds that in the varying situations of our lives there *is* moral value to be recognized and achieved, and it is a practical value that is absolute and apodictic.[82] The point is that good moral judgment is a matter of sensitivity; it is not merely a matter of knowing all the right rules.

Still, if moral rules can have only general applicability, there must be *some* norm beyond them, determining when and how they apply. That norm, if it can be called that, is the moral wisdom of the good man. He is a law unto himself because, through his experience, he has developed the moral sensitivity, the good moral sense to discern in each situation exactly how he should act. But there is no way to formalize the manner in which he makes his judgments, for they are an affective and intuitive exercise of his practical reason. He "feels and acts according to the merits of each case and as reason guides him."[83]

There are serious difficulties involved in the use of moral paradigms.[84] If it is the case, as Aristotle argues it is, that we tend to project our own moral characteristics when we judge the conduct and character of others, then morally evil people, who cannot recognize genuine goodness, will select the wrong men as their models.[85] Morally good and even morally weak people can recognize who has good moral character, but they already know what is right and wrong, so that they normally do not stand in need of paradigms. So we end in a paradox: the recommendation that we look to moral models is either pernicious or useless.

For some, there is no way out of the paradox. If people are morally corrupt, their use of paradigms is pernicious, and if they are morally good, they are autonomous. Paradigms, therefore, have their chief role in moral education, before a person has sufficient experience, before his moral character has firmed. Then paradigms function as guides, and they can do so, because a person does not need to be an expert himself before he can judge who is an expert. The young and immature look to paradigms, and they learn how to act by seeing what others take into account, and how, and why.[86]

Aristotle concludes that the morally good person is the final norm of morality, because the young in fact do learn primarily by emulating the models they adopt, because there is no alternative to the affective judgments of good people in the determination of right action, and because that kind of judgment can be developed only through experience, either personal or vicarious, with the particularities of moral life. He concludes chapter 11 of Book 6, where he discusses moral good sense, with these words:

Therefore, we ought to pay as much attention to the sayings and opinions, undemonstrated though they are, of wise and experienced older men as we do to demonstrated truths. For experience has given such men an eye with which they can see correctly.[87]

From the examination we have made, we know that he meant this advice to be taken seriously and literally.

MORALITY: A SYNTHESIS OF CHARACTER AND OF ACTION

We have studied Aristotle's doctrine concerning the nature, on the outside, of kinds of actions, and we have seen that actions worth doing for their own sake are superior to those which are only instrumentalities, and that, among the former, morally good activities are radically superior to those which are simply pleasurable. We have also studied Aristotle's doctrine concerning, on the inside, kinds of men, and we have seen that the ideal is an internal harmony and integrity, dominated by reason. Practical good, therefore, "has two aspects: it is both an activity [*energeia*] and a characteristic [*hexis*]."[88]

These two aspects of the practical good are sufficiently distinct that we cannot collapse one into the other. In the case of moral excellence, "some men are called 'good' because of a characteristic they have and others because of an activity in which they engage."[89] Which, then, is the more fundamental to morality—having good character or performing right actions? Aristotle acknowledges that it is disputable "whether a man's intention or his performance is the more important element in practical excellence."[90]

We would be seriously mistaken, were we to so emphasize intentions as to ignore the importance of our intentions actually issuing in action. Practice is a matter of affecting others, and without this outer side of action, our practical thinking would be like theoretical thought. Moreover, apart from this outer dimension, there is no way in which to develop character, and there is no way in which to distinguish among kinds of character, to show the difference between idle wishing and efficacious caring, between fradulent and rightful claims to good intentions: "Wishes [*bouléseis*] by themselves are inscrutable, and unjust men also make a pretense of wishing to act justly. . . . if a man cannot perform any actions which display his moral excellence, . . . how else can he show his character?"[91] Finally, if we could say nothing meaningful about the objective rightness of actions, on their surface, we would license men to do whatever they might think right; and such subjectivity destroys morality by permitting men to follow their consciences indiscriminately, however monstrously their character might be formed.

On the other hand, if we neglect the motivation which leads a man to act, again we destroy morality, this time by reducing it to mere legalities which need not be human actions at all. Moreover, there is no single way in which to perform a given action; what gives an action its unity is the intention permeating it. Finally, it is on the inside, in the motives and purposes of men, that the unity of the moral life is accomplished. "Intention [*proairesis*] is the measure of both of the quality of friendship and of moral excellence."[92] For Aristotle, morally good intention consists both in knowing how to act and in having the character to act rightly, and without such intelligent dispositions, a man cannot be a morally good person.[93]

Consequently, although we can distinguish between the inside and the outside of human practice, between good character and right action, we distort the nature of practice if we try to separate what a man does from what he is, or if we take one to be more fundamental than the other.

We can still distinguish between them, because theirs is a contingent relationship which we learn through and from experience, and on any particular occasion we can err. But, as with most claims pertaining to practice, the rule holds generally but not always, that because kinds of activities and kinds of men are correlates, our best clues to a man's character are his pleasures.[94] "A given kind of activity produces a corresponding character," "the end of every activity corresponds to the characteristic that produces it," and "the performance of good deeds is the mark of a good man and of moral excellence."[95]

Ideally, each—a man's character and his activities—is the counterpart of the other. Moral practice is not just one or the other. "It is clear that completeness depends on both."[96] Just as, on the inside, morally good character consists in harmony and integrity, so also morality consists in a harmony and integrity between character and the activities comprising a man's life. The moral life is characterized above all by a wholeness, a unity through which a man finds the fulfillment of his nature.

Notes to Chapter 6

1. See 6. 12. 1144a7-8, 28-37; 6. 13. 1144b31-32.

2. See 3. 2. 1111b11-28; 3. 3; 3. 5. 1113b3-6; 6. 12. 1144a7-8, 20-22;
6. 13. 1145a5-6; 7. 8. 1151a15-19; Eth. Eud. 2. 11. 1227b20-1228a5.

3. In his analysis of deliberation, choice, and wish in 3. 2-5, Aristotle
analyzes all actions as only instrumentally good, and in fact makes the claim
explicit in 3. 3. 1112b33 and 3. 5. 1113b5-6. In the *Ethics* his descriptions of
the 'practical syllogism' typically portray deliberation as an inquiry into
possible means for attaining an ontologically distinct end. (By contrast a
passage in *De an.* does take the possible action as itself the end [3. 11.
434a16-19; see note 30 in chap. 4].) With a sympathetic reading, we might
interpret some of these passages to mean that morally right actions are
"means" in the sense Joachim suggested, "constituent parts of the end" (see
notes 8 and 10 in chap. 3). But it does not seem possible to interpret
everything Aristotle writes about deliberation and choice in this way.

4. See 3. 8. 1117a3-9; 10. 7. 1177a13-16; Eth. Eud. 7. 2. 1235b26-28.
Appetite can aim at the noble only if it is led by reason; cf. 3. 12.
1119b3-19; 6. 3. 1144b8-13.

5. *Metaph.* 1. 1. 981b3-4 (Hope).

6. See 3. 1. 1110a29-b8; 4. 6. 1127a3-6. This interpretation is shared
by Walsh and Allan. See James Jerome Walsh, *Aristotle's Conception of Moral
Weakness*, pp. 128-135, 146-147. Also D. J. Allan, "Aristotle's Account of
the Origin of Moral Principles," *Proceedings of the 11th International Congress of
Philosophy*, pp. 120-7.

7. See note 39 in chap. 4.

8. See "Third Contrast" in chap. 2. Aristotle may never have been as
intellectualistic as Socrates, but he also never completely abandoned that
tradition, as the next section will show.

9. See 3. 8. 1116b4-5; 6. 13. 1144b17-21, 28-30; 7. 2. 1145b23-35;
also Plato *Laches* 199a-b; *Protagoras* 351b-358d; *Hippias Minor* 365d-373e;
Euthydemus 291-2.

10. See *De an.* 1. 1; 1. 5. 411b5-30; 2. 1; 2. 2. 413b13-31; 3. 9.
432a14-b8; also note 26 in chap. 9. In *Eth. Nic.* Aristotle agrees with the
Platonic view that anger is significantly different from and superior to sheer
sensual appetite (see 7. 6. 1149a24-b25). But he does not take that difference
to be great enough to justify thinking, as did Plato, that anger originates in at
least a logically distinct part of the soul. Even righteous anger is a defective
emotion insofar as it is impetuous and lacks rational direction and control.
See 2. 7. 1108b1-6; 5. 8. 1135b19-27; 7. 6. 1149a24-b3; also "Moral
Weakness" in chap. 8.

11. 3. 10. 1117b24.

12. See, e.g., 1. 7. 1098a3-4; 1. 13. 1102a27-28, b12-1103a3; 6. 1. 1139a3-5; 6. 5. 1140b25-27; 7. 14. 1154b21-32; 9. 4. 1166a17-18.

13. See 1. 13. 1102a28-32, b24-25; also 5. 11. 1138a14-20, b6-13; note 1 in chap. 4 above.

14. D. J. Allan also concludes that "the separation of the virtues of character from *phronēsis*, which is a virtue of the mind, is a logical, not a real one" (*The Philosophy of Aristotle*, p. 127). On this interpretation it does not make sense to ask whether moral excellence or practical wisdom has precedence one over the other. But, as we shall see shortly, it *is* important to see that practical excellence, considered *either* as moral excellence *or* as practical wisdom, must be construed so as to give reason precedence over the emotions. If practical wisdom and moral excellence are essentially the same, reason and emotions cannot be ontologically separate in man either. This saves the unity of our agency, but it also creates problems for Aristotle's account of theoretical reasoning, which he describes as an exercise of reason alone. Still, his account of theoretical activity does not exclude all emotional and evaluational considerations; for it is concerned with what is "best" and "valued most highly" and is the "most pleasant" activity in which we can engage; on this see "Living the Good Life" in chap. 9. The problems here indicate again that Aristotle did not bring all his ideas into a coherent whole, at least not in the writings we have.

15. The Greek word *boulēsis* can be translated either as "wish," "aim," or "desire."

16. See 3. 2. 1111b11-13; *De an.* 3. 9. 432b5-7.

17. See *Rh.* 1. 10. 1369a1-5; *Eth. Eud.* 2. 7. 1223a27-28; *De an.* 2. 3. 414b2-3; 3. 10. 433a23-26; *Motu an.* 6. 700b23-25.

18. *Rh.* 1. 10. 1369a2-3 (my translation).

19. 3. 2. 1111b19-20. See "Deliberation and Choice" in chap. 4.

20. 3. 2. 1111b27-30; see also 3. 4. 1113a15; *Eth. Eud.* 2. 10; also note 15 in chap. 4.

21. See 6. 2. 1139a17-27.

22. The role of emotions in wishes keeps this kind of thought from being theoretical.

23. That this is Aristotle's doctrine is shown by his claim that choice is a reliable criterion for judging character; see, e.g., 3. 2. 1111b5-7; 8. 13. 1163a21-23. If practical reasoning were limited to choices of means, it could be judged only by the norm of effectiveness and Aristotle's claim here would not stand up.

24. 1. 2. 1094b7, a24-25, 7. 11. 1152b2-3, and 1. 3. 1095a10-11. Cf. 1. 2; 6. 7. 1141b21-23.

25. In both its practical and theoretical uses reason is perfected by the attainment of truth; see 6. 2. 1139a18-30, b12-13; 6. 5. 1140b4-5; 6. 6.

1141a3-6; 6. 8. 1142a21-22; 10. 5. 1176a2-23; *Metaph.* 12. 7. 1072a20-25; *De an.* 3. 11. 434a16-22.

26. 6. 12. 1144a34; cf. 3. 4. 1113a22-b2; 6. 5. 1140b4-21; 10. 9. 1181a1-b12; *Eth. Eud.* 2. 10. 1227a28-31.

27. 3. 5. 1114a9-11. For a discussion of moral education, see chap. 7.

28. See 3. 5. 1113b6-14, 1114a3-30, b20-1115a3. Aristotle also states that maturation is not necessarily dependent on age; see 1. 3. 1095a2-8.

29. See, e.g., 3. 4; 3. 5. 1114b25-30; 3. 12. 1119b3-19; 6. 2. 1139a27-30; 6. 5. 1140b12-20; 6. 12. 1144a34-37; 6. 13; 10. 8. 1178a15-18; *Pol.* 1. 5. 1254b4-9; *De an.* 3. 10. 433a13-30; 3. 11. 434a10-14; *Metaph.* 12. 7. 1072a25-30.

30. 3. 11. 1119a20-21; cf., e.g., 3. 3. 1113a7; 3. 7. 1115b11-13, 20-21; 3. 12. 1119b15-18; 6. 13; 9. 8. 1168b30-31; *Pol.* 7. 14. 1333a17-23.

31. 3. 12. 1119b3-16. It seems to me that D. J. Allan must be wrong when he interprets Aristotle as saying only that we need "to try to establish some sort of harmony between the powers in our highly complex souls. . . . such that neither partner [reason or appetition] submits to the other" (*The Philosophy of Aristotle*, pp. 48, 135). Allan then concludes that Aristotle's delineation of the relation between reason and emotions is one significant way in which "the plan of the whole treatise is weak" (p. 136).

32. 7. 9. 1152a3; cf. 1. 8. 1099a7-22; 3. 7. 1115b12-21; 3. 11. 1119a12-21; 6. 13. 1144b17-32.

33. This doctrine follows from his conviction that reason is the highest and best power a man has, and his doctrine that what is superior is meant by nature to rule over what is inferior, just as what is inferior exists to serve what is superior. See, e.g., *Pol.* 1. 5. 1254a34-36; 1. 13; 7. 14. 1333a17-23.

34. 9. 8. 1168b19-20, 1169a4-6, and 10. 9. 1180a10-13.

35. See 2. 3; 3. 4; 3. 5. 1114a3ff.; 6. 13. 1144b1-13. At an earlier stage in his thinking, Aristotle held that since wishing is a rational activity, its object must always be what is genuinely good, and the apparent good is the object only of sensual appetite; see, e.g., *Metaph.* 12. 7. 1072a26-30.

36. 1. 13. 1102b13-18; cf. 9. 8. 1168b33-35.

37. 1. 13. 1102b27-28.

38. See 1. 13. 1102a13-25.

39. See, e.g., 1. 3. 1095a4-11.

40. See, e.g., 1. 3. 1094b13-27.

41. See note 25 in chap. 7.

42. Perhaps the harshest recent interpretation of Aristotle's methodology is given by Whitney J. Oates in his *Aristotle and the Problem of Value*. Oates maintains that Aristotle invokes various "sanctions for value," and lists some eleven different ones, with no effort to relate these into a coherent whole (see pp. 352, 370). A superior analysis can be found in J. Donald

Monan's *Moral Knowledge and its Methodology in Aristotle*, to which my interpretation in this section is indebted even though it diverges from Monan's.

43. 6. 8. 1142a13-16; cf. 2. 9. 1109b23; *Metaph.* 1. 1. 981a16.

44. 1. 4. 1095a31-b8 (my translation).

45. See, e.g., 1. 3. 1095a2-4; 10. 8. 1179a17-22.

46. See, e.g., 1. 8. 1098b26-29. Aristotle may seem to go too far when he writes: "What all believe to be true is actually true; and anyone who challenges that basic belief will hardly gain more credence by propounding his view" (10. 2. 1172b36-1173a2). Such statements simply reflect Aristotle's profound respect for "common sense." As Henry Veatch writes, "Aristotle's consistent reaction was that any philosophical view that appeared patently to fly in the face of the common sense judgment of mankind simply could not be true;" see his *Aristotle: A Contemporary Appreciation*, p. 17.

47. Douglas Browning, "The Region of the Mental," *The Southern Journal of Philosophy*, 12 (1974), p. 300; cf. pp. 298-300.

48. For a few examples, see 1. 12. 1101b12-32; 1. 13. 1103a5-10; 2. 5. 1105b28-1106a8; 2. 6. 1106b23-35; 2. 9. 1109b17-20; 3. 1. 1100a19-26; 3. 5. 1113b22-1114a3; 3. 6. 1115a31-32; 3. 10. 1117b31-1118a1, 7-12; 3. 11. 1118b29-33; 4. 1. 1120a15-17; 6. 5. 1140a24-32. For descriptions of the moral culture and language of Greece before and during Aristotle's lifetime, see: K. J. Dover, *Greek Popular Morality in the Time of Plato and Aristotle*; H. D. F. Kitto, *The Greeks*; and Hugh Lloyd-Jones, *The Justice of Zeus*.

49. 6. 5. 1140a24-25 (emphasis mine).

50. See Immanuel Kant, *Groundwork of the Metaphysic of Morals* 24/405.

51. There are many reasons for these differences. One that should not be overlooked is the fact that people tend to pay more attention to what they do not have than to what they do have; see 1. 4. 1095a23-25.

52. See 1. 8. 1098b9-12.

53. See, e.g., 1. 4. 1095a14-30; 10. 6. 1176b19-27.

54. 10. 9. 1179b15-16; cf. 1. 5. 1095b13-22.

55. 7. 2. 1146b6-8.

56. See 7. 1. 1145b3-7; 10. 1. 1172a34-b7; 10. 9. 1181b12-24; *Top.* 1. 1. 100a30-b23. Aristotle typically used the dialectical method when beginning any inquiry in which previous opinions had been expressed, to set out the main problems and to help organize his own thinking. The *Politics*, the *Metaphysics*, and most of his scientific works begin with a survey of opinions, especially the theories of his predecessors. For a detailed analysis of Aristotle's use of the dialectical method in Book 6, see L. H. G. Greenwood, *Aristotle: "Nicomachean Ethics" Book Six*. See also John Burnet, *The Ethics of Aristotle*, p. v.

57. Only morally good people will know what to look for and how to interpret what they find. See 1. 3. 1094b28-1095a13; 1. 8. 1098b15-16; 10. 5. 1176a10-23; 10. 6. 1176b19-27; 10. 8. 1179a10-17; 10. 9. 1180b35-36, 1181b1-12; *Top.* 3. 1. 116a1-20. We cannot examine moral data as we might, for example, examine scientific activity. We can do the latter without being scientists ourselves (and many philosophers of science do just that), but we bring our personal history and the moral character shaped by it to our reflections on the nature of morality.

58. 10. 8. 1179a17-22; cf. 2. 7. 1107a28-33.

59. 7. 2. 1145b27; see also 1145b23-35; 6. 13. 1144b14-21. There are many instances in which Aristotle disagrees with common opinions; see, e.g., 1. 5. 1096a6-10; 5. 9. 1137a14-25; 6. 8. 1141b29-1142a10.

60. See e.g., 1. 4. 1095a28-b8; 1. 5. 1095b13-15; 1. 8. 1098b8-1099a7; 6. 8. 1142a12-20; 7. 1. 1145b2-7; 9. 8. 1168a28-b3; 10. 1. 1172a18-b7; 10. 8. 1179a10-22. Aristotle organizes the insights of his dialectical inquiry through his discussion of the constitution of the human *psuche*, and through his use of notions such as nature (*phusis*), function (*ergon*), activity (*energeia*), and excellence (*arete*).

61. See 1. 4. 1095a31-b3; 1. 7. 1098b1-4; 2. 9. 1109b13-23; 6. 3. 1139b27-35; 6. 6; 6. 8. 1142a13-18, 23-30; 6. 11; *Metaph.* 1. 9. 992b24-35; *Rh.* 2. 23. 1398a32-b19; *An. pr.* 2. 23; *An. post.* 1. 1. 71a1-17; 1. 3. 72b5-33; 1. 18. 81a37-b9; 2. 3. 90b13-14; 2. 19. 100b3-18. When Aristotle writes that "some fundamental principles can be apprehended by induction [*epagoge*], others by perception [*aisthesis*], others again by some sort of habituation [*ethismos*]," he should not be interpreted as meaning that these methods are mutually exclusive (see 1. 7. 1098b3-4). Learning moral principles requires all three.

62. For Aristotle's analysis of the nature of experience, see *Metaph.* 1. 1. 980a21-981b9 and *An. post.* 1. 3. 72b5-33; 2. 19. 100a3-8. Experience involves not only knowing particulars but also, for rational experience, the abstraction from particulars of universals, which are used in all rational activity. Although we come to know particulars only through immediate apprehension, we can come to know about them through knowing universals which they instantiate; see *An. post.* 1. 1. 71a19-22; *Metaph.* 7. 10. 1036a2-12.

63. See 6. 8. 1142a12-18, 23-31. *Nous* (intuitive thought) is common to both theoretical and practical reason and equally important to both; see 6. 6; 6. 7. 1141a16-19, b3-4; 6. 11. 1143a33-b5. Theoretical intuition grasps universals so ultimate they cannot be attained deductively, though they make deduction possible; practical intuition senses the facts relevant to accepted rules of conduct, and the rules, in turn, are inferred from experience with the facts of moral life (*ta kath' eschata*). Whereas deductive thinking

begins with universals, induction is 'dialectical' (*dialektikos*), proceeding from particulars. See *Top*. 1. 12. 105a10-19; *An. post*. 1. 1. 71a1-11. In the *Topics* Aristotle appeals to intuition to distinguish between ethical, theoretical, and logical questions and claims (see 1. 14. 105b19-29).

64. D. J. Allan has pointed out the similarity between Aristotle's doctrine here and Plato's analysis of the operation of *technē* in the *Phaedrus* 268a-272a: the application of universals to particulars requires a kind of perception or feel (*aisthēsis*); see D. J. Allan, "The Practical Syllogism," in *Autour de'Aristote*, pp. 331-332.

65. See 3. 5. 1114a31-b12; 6. 11. 1143b6-10. This is consistent with Aristotle's metaphysical claim that actuality is and must be logically and also, in a sense, temporally prior to potentiality. Potentialities are always potentialities for something, and that something has a definiteness which the potentiality lacks because it is only a possibility; yet potentialities are not completely indefinite, because they are potentialities for something, not for everything. The immature human being must have the potentiality to discern practical good before he can begin to discern it (see 2. 1. 1103a26-30; *Metaph*. 9. 8). In general, all our powers are either innate or acquired by practice (see 2. 1. 1103a30-b2; *Metaph*. 9. 5. 1047b31-35); the latter cannot arise out of nothing but presuppose potentiality.

66. 6. 11. 1143b8-9; cf. 1143a18-b10. Since we are dependent on nature, we are only responsible *to an extent* for our moral character; see 3. 5. 1114a32-b25. Because morality is a social phenomenon, Aristotle also calls good moral judgment 'consideration' (*sungnōmē*), that is, sensitive, empathetic judgment about the just and equitable in our dealings with others; see 6. 11. 1143a18-24.

67. See 1. 3. 1095a3-4; 2. 9. 1109b21-23; 3. 4. 1113a24-35; 3. 5. 1114b7; 4. 5. 1126b3-4; 6. 5. 1140b8-10; 6. 8. 1142a23-30; 6. 11. 1143a35-b5, 13; 7. 3. 1147a25-26; *De an*. 2. 6. 418a7-27; *An. post*. 2.19.

68. See 6. 8. 1142a27-28. Of course sense perception necessarily also is involved in moral sensitivity.

69. He was well acquainted with Plato's doctrine in the *Phaedo* that knowledge can only be attained through dialectical examination and criticism.

70. Practical reasoning can take the form of deliberation (*bouleusis*), wishing (*boulēsis*), dialectical examination (*dialektikē*), or choosing (*proairesis*); and its "achievements" include the characteristics of slyness (*panourgia*), cleverness (*deinotēs*), skill (*technē*), good judgment (*sunesis*), and practical wisdom (*phronēsis*). They all depend on intuition.

71. See note 28 in chap. 4.

72. Aristotle is commonly criticized for defining man's distinctiveness in terms of his rationality; there is, the argument goes, no single conclusive

scientific way in which to describe human uniqueness. Others have thought that Aristotle also falls into what sometimes is called "the naturalistic fallacy," by trying to derive value judgments from scientific and 'value-neutral' descriptions. But if we accept Aristotle's analysis of his own procedure, these criticisms do not touch him. His philosophic psychology as well as his theory of action are, from the beginning, valuative, moral analyses with the function of providing the rationale for viewing human practice through specifically moral categories. If there is an ineluctable circularity in doing moral philosophy, it is not necessarily vicious and cannot be helped. The inquirer's moral character will always affect his inquiry; see 1. 5. 1095b13-15. Aristotle therefore controverts the claim of many modern metaethicists—that ethical philosophy can and ought to be a purely theoretical enterprise. Ethics, according to Aristotle, also ought to help a person attain practical wisdom, and "practical wisdom is concerned with action" (6. 7. 1141b21; cf. 2. 2. 1103b26-28).

73. See chap. 7.

74. Therefore a teacher of morals needs himself to be a morally good man. (He will have a right understanding of the subject even if he is morally weak, but if his students see him in his moments of weakness, they will believe his actions rather than his words; see 10. 1. 1172a35-b8). Since the *Ethics* is itself an exercise of practical reason, Aristotle cannot expect us to respect his claims without at least implicitly claiming he is himself sufficiently experienced and sufficiently good to deserve our respect; see, e.g., 1. 4. 1095b1-13; 10. 9. 1181a1-b23. But it would be gauche for him to make the claim explicit, and first person references are conspicuous for their absence. See also note 97 in chap. 9.

75. 1. 7. 1098b1-3 (my translation).

76. *Metaph.* 4. 4. 1006a6-8 (Hope).

77. "A man whose life is guided by emotion will not listen to an argument that dissuades him, nor will he understand it" (10. 9. 1179b27-28; cf. 1. 3. 1094b28-1095a13; 1. 4. 1095b4-12; 10. 3. 1173b28-30; 10. 5. 1176a10-29; *Rh.* 2. 12. 1389a2-b11).

78. See, for example, D. J. Allan, *The Philosophy of Aristotle*, p. 136.

79. See 2. 4. 1105b5-8; 2. 6. 1106b36-1107a2.

80. C. J. Rowe, *The Eudemian and Nicomachean Ethics: A Study in the Development of Aristotle's Thought*, pp. 112-113.

81. See, e..g., 4. 2. 1122a25-33; also the last section of chap. 3.

82. J. Donald Monan puts it well when he writes: "Aristotle's situating of the norm in the action of the *phronimos* is no crude affirmation of subjectivism or of an absolute autonomy of the individual in forming moral judgments. . . . It rather asserts that intuitive moral judgments are the meeting point or the expression of encounters between factors both interior

to the agent and independent of him. . . . the reason why Aristotle introduced the *good* man in Book III, 5 was *not* because all goods are purely relative, but because it is only to the good man that the genuine good will appear." See J. Donald Monan, *Moral Knowledge and its Methodology in Aristotle*, pp. 84-85.

83. 3. 7. 1115b20-24.

84. See "Making and Doing" in chap. 3.

85. See 1. 5. 1095b14-23; 2. 8. 1108b18-26, 1109a13-18; 9. 12. 1172a8-13.

86. Mature and morally good men can also find themselves in novel and perplexing situations, and then they need the help of other good men who are experienced in such situations. Paradigms also have a role in quickening moral principles. Morally weak persons do not need models to learn the right moral principles; they know them already. But they do need the moral suasion that the example and encouragement of others can help provide.

87. 6. 11. 1143b10-13; cf. 9. 12. 1172a11-13.

88. 7. 12. 1152b33; see also 2. 6. 1106a15-23.

89. 8. 5. 1157b5-6.

90. 10. 8. 1178a34-35 (my translation).

91. 10. 8. 1178a30-34 (my translation).

92. 9. 1. 1164b2-3 (my translation).

93. See chap. 5.

94. See 2. 3; 10. 4. 1175a13.

95. 3. 5. 1114a7, 3. 7. 1115b21-22, and 9. 9. 1169b12-13; cf. 2. 1. 1103a26-b25; 2. 2. 1104a11-b2; 6. 12. 1143b23-27.

96. 10. 8. 1178b1. Because Aristotle so often stresses the importance to morality of enduring moral qualities of character (excellent *hexeis*), he is sometimes described as offering an "ethics of character," and on that basis a contrast is drawn between him and philosophers like Immanuel Kant, who are said to stress the importance of individual choices (or actions). This is a misinterpretation of Aristotle. Again and again he insists that practical excellence concerns *both* a person's character *and* his actions (see, e.g., 2. 6. 1106a15-23, b15-16, 24-25, 1107a4-11; 2. 8. 1108b15-18; 2. 9. 1109a19-23; 3. 1. 1109b30-31; 7. 12. 1152b33). Character and activity are counterparts of each other, for actions are the expressions (*energeiai*) of character which has been formed by other, similar actions (see, e.g., 2. 1. 1103b21-22; 2. 2. 1104a27-29; 2. 3. 1105a13-16; 3. 5. 1113b12-14; 5. 1. 1129a7-10; 5. 5. 1134a1-8; *Eth. Eud.* 2. 1. 1219b8-11; *Pol.* 7. 12. 1331b27-28). Moreover, if one *must* be taken as more fundamental and important than the other, for Aristotle it is activity and not character. In discussing the qualities and constituents of the good life, Aristotle rejects the view that the good life consists in the possession of good qualities and argues it must rather consist

of activities (see 1. 5. 1095b31-1096a2; 1. 8. 1098b12-19, 29-1099a7; 2. 3. 1104b19-21; *Eth. Eud.* 2. 1. 1219b8-25; also note 8 in chap. 9 below). The main reason is that human life *is* activity, and capabilities and characteristics are important only for what they enable us to *do* (see 10. 4. 1175a12). Consequently, characteristics are defined by their activities, and the activities themselves, not the characteristics, are the end; see 4. 2. 1122b1-2; 8. 5. 1157b5-12; 9. 7. 1168a5-8; 9. 9. 1170a17-18; *Metaph.* 6. 8. 1050a8-11.

Unfortunately, in 1. 12 of *Eth. Nic.*, Aristotle claims that honor (*timē*), which is appropriate only to the best and the standard for all else, should be given to the divine, to the good life, and (perhaps) to pleasure; praise (*epainos*) is rightly given to things good only in relation to those things honored, namely, to skillful and morally good men alike. This is completely incompatible with the doctrine that moral goodness is far superior to skill and with the fact that it is the individual person who performs morally good actions and lives the good life. Perhaps this chapter belongs to an early stage in Aristotle's career; it seems clearly contradicted by passages such as 4. 3. 1124a20-b5 and 10. 5.

7

The Political Genesis
and Political Nature of Morality

We have not yet achieved an adequate understanding of the nature of our moral life. So far, that life has been depicted primarily as a personal phenomenon with only a mention here and there of the fact that, as Aristotle sees it, there is no such thing as a radically individual human person. We do not have a self-sufficing nature. There may be other beings who can live totally apart from others, but they are either gods or beasts. We cannot survive, much less achieve any degree of excellence, apart from others—our family, our friends, and our fellow men. "Hence it is evident that the state is a creation of nature, and that man is by nature a political animal [*phusei politikon zōon*]."[1]

The family is the smallest societal unit, but it is too small to provide for all our needs. Its nature, in fact, is partly defined by the larger society of the state, which can provide a structured community within which men can have the leisure and education necessary for the good life. Societal and political life is not only the most efficient way to provide for the necessities of life; it is also a good in itself. There is hardly any pleasure greater than the pleasure of friends; and political life gives us the opportunity to engage in morally good activities. The life of a citizen, therefore, is worthwhile for its own sake, and it is an essential part of our nature as men to be active members of a state.[2]

We have no cause to resent our dependency on the state into which we were born and within which our self is shaped and formed. For we can develop and achieve excellence only within the acculturation provided by societal institutions which pass along to us the accumulated wisdom of centuries, rules and ideals tested in the fire of vast experience.[3]

We need to define ourselves in terms of our citizenry, but we are not completely limited by our own time and place with its special arrangements. Aristotle traveled widely, and he was acutely aware that different cultures do not stress the identically same values and that there are varying institutional arrangements for transmitting values. He recommends we study how others live and have lived. Doing this expands our experience so that we can better understand the strengths and weaknesses of our own social and political structures.

Attending to the socio-political nature of man helps complete Aristotle's delineation of our moral life by the addition of three significant doctrines. First, moral education is fundamentally political education. Secondly, the moral ideal demands an integrity between the inner, the individual, and the socio-political aspects of a man's life. Finally, and perhaps most importantly, the institutions and laws of a state are, in fact, a systematic and concrete expression of the moral ideal, for they reflect a conception of the good life, developed and tested for decades and even centuries. (Tyrannies are an exception to this claim).

These three doctrines also help complete the discussion of moral epistemology. In the last chapter we saw one reason for Aristotle's frequent appeals to the language of praise and blame: that language reflects and enunciates common moral experience. There is another and equally important justification for such appeals: only within the whole context of the complex and interrelated customs, laws, and institutions of a state do specific moral rules take on their full meaning. Aristotle does argue that there is a universal foundation for moral value in the nature of man and the nature of kinds of activities, but this foundation is not so determinate as to not allow some leeway in the ways in which the morally good life can be constructed. Consequently, there is no way in which Aristotle can discuss specific moral virtues nor specific ways of acting, without a tacit appeal to familiar conventions, institutions, and laws. Yet his comparative studies of other constitutions and other states enable him to argue, even within the context of the Athenian life, that some prevalent views in that life are mistaken and need amendment.

Since our own chief cultural heritage in the Western world is Greco-Roman, many of Aristotle's more particular claims seem obviously right even today. But we are not just modern Greeks, and that is why, for example, Aristotle's description of the 'great-souled' man in 4. 3, a man with a deep sense of self-respect, seems ludicrously pompous and self-righteous to us, and why Aristotle's defense of slavery and of an inferior status for women are downright offensive.

THE STATE: MASTER PARADIGM AND MORAL EDUCATOR

We have seen the great stress Aristotle places on the role of the man of high moral standards (the *spoudaios* or *phronimos*) as the ultimate model or paradigm in moral matters. He also gives more space to his discussion of kinds of friendship—*philia*—than to any other single topic. Yet he devotes practically no space at all to the dynamics of the personal relationship of moral instructor to pupil.[4] Like Plato, Aristotle is far more concerned about the political context within which moral education must take place; morality and political life cannot be separated from one another. A person can hope to attain practical excellence only within a state, and the most important and influential moral paradigm is the person of the state, its wisdom as found in its laws and customs and as epitomized in its leaders.

Like the family, the state is not a merely conventional aggregate of individual men; it is a natural society, with its own proper function (*ergon*): to embody, through its citizens and their activities, the ideal human life. The morally significant activities of individual citizens consist primarily in their participation in the affairs of the state and in its social institutions, such as the family.[5] Because the fit between them is so close and because individual citizens and the state share the same goal, "the highest good attainable by action [*praxis*]," "the virtue of the good man is necessarily the same as the virtue of the citizen of the perfect state."[6]

Given this view, there is no sense to the contemporary belief that morality cannot and should not be legislated; most crimes, for example, can be traced to the morally defective character of law-breakers.[7] Therefore, "the main concern of politics is to engender a certain character in the citizens and to make them good and disposed to perform noble actions."[8] The means of doing this is public education:

> Since the whole city has one end, it is manifest that
> education should be one and the same for all, and that it
> should be public. . . . in the same manner, and by the same
> means through which a man becomes truly good, he will
> frame a state . . . , and the same education and the same
> habits will be found to make a good man and a man fit to be
> a statesman or king.[9]

Aristotle is not thinking only of formal education here, for much of
the state's educative function consists of good laws to promote
exemplary moral conduct.[10]

The educational system Aristotle sets out seems almost a
restatement of Plato's proposals in the *Republic* for the training of the
Guardians.[11] Following Plato, Aristotle holds there are three elements essential to moral achievement: nature, nurture, and instruction.[12]

A child's natural temperament concerns the pleasures to which
he is attracted and the pains to which he is most sensitive. A child
born with a "naturally good nature" is gifted both with the potentiality to reason rightly and with a temperament which can develop
into morally good character.[13] But moral goodness itself is "im-
planted in us neither by nature nor contrary to nature. . . . We do
not by nature develop into good or evil men"; we must *learn* how to
live rightly and well.[14] That learning takes place in two stages:
nurture and instruction.

Nurture consists primarily in physical and emotional training.
The development of many capacities (*dunameis*) depends on practice; learning how to act rightly can only be done by doing, by
habituation (*ethismos*), whether a person is following his own decision or the directions of others.[15] Moreover,

> it is pleasure that makes us do base actions and pain that
> prevents us from doing noble actions. For that reason, as
> Plato says, men must be brought up from childhood to feel
> pleasure and pain at the proper things; for this is correct
> education. . . . Hence, it is no small matter whether one
> habit or another is inculcated in us from early childhood; on

the contrary, it makes a considerable difference, or rather, all the difference.[16]

The process of learning self-control is not always pleasurable, but good laws and customs will enforce right behavior, and, since an adult's pleasures are not definitely set at birth but are mostly learned, nurturing must make an ally of pleasure, so that children learn to enjoy acting rightly.

It might seem that training, indoctrination, and habituation are precisely the educational techniques to be avoided if the aim is to develop persons who are a law unto themselves. But this is Aristotle's solution to the problem first mentioned in Chapter 5, "Moral Excellence": if moral excellence and practical wisdom presuppose each other, how is it possible to generate practical excellence? We also have seen the answer: only through the right experiences, experienced rightly, and only by acting as good men act, until one becomes a good person.

"It is clear that in [moral] education practice must be used before theory, and the body be trained before the mind."[17] Children have biological and emotional needs and drives long before they can reason in the full sense; therefore, psychological conditioning, and physical training which can support it, must be begun in early childhood. A person's actions not only have an outer direction but also an inner bearing on the formation of his character. When he does the same actions over and over, he can generally do them better, more easily, and more quickly.[18] But more importantly, he begins to take on personal characteristics (*hexeis*) appropriate to those kinds of activities.[19]

Although moral excellence presupposes habituation, it should not be identified with it, for good emotional qualities deserve to be called morally excellent only when they are united with and informed by principles of reason.[20] Emotional dispositions are not traits of moral character until a man acts from his own choices and not merely as a machine programmed by someone else.[21] That is why the goal of nurture is not moral excellence itself but a shaping in the direction of moral excellence, "a character that somehow has an affinity for excellence or virtue, a character that loves what is noble and feels disgust at what is base."[22]

The second stage of moral education, instruction, aims at

cultivating "the power of forming right judgements, and of taking delight in good dispositions and noble actions."[23] Because practical wisdom (*phronēsis*) is, in part, an intellectual excellence, its development requires instruction.[24] But because it is not whólly intellectual, instruction in the principles of right action will be effective only when students have had the right kinds of experience, only when they already are "truly enamored of what is noble."[25] It is impossible to convince a person of the rightness of a practical principle by argumentation; he can grasp its rightness only when he already is in a position to adopt it as his own. Instruction, therefore, both presupposes good nurture and aims to transform emotional traits into intelligent dispositions of good character. It also aims to make the connectedness between the inner and outer dimensions of a man's practical life as perfect as possible.

Although instruction consists in discussions about the rational principles a good man might use, the student still needs to learn for himself how to apply those principles to his own circumstances. Learning rules does not mean parroting them. At this stage of moral education, the student should no longer be encouraged simply to imitate others. He must learn to deliberate correctly, to determine *for himself* what is the best way for him to act in the situations of his life.

Although Aristotle does not offer us a systematic exposition of this final stage of moral education, his own *Ethics* exemplifies it. What he points to is a transition from patterns of conduct and attitudes based on authority to a critical understanding of and appreciation for the rationale behind them, so that the mature person can move about in the practical world of pleasures, ideals, and paradigms with self-imposed discrimination. At this point moral education is more of a making available to than an imposing; and it can be no other way if a man is to assume responsibility for the moral quality of his own life. If he is to be, in the fullest sense possible to him, the *archē*, the source of his own activities, they must arise out of *his* conception of what is good.

Beyond the State

Thus far we have seen Aristotle's view of the ideal—the ideal citizens ideally educated in an ideal state. States, even when they are the best possible relative to conditions obtaining in the world, rarely realize the ideal. Moral philosophy must depict the absolute ideal, which will stand above and measure all attempts to approximate it. But moral philosophy must also deal with the best open possibilities; it should not become so abstract as to be no longer practical.[26]

Since the state is prior to the individuals, Aristotle lays down the principle that "the citizen should be moulded to suit the form of government under which he lives."[27] The only hope for the good life is within a state, and a state can only survive if its constitution is upheld. Consequently,

> that which most contributes to the permanence of
> constitutions is the adaptation of education to the form of
> government. . . . The best laws, though sanctioned by every
> citizen of the state, will be of no avail unless the young are
> trained by habit and education in the spirit of the
> constitution.[28]

The ideal government, as Aristotle sees it, is a monarchy.[29] But, given the actual number of superior men in a country, the way wealth is in fact distributed, and the manner in which the people conceive of the best way to live, timocracy is often the best form of government possible. Usually power drifts into the hands either of a very few or of a very many, so that most governments end up either as oligarchies or democracies.[30] Since civil laws are written so as to conform to the constitution in effect, the definitions of, for example, just acts and just men will vary somewhat from state to state, and then what makes a man a good citizen may not be sufficient for his also being a morally excellent person.[31] Again Aristotle shows that his objectivism does not lead him into absolutism: there are various ways of constructing the good life, given the circumstances obtaining, with their special possibilities and limitations.

Likewise, not many persons achieve the status of moral excellence. Aristotle's observations lead him to believe that most people end up with a temperament which finds sensual pleasures to be the only pleasures and which reacts more strongly to fear of punishment than to a sense of moral shame.[32] The main reason is that most states fail to educate their citizenry adequately; most men are not "conditioned by habits to the right kinds of likes and dislikes."[33] Aristotle then concludes that the majority of men live "under the sway of emotion. . . . [and] do not even have a notion of what is noble and truly pleasant, since they have never tasted it."[34] When this is the case, then generally "emotion does not yield to any argument but only to force."[35] Civil law cannot compel men to act from morally good motives, but it can and should habituate them, under threat of punishment, to avoid acting wrongly and to perform the right actions.[36] There is always the hope, once men have become habituated to doing the right actions, that some will eventually develop good character.[37]

Aristotle feels forced, therefore, to replace individual moral responsibility with externally enforced behavioral norms. If most men are incapable of genuinely moral action, at least their behavior can be regulated, even if moral education by the state does not progress beyond conditioning and indoctrination. Aristotle clearly is not happy with this conclusion, but he sees no alternative to giving license to a few to coerce a majority incapable of understanding what is in their real and best interest. This is not invidious if it is done under the rule of law and if the law reflects the best deliberations of the best men.[38] Nonetheless, many thoughtful men have argued that this is too dangerous a doctrine; it is too open to abuse. It provides too easy a rationale for governments of the worst kind, and it self-servingly prevents any challenge.

What we need now are norms or criteria for judging the moral acceptability of kinds of states. If all laws are relative to an existing constitution, and if that constitution is the moral ultimate, we are surely left in cultural relativism. But Aristotle does provide us with four such criteria. The first of these criteria, justice, is discussed at length in Book 5 of the *Ethics*. Since the fundamental bond within a community is the fulfillment of common needs and the fundamental activity of a community is exchange, the fundamental condition of exchange and so of community is reciprocal justice.[39] Justice concerns not only material goods but also the manner in which people treat each other, and Aristotle's famous dictum here is that equals should be treated equally and unequals unequally.[40] There is another, higher form of justice incumbent on the state and not definable simply in terms of the laws of the state, and that is justice in the sense of moral excellence. This kind of justice implies all other moral qualities and also provides the norm that those in power should rule for the advantage of all the citizens, not just for the private gain of the rulers.[41]

The other three criteria are delineated, strangely enough, mainly in negative terms, in Aristotle's criticisms of tyranny, the worst form of government. In order to render his subjects incapable of rebellious actions, Aristotle writes, the tyrant does everything possible to destroy their sense of personal dignity, their sense of community and mutual trust, and their freedom.[42] If we reverse the perversions of tyranny, we find three fundamental moral ideals legislating for the moral acceptability of any constitutional arrangement of institutions and power: respect for the dignity of all men, including one's self; a sense of moral community with other men; and moral freedom.

Insofar as a particular form of government does not recognize and promote freedom and a sense of individual dignity and of community, to that extent it is immoral, regardless of the arguments it may try to use to defend its policies. Principles incorporating these criteria should be part of the constitution of any state, and only those laws are good which conform to them. Aristotle does not himself develop these ideas any further, and at this point his moral-political philosophy needs supplementing and elaborating.

Aristotle, however, does provide the ontological foundation for these ideals. Human dignity and moral freedom are demands which follow from what we are: agents capable of self-determination, agents whose own reason can and should dominate the exercise of our power to affect others and, in doing so, will shape our own character.[43] Justice and a sense of community are also demands based on our nature, for we are social beings, and our practical reason can develop and achieve excellence only within a community with our fellow men.

Notes to Chapter 7

1. *Pol.* 1. 2. 1253a2-3 (Jowett); cf. 3-38; 3. 6. 1278b20; *Eth. Nic.* 1. 7. 1097b11; 9. 9. 1169b17-22.

2. See 1. 2. 1094a26-b12; 1. 7. 1097b7-11; 6. 8. 1142a7-10; 8. 1. 1155a3-31; 8. 5. 1157b20-24; 8. 6. 1158a22-27; 8. 9. 1160a9-30; 8. 12. 1162a16-29; 9. 9. 1169b17-1170a20; 10. 7. 1177a28-b1; *Pol.* 1. 2. 1253a2-28; 3. 6. 1278b15-29. What differentiates citizenship from both coexistence and gregariousness is the fact that citizens share common goals (*erga;* see 9. 9. 1170b10-13; *Hist. an.* 1. 1. 488a9). Men unite first to have the bare necessities of life—food, clothing, shelter, and security, then to secure what is necessary for living well, e.g., moderate wealth, freedom, and education, finally to actually live the good life (see 8. 12. 1162a16-27; *Pol.* 2. 6. 1265a18-27; 4. 11. 1295a35-b1; 7. 8. 1328b3-23). The state, therefore, is composed of men with different functions, all contributing to the social harmony within which it is possible to achieve the good life (see *Pol.* 4. 4. 1290b24-1291b1). In Aristotle's view negative utilitarianism, which justifies only a minimal state (for the sake of survival and fundamental needs), has a radically inadequate conception of the purpose and nature of the state; see *Pol.* 3. 9. 1280a26-1281a10; 7. 10. 1329a23-24.

3. "Men should not think it slavery to live according to the rule of the constitution; for it is their salvation" (*Pol.* 5. 9. 1310a34-36; Jowett). "Neither must we suppose that any one of the citizens belongs to himself, for they all belong to the state, and are each of them a part of the state, and the care of each part is inseparable from the care of the whole" (*Pol.* 8. 1. 1337a29-31; Jowett).

4. Aristotle does say a few things about this. See, e.g., 8. 3. 1156b9-10; 9. 3. 1165b18; 9. 4. 1166a3-4; 9. 9. 1170a11-12; 9. 12. 1172a12-13; 10. 9. 1180a31-32. But he does not discuss what is a common phenomenon today—moral crisis precipitated by a sudden realization of inadequacies and inconsistencies in one's models. If Aristotle is right about the role of paradigms, the agony of the person in moral crisis will ease only when other, different models have been found; but Aristotle does not tell us how this transition can be made.

5. See 1. 4. 1095a14-16; 5. 1. 1129b13-35; 6. 13. 1145a6-9; *Pol.* 1. 1. 1252a5-6; 3. 1. 1275b20-21; 3. 9. 1280b30-1281a8; 7. 2. 1324a23-35; 7. 7. 1328a36-37, b16-22; 7. 9. 1329a2-24; 7. 13. 1332a3-7; 7. 14. 1333b37-38. Aristotle defines the notion of a state by means of three concepts. A *citizen* is a member of a state; he is governed by the state and he also shares in the governing, either by deliberating over or by administering its laws (see 5. 6. 1134b13-15; *Pol.* 3. 1. 1275b18-20; 3. 13. 1283b45-1284a3). The *constitu-*

tion of a state determines the manner in which power is divided, by whom it is exercised, and toward what end. The constitutional arrangement of offices determines the form of government, and there are as many forms as there are ways of arranging these offices (see *Pol.* 4. 1. 1289a15-17; 4. 3. 1290a8-12; 7. 9. 1328b22-32). The *laws* of a state should not be confused with the principles of the constitution. Laws are specific rules according to which citizens fulfill their functions; "law is order, and good law is good order" (*Pol.* 7. 4. 1326a30; Jowett). The rightness of any law is relative to the constitution in effect (see *Pol.* 4. 1. 1289a13-15).

6. 1. 4. 1095a17 and *Pol.* 3. 18. 1288a38. Even in the perfect state this claim is qualified; see *Pol.* 1. 13. 1259b33-1260a33; 3. 4. 1277a13-b33; 3. 5. 1278b1-5; 4. 7. 1293b5-8; 7. 14. 1333a11-12; *Eth. Nic.* 1. 2. 1094b7-11. Aristotle's political philosophy echoes Plato's view that the state is a macrocosmic counterpart to man, with the same activities as its intrinsic good and the same qualities, if it is a good state, as the good man. See, e.g., *Pol.* 1. 13. 1260a3-7; 3. 4. 1277a5-10; 4. 4. 1290b21-1291b8; 4. 11. 1295a35-b1; 7. 1. 1323b34-36; 7. 3. 1325b14-31; 7. 13. 1332a3-7; 7. 14. 1333b37-38; 7. 15. 1334a12-36; also Plato *Republic*, esp. chaps. 6, 12-14. This is a dangerous doctrine, for it too easily leads to the view that some people within a state correspond to the vegetative soul (they can be slaves, with no share in citizenship or the good life); others correspond to the emotions, and they need only to be obedient, particularly in matters pertaining to their functions within the state; and the only people needing practical wisdom are the elite, who rule as reason rules the individual. Aristotle in fact takes this very view; see citations above, also 3. 4. 1277a10ff. Because he did not free himself of the Platonic model, Aristotle frequently makes claims in the *Politics* which are completely incompatible with his analysis of moral personality in the *Nicomachean Ethics*. Even in the *Ethics*, Aristotle holds there is an essential difference between the practical wisdom of the individual and the political wisdom (*politikē*) of the ruler, even though their fundamental operations seem the same; see 6. 8. 1141b23-1142a11; also 1. 2; 1. 4. 1095a16.

7. See *Pol.* 2. 5. 1263b15-23; 2. 7. 1267a5-14; 2. 9. 1271a16-17. The two main causes of civil unrest and crime are inequity in the distribution of property and the desire for the 'necessary' pleasures. The state can help remedy the first by prospering a large middle class (see *Pol.* 4. 12. 1296b35-1297a8). Legislators must pass laws which will teach young citizens to control their desires for the 'necessary' pleasures, for such desires are insatiable if left unchecked. See 2. 3. 1105a1-13; 10. 9. 1179b31-1180b31; *Pol.* 2. 7. 1267a8-14.

8. 1. 9. 1099b30-32; cf. 1. 2. 1094b7-11; 1. 13. 1102a7-26; 2. 1. 1103b3-6; 5. 1. 1129b17-18; 5. 2. 1130b22-25; 7. 11. 1152b1-3; *Pol.* 8. 1.

1337a9-10. The state therefore must help make leisure possible; see *Pol.* 2. 7. 1273a8-b7.

9. *Pol.* 8. 1. 1337a21-23 and 3. 18. 1288a39-b3 (Jowett); cf. 7. 14. 1332b41-1333a16.

10. See 2. 1. 1103b2-6; 10. 9. 1179b32-1180b31.

11. See Plato *Republic* 374d-404, 521-541.

12. See 10. 9. 1179b20-32; also 1. 7. 1098b3-4; 1. 9. 1099b8-34; *Pol.* 7. 13. 1332a39-b11; 7. 15. 1334b7-28. Socrates had been preoccupied with the frequency with which moral education fails; the best men in Athens could not transmit their excellence of character to their friends nor even to their own children (see 10. 9. 1181a1-9). Aristotle concludes that moral training will fail if either nature, nurture, or instruction is seriously defective.

13. See 3. 5. 1114a31-b11; 6. 11. 1143b6-10; 6. 13. 1144b4-9; 10. 9. 1179b20-23; *Pol.* 3. 13. 1283a33-37. For various senses of the term 'nature', see chap. 3, note 5. Here 'naturally' means "that which is found with us as soon as we are born" (*Eth. Eud.* 2. 8. 1224b31; Solomon), and 'nature' refers primarily to the *psuchē*, the form of humanness, but also, since it is necessary to the moral life, to the child's physical body as well.

14. 2. 1. 1103a24 and 2. 5. 1106a10; cf. 2. 1. 1103a17-25. Because potentialities (*dunameis*) are by themselves morally neutral, merely capacities for opposites, whether a child eventually becomes good or evil depends on the manner in which his potentialities are developed; see *Metaph.* 9. 9. 1051a3-21. This doctrine differentiates, in a fundamental way, Aristotle's moral theory from others, such as Immanuel Kant's, which begin with a view of human nature as radically and innately depraved. For Aristotle, as Sir David Ross writes, "Evil . . . is not a necessary feature of the universe but a byproduct of the world-process, something that casually emerges in the course of the endeavor of individual things to reach such perfection as is open to them"; see his *Aristotle*, 5th ed. rev., p. 178. This doctrine of the moral neutrality of individual potentialities needs to be balanced by the doctrine that man's psyche as a whole does have certain entelechies toward which his nature will tend if not impeded, so that there is a proper way in which human potentialities should be developed; see, e.g., *Part. an.* 1. 1. 640a33-b4.

15. See 2. 1-4; *Metaph.* 9. 5. 1047b31-35; 9. 8. 1049b29-32; *Pol.* 8. 1. 1337a19-21.

16. 2. 3. 1104b10-13 and 2. 1. 1103b23-25; cf. 2. 1; 2. 2. 1104a12-b2; 2. 9. 1109b2-12; 10. 1. 1172a18-25; 10. 5. 1175b2-23; 10. 9. 1179b20-1180a2. So much depends on the kinds of pleasures to which we become accustomed, that the entire development of character depends on children learning to feel joy and pain in the right way; see, e.g., 2. 3. 1104b28-

1105a17. This part of education cannot be left until later, for "children live as their appetite directs them, and the desire for pleasure is especially strong in them"; since "the desire for pleasure is insatiable" if not checked, a child's appetites must be "pruned" if they are to be able to listen later to the guidance of reason (3. 12. 1119b5-10; cf. 6. 13. 1144b8-30). In the concluding pages of the *Politics*, Aristotle offers three rules for nurture: (1) Do what is possible (*to dynaton*); nurture must build on the abilities a child has at each stage of his development; (2) Do what is suitable (*to prepon*); the strengths and weaknesses of each child should be taken into account, and his education tailored to him; (3) Promote the mean (*to meson*), for that is the goal of dispositional training. See *Pol.* 8. 7. 1342b18-19, 33-34; see also 7. 15. 1334b7-28; 7. 17. 1336b35-1337a2; *Eth. Nic.* 10. 9. 1180b7-14.

17. *Pol.* 8. 3. 1338b5-6 (Jowett); cf. 1337b23-1338b4; 8. 5. 1340b10-19; 7. 5. 1334b7-28; 8. 7. Education begins with physical exercise and progresses to training in basic skills.

18. See "Pleasure and Kinds of Pleasure" in chap. 3. "Teachers consider that they have attained their end when they have exhibited their students actually performing their training" (*Metaph.* 9. 8. 1050a18-19; Hope). Those engaged in nurturing can measure their success in terms of behavioral characteristics only.

19. See 2. 1. 1103b21; 2. 2; 2. 4. 1105a17-26; 3. 5. 1114a3-30; 6. 12. 1143b22-23.

20. See 2. 6. 1106b37-1107a2; 3. 7. 1115b22-23; 3. 8. 1117a3-9; 6. 13. 1144b2-30.

21. See 2. 4. 1105a17-b8; 6. 12. 1144a13-19, 24-37; *Ph.* 3. 3. 202a30-b7.

22. 10. 9. 1179b29-31; cf. 6. 13. 1144b1-30.

23. *Pol.* 8. 5. 1340a17-18 (Jowett).

24. See 2. 1. 1103a15-17.

25. 10. 9. 1179b8; cf. 1. 3. 1094b28-1095a11; 1. 4. 1095b1-12; 1. 7. 1098b1-4; 2. 1-4; 6. 12. 1143b23-28; 10. 9. Good moral reasoning involves a personal commitment toward acting rightly, and that is incommunicable by discussions, arguments, or lectures (see 2. 4. 1105b13-17). Aristotle makes this point as strongly as he can when he writes that knowledge is of little or no help in *learning and developing* the right moral dispositions (see 2. 4. 1105b3-5; 7. 8. 1151a15-20). Socrates was wrong in thinking he could make men good only by enlightening them about their best good (see 3. 8. 1116b4-5; 6. 13. 114b17-21): "Our ability to perform such actions is in no way enhanced by knowing [about] them, since the virtues are characteristics. . . . [just as] our ability to perform actions (which show that we are healthy and well) is in no way enhanced by a mastery of the science of

medicine or of physical training" (6. 12. 1143b23-27). But Socrates did understand that we cannot fully understand good practice if we have no love for it. We must already be on the inside of good practical activity before we can engage in meaningful discussions about it. Plato had a similar difficulty trying to explain the Good to those lacking experience of it; see Plato *Republic*, chap. 23 and *Symposium* 210-211. See also *Rh.* 2. 12. 1389a2-b11 where Aristotle describes youth as regulating their lives "more by moral feeling than by reasoning" (Roberts).

26. See 2. 9. 1109a30-b1; *Pol.* 4. 1. 1288b21-40; 4. 11. 1296b3-12.

27. *Pol.* 8. 1. 1337a13-14 (Jowett).

28. *Pol.* 5. 9. 1310a13-17 (Jowett).

29. Again following Plato (see the *Statesman* 291a-292a, 300e-303b), Aristotle argues there are three "true forms" of government: kingly rule (the rule of one), aristocracy (the rule of a few), and timocracy (the rule of many, with a constitutional property requirement). Of these monarchy is "the first and most divine," for there ideally should be only one ruler just as in the individual there is but one ruler, reason. Timocracy is the least good of the true forms, because it bases the right to rule on the possession of property, not on personal excellence. There are three corresponding perverted forms of government—tyranny (the worst because it is a perversion of the best), oligarchy ("a little better"), and democracy ("the most tolerable of the three"). They are perverted, because those in power look out only for their own advantage rather than for justice. See 8. 10. 1160a31-b22; also 5. 1. 1129b14-17; 5. 3. 1131a25-28; 5. 7. 1135a3-5; *Pol.* 3. 6-18; 4. 1-10.

30. See 8. 10-11; *Pol.* 4. 11. 1295b35-1296a37.

31. See 5. 2. 1130b28-29; *Pol.* 3. 4. 1276b15-1277a13; 3. 5. 1278b1-5; 5. 9. 1309a33-b8.

32. See 1. 5. 1095b19-22; 3. 4. 1113a34-b2; 7. 13. 1153b33-36; *Pol.* 1. 6. 1255b1-3; 7. 13. 1331b39-1332a3.

33. 10. 9. 1179b25-26; cf. 1180a25-33; *Pol.* 5. 9. 1310a13-14.

34. 10. 9. 1179b13-16; see also 1. 5. 1095b16-17, 19-22; 8. 13. 1162b35-36; 8. 14. 1163b27-28; 9. 8. 1168b15-21; 10. 8. 1179a15-16; *Pol.* 7. 8. 1328a38-39. Aristotle has been faulted, not unexpectedly, as a moral aristocrat for such comments.

35. 10. 9. 1179b27-28; cf. 1180a1-10. People with an "inferior" sort of nature "must be kept down, but not ill-treated" (*Pol.* 2. 7. 1267b9; Jowett).

36. See 2. 1. 1103b3-4; 10. 9. 1180a1-17; *Eth. Eud.* 1. 3. 1215a1-3; *Pol.* 2. 7. 1267b5-9; 2. 8. 1269a12-23; 4. 11. 1295b19-21; 5. 8. 1307b30-40. Malfeasance should be punished by the infliction of pain opposed to illicit pleasures, and incorrigibility by exile (see 2. 3. 1104b13-18; 3. 5. 1113b22-27; 10. 9. 1180a8-13; *Eth. Eud.* 2. 1. 1220a35-37. Aristotle takes the

primary purpose of punishment to be rehabilitation and deterrence, not revenge (see *Rh.* 1. 10. 1369b13-14). Note the parallels between punishment and moral education; see 2. 9. 1109b2-7.

37. See 10. 9. 1180a1-8.

38. See 10. 9. 1180a21-24.

39. See 5. 2; 5. 5. 1133a2-b6; 5. 6. 1134a26-27.

40. See 5. 3. 1131a21-25; *Pol.* 3. 9. 1280a22-23.

41. See 5. 1. 1129b26-1130a13; *Pol.* 3. 13. 1283a37-40.

42. See *Pol.* 5. 11. 1313a34-b32.

43. See 4. 8. 1128a33; 9. 4. 1166a10-29. Emotions deserve respect only when reason judges them worthy of respect.

8

When Practice Goes Amiss

A crucial test of the adequacy and coherence of any analysis of practical reason is the ability of that analysis to help us understand both excellent and defective instances of the exercise of our agency. In Chapter 6 a brief discussion of Aristotle's construction of the difference between morally good and morally bad persons helped to clarify the role of moral reasoning in assessing the ends of actions. We now need to see in a more detailed way how Aristotle construes cases in which our practice goes astray.

In Chapter 2 we saw that the outside of an action consists of a matrix of contingent items, and in Chapter 3 'right action' was defined in terms of those particulars, as the doing of the right kind of action in the right manner toward the right people and so on. Because the arrangement of those facts can vary indefinitely from situation to situation, there is also an indefinite number of ways in which any individual action can be defective. All practical errors, however, are of two general kinds, depending upon whether an error concerns the principle of an action (its 'major premise') or the particularities involved in an action. This difference corresponds to the difference between the norm of moral acceptability and the norm of effectiveness.[1]

Although Aristotle does not agree completely with Socrates' analysis of malpractice, he does believe that Socrates is, in the main, right in thinking that no one willingly does what he thinks is wrong. Practical error of any kind must finally be traced to ignorance; since every rational person wants what is good for himself, a person will act badly only if he does not know what is the right way in which to act. Simple error about the circumstances of an action is caused merely by the absence of knowledge, while moral ignorance is caused by malformed dispositions which pervert the functioning of practical reason. A morally evil person may or may not reason effectively about how to get what he wants; what makes him morally wrong is the fact that he does not aim at the right kinds of goals.[2]

In order to understand Aristotle's doctrine concerning the nature of moral error, we need to keep in mind that his analysis in the seventh book of *Eth. Nic.* is not his complete doctrine, or, more accurately, his analysis there presupposes his previous discussions of the nature of practical reasoning. Consequently, when he explains morally defective practice as a kind of ignorance, he is using the term 'ignorance' (*agnoia*) in a special, technical sense. It clearly is not merely not knowing nor just forgetting.[3] If we were to take practical knowledge to be a sort of theoretical knowledge, we would be tempted to attribute to Aristotle the very doctrine for which he took Socrates to task: an excessively intellectualistic view, making it impossible for a person freely and intentionally to act wrongly.[4] Likewise, if we were to ignore the distinction between the norms of morality and sheer effectiveness, we would not understand why Aristotle does not take moral error to be simply a lack of skill or of cleverness.[5] Aristotle has already given us ample indication of the special nature of moral ignorance when he defined practical reasoning as a synthesis of thought and desire and stated that our practical reasoning will not be right if our desires are not correct:

> It is through pleasures and pains that men are corrupted, i.e., through pursuing and avoiding pleasures and pains either of the wrong kind or at the wrong time or in the wrong manner. . . . The pleasant and the painful do not destroy and pervert every conviction we hold—not, for example, our conviction that a triangle has or does not have the sum of its angles equal to two right angles—but only the convictions we hold concerning how we should act.[6]

'Moral ignorance', then, is Aristotle's term to denote the condition of a person who pursues morally evil ends because his practice is dominated by appetition rather by reason. The term can be translated accurately either as "morally bad judgment" or as "moral insensitivity."

SIMPLE ERROR

Simple practical errors are errors which an agent does not *mean* to make but errors which he in fact does make, about the person affected by his action, about his action itself or the instruments used in the action, or about the results of his action. Aristotle describes all such errors as "involving ignorance" (*met' agnoias*), but an ignorance which does not reflect or reveal the agent's character, precisely because the element of deliberateness is lacking. Aristotle divides such errors into three different kinds.[7]

The first two are differentiated from each other by the presence or absence of factors which could not possibly be foreseen.[8] In the case of mishaps or accidents (*atuchēmata*), the cause lies not with the agent or with his calculations but with some other agency, and for that reason the agent is not held responsible. If, for example, a person exercises all reasonable precautions while driving but strikes a child who darts out from between two parked cars, that is a mishap, and the driver is not held responsible for it. If a person, however, errs in his deliberations about matters he could have foreseen or known, that is a mistake (*hamartēma*).[9] The initiative for the action lies with the agent; the mistake is his, and the responsibility is his. Even so, his action, if it was wrong, is without malice, for his mistake was not deliberate. Consequently, neither the action nor the mistake necessarily reflect his character. He blundered, not because he did not know, in general, how to act rightly, but because, for various nonmoral reasons, he did not know how to act rightly in one particular instance. If, for example, a person violates a traffic law and causes an accident because of his tiredness, it is his mistake and he is responsible for it, but that does not give us reason, by itself, to blame the mistake on some defect in his character.

This, of course, is not to say that the outside dimension of action has no moral significance; nor is it to offer a license for stupidity or incompetence. The good man's decisions should initiate the right kinds of actions. Still, even in familiar situations various personal deficiencies—a slip of memory, worries, illness, and so on—can lead even a good man to fail to take into account some fact in his situation, without any reflection on the moral quality of his character. Moreover, in practical matters, there comes a time when we must act, and even though all the possible consequences of an action have not yet been taken into account, we simply do not have time to do so.[10] For these reasons, we generally feel sorry for a person when he makes an "honest mistake," and, although he may still be held civilly liable for what he has done, we do not infer from his action that he is a morally reprehensible person.[11]

Aristotle lists a third type of malpractice in which the conditions are not present for the possibility of a person acting "in character"; these are actions committed in anger, when the anger has been provoked by someone else.[12] As in the case of mishaps, the cause lies outside the agent, and to that extent he is not morally responsible for what he does, although the extent of responsibility may need to be settled in a court of law.

A man does show his character by the way in which he reacts, once he realizes his error. Again we see that character is often best revealed not by what a person does but by his pleasures and pains. The good man feels regret; he would not have acted as he did, had he known all the facts.[13] The morally evil person feels no such regret.

Moral Evil

The situation is radically different in cases of moral ignorance, which may also involve ignorance of the circumstances of an action. If, for example, a person does not know what he is doing while he is drunk and, while drunk, harms another, we hold him morally responsible for what he has done.[14] His initiative was not taken from him, and he had the power to stay sober. Like the man who simply makes a mistake, this person could have and should have known what he was doing, but, unlike the man who simply makes a mistake, this person did not *care* about how he might act while drunk.[15] Likewise a man is morally responsible for insouciantly violating a law he should and easily could have known.[16] In both cases, negligence was caused by the kind of character the agent had; in both cases the agent acted as he did because he was that kind of a person.

These two examples show the nature of moral evil (*kakia*): a person freely chooses to act as he does and he acts wrongly, "with malice aforethought," because his character is misshapen.[17] He does not love what he should love nor hate what he should hate; for his reason is blinded to what is genuinely good.[18] No matter how effectively he might deliberate, insofar as he is morally corrupt he systematically errs in his practical principles (the major premise of the practical syllogism), in which the ends he sees as good are set out.[19]

Moral evil, therefore, is analyzed by Aristotle as a radical failure of practical reason, which cannot recognize that what seems good is not genuinely good. This lack of practical truth is what Aristotle refers to as moral ignorance. A morally evil person acts *in* ignorance, but his actions are not *due to* ignorance; they are due to his character.

> Now every wicked man is in a state of ignorance as to what he ought to do and what he should refrain from doing, and it is due to this kind of error that men become unjust and, in general, immoral. But an act can hardly be called involuntary [*akousion*] if the agent is ignorant of what is beneficial [for him as a human being]. Ignorance [i.e., deliberate ignorance of the particular facts] does not make an act involuntary—it makes it wicked; nor does ignorance of the universal, for that invites reproach.[20]

The relation between emotions and reason is ordered in just the wrong way in the morally evil person: his reason serves his desires rather than being served by them.[21] Just as, for Aristotle, the paradigm of moral goodness is self-control (*sōphrosunē*), so the paradigmatic form of moral evil is self-indulgence (*akolasia*). Self-indulgent people are not overwhelmed by a compulsion for pleasure, but they are misled into believing that their highest good consists of such pleasures.[22] They go wrong by restricting the compass of their ends to those which men share with brute animals. As a consequence, they enjoy

some things that they should not, because they are
detestable things, and if there are any such things that ought
to be enjoyed, they enjoy them more than they should or
more than most people do. . . . [A man] is called
"self-indulgent" for feeling more pain than he should at not
getting his pleasure (so that it is pleasure which makes him
feel pain) . . . [He] has appetite for everything pleasant or
for what is most pleasant, and he is driven by his appetite to
choose pleasant things at the cost of everything else.[23]

By contrast, the man who is self-controlled (is *sōphrōn*) does not try
to avoid all sensual pleasures, but he avoids excesses in them, he
does not find abstinence painful when morality demands it, and he
does not try to avoid physical pain when enduring it is necessary if
he is to act morally well.[24]

Because his practical reasoning is chronically corrupt, the
morally evil person is "not aware of his vice."[25] Because his choices
are made in moral ignorance, he finds no cause to feel remorse for
his way of acting. He does not *wish* to change, and unless some great
trauma intervenes, his character is incorrigible.[26]

MORAL WEAKNESS

It is easy to confuse the self-indulgent man with the person who is
morally weak (*akratēs*); each is "the kind of person who pursues
bodily pleasures to excess and contrary to right reason."[27] But the
self-indulgent person thinks it is right to do so, and the morally
weak person does not.[28] The marks of moral weakness (*akrasia*),
therefore, are internal conflict and the remorse such a man feels
after he has yielded to his moral weakness:

[Morally weak people] are at variance with themselves and
have appetite for one thing and wish for another . . . instead
of what seems good to them they [do] what is pleasant and
actually harmful. . . . their soul is divided against itself, and
while one part, because of its wickedness, feels sorrow when
it abstains from certain things, another part feels pleasure:
one part pulls in one direction and the other in another as if

to tear the individual to pieces. If a man cannot feel pain and pleasure at the same time, he can at least after a while feel pain for having felt pleasure at a certain object, and he can wish it had not been pleasant to him. Bad people are full of regrets.[29]

Aristotle's explanation of the conflict is, as we would expect, in terms of a man having two kinds of desires—some are united to and led by reason, others are opposed to it and, in a sense, tend to seduce reason to their ends:

> Appetites [*orexeis*] may conflict, and this happens whenever reason [*logos*] and desire [*epithumia*] are opposed, and this occurs in creatures which have a sense of time (for the mind advises us to resist with a view to the future, while desire only looks to the present; for what is momentarily pleasant seems to be absolutely pleasant and absolutely good, because desire cannot look to the future).[30]

Excessive attachment to sensual pleasures is base, and moral weakness deserves blame; but since he is not persuaded that he should act in a morally evil fashion, the morally weak man is not as bad a man as he would be if he were self-indulgent.[31] In fact, if he were not a good man (though not wholly good), he would not have a correct understanding of and appreciation for the right moral principles.

It is this mixed nature of moral weakness which makes it difficult to account for its very possibility. We have seen that a man cannot be practically wise without also being of excellent character: that his reason is wise *means* that he has the moral sensitivity to know how to act rightly, and that it is practical *means* that he in fact acts on the basis of his moral judgments.[32] But the morally weak man apparently knows how he should act and apparently even wishes to act rightly, but still has moral lapses, acting as he ought not to act.[33] If Socrates is right in saying that a man cannot rationally seek what he believes is base and harmful or reject what he believes is good, how can the Socratic conclusion be wrong, that moral weakness must be an illusion? Yet it must be wrong, because it conflicts with "the observed facts."[34]

Aristotle's own analysis leads him to a position very close to that of Socrates: when a man does not do what is in his own best interest, at that moment he does *not* know what is his own best good, no matter what he may say.[35] When it is the case that a man acts contrary to his own wishes by doing what he knows he ought not to do, then either his reason must somehow fall into error or, if it does not, it is somehow not practical.[36] In either case we need to resort to a distinction between two ways in which a man can 'have' any characteristic (*hexis*)—here, practical knowledge.[37] A man 'has' knowledge in one way when he is actually using or exercising (*energein* or *chrēsthai*) what he knows; and if it is practical knowing, then using his knowledge means that he is "keeping his attention on" what he knows so that it efficaciously influences his acting. A man 'has' knowledge in another way when he does possess it but is not adverting to and using it, e.g., when he is asleep, drunk, or preoccupied with other things. In this second case it also makes sense to say that a man does not then have knowledge, for it is not operative at that moment.[38]

Aristotle uses the "tremendous difference between these two ways of knowing" to argue that, at the moment of his acting in a morally weak fashion, a man both does and does not know how he should act.[39] The feelings of guilt which follow upon instances of moral weakness show that this kind of "not knowing" is not merely a case of simple error. It is, instead, a failure in the second function of practical reason, a failure to apply the right rule as one should to the particulars in one's situation. The morally weak man acts as he does, not because he is inept or because he makes an innocent mistake; rather, he does not always *want* to know how he should act, and this failure to keep his desires under the control of his reason shows his defective character.

Aristotle typically explains all practical error on the side of reason in terms of defective practical syllogisms, and he follows this method by proposing three different ways in which moral weakness can occur.[40] In each of the three cases, the agent has possession of the appropriate principle of morally acceptable action (the major premise). But in the first case, he fails to formulate the minor premise correctly (concerning the particulars of his situation); in the second he formulates the minor correctly and reaches the right decision, but then does not keep his mind on it; and in the third, he also knows a pleasure principle, and it is to this that he attends, formulating the relevant minor and acting on it.[41]

Although some of the details necessarily differ, in all three cases the morally weak man is a man who, at the moment of his moral weakness, both knows and does not know how he should act. He does keep possession of the principles of morally good actions (in this sense appetite cannot corrupt *logos*, our faculty of principles), but at some stage of his deliberation, his emotions distract and blind him so that his moral reasoning loses its practical perceptiveness, and he does not know how *he* should act *here* and *now*. He then acts in ignorance, but not due to ignorance. He is not overcome by passions which no man could resist; he could and should know what he is doing, but he does not want to know. The fault lies in his character, for which he is responsible. Again, during his moral lapse, he still 'has' knowledge of how to act rightly. He may even be able to reel off the right moral rule and apply it to himself in his situation, but he does this like an actor reciting lines or like a man speaking while drunk or asleep. The meaning of his words is not his in the sense of active knowledge, and he still can be said not to know how he should act.[42]

The third case, in which the agent acts on a pleasure principle, presents special complications. The morally weak person is not persuaded to adopt that principle as a moral rule (and this sets him off from the self-indulgent person); he apparently takes it simply as an effective rule for gaining the object of his desire. The conflict in this case is therefore not between two practical rules but between the moral rule and the agent's desire, and it is this opposition which makes his adoption of the pleasure principle immoral. Furthermore, the morally weak person does deliberate correctly in the sense that he reasons effectively about how to get what he wants, but because what he wants is morally unacceptable, he is, at best, clever and not practically wise.[43]

Once a moral lapse is over and desires have been satisfied, they lose their strength and, if nothing else distracts the morally weak person, he becomes aware of how he should have acted, like someone wakening from sleep. Moral lapses are intermittent, and a person with this kind of character does recognize and feel shame for his moments of weakness. He can do this only because he does not deny the rightness and the binding force of moral principles. Consequently there is hope that his moral illness can be cured.[44]

Like other moral dispositions, moral weakness concerns primarily the pursuit of sensual (or 'necessary') pleasures, especially those of touch and taste.[45] Other pleasures—those accompanying the exercise of our abilities to perceive, to think, and to act—are not subject to deficiencies and so are not susceptible to excess.[46] Nonetheless, even the best kinds of activities can become bad for a particular person in certain situations, and then a person would be wrong to engage in such activity.[47] For want of a better way to characterize this kind of fault, we might call it a form of moral weakness, but it is not moral weakness in the usual sense. It is only something like it.[48] It is also like a mistake, for people who err in this way are not morally evil; they err only because they are the kind of persons who love and engage in good activities.

Impetuosity (*propeteia*) is another defect of character analogous to moral weakness. The impetuous man is easily excitable; he tends to be "driven on by emotion" and led on by his imagination; although he does not deliberate sufficiently before acting, he is a better man than the morally weak person, for he still in a sense follows reason and he acts as he thinks he ought. Impetuosity, therefore, is not moral weakness in the strict sense, though it is like it in some ways.[49]

Moral Strength

We can best understand moral strength (*enkrateia*) by contrasting it with moral weakness. The morally strong man (*ho enkratēs*) also experiences a conflict between his moral principles and some desires which are either deficient or, more commonly, excessive, but he is a better man than the weak man because his wish to be morally good will always dominate the recalcitrant emotions which tempt him. He is not as good a man as the morally excellent man, however, because he lacks internal harmony. He needs to be suspicious of every attraction to sensual pleasure, and his good choices often require special effort.[50]

The morally strong man is not to be confused with the obstinate man. The former will not deny his moral principles in the face of conflicting emotions, and he is open to rational arguments. The latter is almost immune to argumentation because he is emotionally a stubborn person; so he actually is closer to being morally weak then morally strong.[51]

BRUTISHNESS

There is another form of morally reprehensible character—brutishness (*thēriotēs*)—which consists in enjoying actions which men naturally find utterly repulsive, such as cannibalism, disgusting appetites, utterly irrational phobias, and sexual aberrations.[52] In a sense brutishness lies "outside the limits of vice," for vice is a perversion of practical intelligence, whereas the brutish person acts so repulsively that his actions seem outside the pale of intelligent behavior.[53] His behavior is all the more horrifying because it originates in a being of whom we expect intelligent conduct. The mastering of such appetites is not to be considered morally good for that only brings a man to the threshold of human conduct.[54]

CONCLUSION

Despite its initial implausibility, the Socratic analysis of practical error is at least partly correct: because no one can be an intelligent agent and still deliberately harm himself, no one ever acts badly when he has practical knowledge in the full sense. In cases of simple error, a man misapprehends one or more of the particulars involved in his action. In cases of moral error, a man acts badly because he is not, at least at the moment of his error, in *full* possession of the right principle of conduct. Socrates was right in arguing that when the outside of action is defective, the explanation lies on the inside; he was also correct in believing that knowledge in the full sense cannot be corrupted by emotion, for, even at the moment of his moral weakness, a man still does not deny the rightness of his moral principles. But Socrates was wrong in neglecting the appetitive nature of moral thinking; and because he did, he also did not sufficiently realize that moral ignorance is an affective as well as an intellectual state.[55]

Just as our practice cannot be accounted for except in terms of both thinking and desiring, so also good practice and malpractice must involve both. One requirement for good practice is harmony between thinking and desiring, but that is not sufficient by itself, since the thoroughly evil man may achieve internal harmony by making his practical reasoning subservient to the demands of certain of his desires. What is also necessary for moral goodness is the proper ordering of appetition by the principles of reason.

The existence of internal conflict is evidence that neither appetition nor reasoning is completely corrupted, and then there is still hope for the attainment of excellence. The morally strong man has a better character than the morally weak man precisely because, when conflict occurs, the morally strong man is committed to what is morally good, even if it means yielding pleasure. What is lacking in both men is the affective influence of a sufficiently good character. Neither is genuinely, thoroughly evil, for if they were they would not have possession of the principles of morally right practice. But they are not completely good either. They are, like most men, some of each.

Aristotle's analysis of character which is neither completely good nor completely evil is important to our understanding his view on the ancient question of whether morally good character is a single phenomenon or whether it consists in many distinct character traits. In the *Republic* Plato had described good character in terms of a single overriding quality which he called 'justice'.[56] Yet this view has obvious problems, for one of the "actual facts of life" seems to be that most men have various character traits in various degrees.[57] The resolution of this question can have enormous consequences for the manner in which moral education is carried out, and it is this fact which has interested some contemporary psychologists in the problem.[58]

In the *Nicomachean Ethics*, especially in Books 3 through 5, Aristotle discusses several different character traits and implies that, since such traits are relevant only in certain kinds of situations, they apparently can be taught only in those kinds of circumstances. Courage, for example, is called for primarily in dangerous situations.[59] This, however, should not be taken as evidence that Aristotle thought of good character as anything but an organic whole. The really good man, as we have seen, acts as he should in every situation. As we have also seen, Aristotle echoes the Platonic description of moral integrity when he describes justice, in its most comprehensive sense, as "not part of virtue but the whole of excellence or virtue, and the injustice opposed to it is not part of vice but the whole of vice."[60]

The man of practical wisdom and moral excellence is the ideal, but an ideal not achieved by most men, and that is why even normally good character traits like courage can become bad.[61] That is also why moral education consists, for Aristotle, both in teaching the young how to react rightly in various kinds of situations and in trying to provide a foundation for the development of practical wisdom. Right reactions are not enough, nor are individual virtues by themselves; and that is why the unity of moral personality requires the integrity called practical wisdom. "As soon as [a person] possesses this single virtue of practical wisdom, he will also possess all the rest."[62] Anyone who has participated in the moral education of children knows the difficulties involved in that effort, and Aristotle should not be faulted for believing we should try to achieve what we can in moral education, even if we cannot always achieve all we would wish.

Notes to Chapter 8

1. See 3. 5. 1114b3-5; 6. 5. 1140b4-19; 6. 8. 1142a21-23; *Eth. Eud.* 2. 11. 1227b20-23; also citations in chap. 2, note 74. As we have seen, practical wisdom cannot be reduced to the norm of effectiveness but surely includes it.

2. See 2. 3; 3. 4-5; 6. 2. There are similarities in Plato's analysis; see *Republic* 444a ff.; *Timaeus* 86a-87b; *Laws* 860c ff.

3. See 6. 5. 1140b20-30; 7. 2. 1145b28-30; 7. 3. 1147b6-17.

4. An example of this criticism occurs in Ronald D. Milo's *Aristotle on Practical Knowledge and Weakness of Will*, pp. 75ff. Milo argues that, for knowledge to *be* practical, it is sufficient that it be *about* practice, and concludes that Aristotle misconstrues both the nature of practical wisdom and the nature of moral weakness.

5. See chaps. 5 and 6.

6. 2. 3. 1104b21-23 and 6. 5. 1140b13-16.

7. See 5. 8. 1135b12-16. |A rather long digression is necessary here, however though in the end it does not significantly advance Aristotle's analysis. In 3. 1. 1110b25-27, Aristotle makes what seems to be an important distinction between actions *due to* ignorance (*di' agnoian*) and actions done *in* ignorance (*agnoounta*). Under the title of "actions done in ignorance but not due to ignorance" he classifies all actions explicable by (because they are due to) the agent's morally defective character. This ignorance always involves ignorance of the right rule on which the agent should have acted and often, because of this, also ignorance of important circumstances (not taking them into account correctly or at all; see, e.g., 3. 1. 1110b28-34; 3. 5. 1113b30-1114a30).

The problem here involves the range of actions Aristotle meant to include under the description "due to ignorance." He does not himself directly address this question, and we are left to ourselves to construct an interpretation congruent with his apparent intent. Initially at least, it seems we should classify all three kinds of "simple errors" as due to ignorance. Aristotle prefaces all three with a common introduction (see 5. 8. 1135b12-17), and states that none of them are caused by the agent's having a morally defective character. But this proposed classification does not seem to stand up under scrutiny.

In the case of both accidents and actions provoked by another, what exonerates an agent of responsibility is the intervention of another agency, just as in the case of coerced actions. (The only difference is that Aristotle defines coerced action as action in which the coerced person "contributes nothing;" see 3. 1. 1110b2-3, 16-17). What goes wrong, then, is not due to ignorance but due to other agencies; there seems no good reason to consider ignorance to be *the* crucial feature in their not being voluntary, even when ignorance is involved.

Mistakes now seem to be the only cases of errors committed "due to" ignorance. They are mistakes only about the particulars involved in an action and not about the right principles of action, and this is just the kind of mistake Aristotle describes as "due to ignorance" and as diminishing or destroying the voluntariness of an action, making it pardonable (see 3. 1. 1111a16-20; 5. 8. 1135a15-b11, 1136a5-9). This interpretation also agrees with Aristotle's analysis of mistakes as not due to malice, i.e., as not caused by defective character (see 5. 8. 1135b16-17).

But mistakes do not really fit under the classification "due to ignorance" either. For in 3. 5. 1113b24-25, Aristotle defines "due to ignorance" as an ignorance for which the agent is *not* responsible, while claiming that, in the case of mistakes, "the source of responsibility lies *within* the agent" (5. 8. 1135b17).

Now we are left with an empty class of actions due to ignorance. This conclusion is compatible with the claim that all ignorance is caused by something else, namely, the agent's character, and so also with the claim that when an agent acts badly because he acts in ignorance, he is morally culpable for doing so. There is another class of actions in which malpractice occurs due to the uncontrollable intervention of others. However, this claim is clearly contrary both to Aristotle's own claims that there are in fact actions due to ignorance and that there are actions which are not voluntary, and to our common sense belief that men do make mistakes which do not reflect on their character.

If we want to be very generous toward Aristotle, we might interpret the class of actions involving the intervention of others as due to ignorance in the sense that, if the agent could have foreseen what others were going to do, he would have taken their actions into account. But then the knowledge necessary for fully voluntary action apparently would need to be so extensive that we might wonder whether *any* human actions should be considered to be voluntary.

The confusions are further compounded by the fact, as we have already seen, that Aristotle's definition of voluntariness is defective and that it also causes systematic difficulties because it includes disparate elements (see notes 20 and 21 in chap. 2). Moreover, in the original Greek text, Aristotle himself does not consistently use terminology which clearly respects the distinction between "in" and "due to." The entire topic is so muddled that I have mainly ignored it in the text above. I do not think doing so obscures the main distinction Aristotle seems to want to make: ignorance in an action is sometimes caused by an agent's character and that makes the ignorance morally reprehensible; and sometimes people simply make mistakes which do not reflect on the quality of their character (character is not *that* pervasive).

8. See 5. 8. 1135b17-18.

9. See. 5. 8. 1135b18.

10. See 3. 3. 1113a3; 6. 9. 1142b26-27.

11. See 6. 12. 1144a13-18. Of course the agent *might* be a morally bad person, for such people also make mistakes. Mistakes are mistakes precisely because they do not reveal character. If a person commits them frequently enough, they may then begin to reflect character traits. But this is not necessarily so; I may often strike the wrong keys while typing simply because I am spastic.

12. See 5. 8. 1135b26-36.

13. This claim seems to apply to mistakes only if we take them to be due to ignorance and therefore not done voluntarily but done only 'incidentally' (see 3. 1. 1109b35-36, 1111a16-20; 5. 8. 1135a15-35; 6. 12. 1144a13-17). (If they are done in ignorance but not due to ignorance, it seems they would be cases of moral weakness rather than just mistakes.) When an agent does not regret what has happened, Aristotle suggests we say his action was "not voluntary" (*ouch hekousion*) rather than "involuntary" (*akousion*), or, in more contemporary terms, "not intentional" rather than "unintentional" (see 3. 1. 1110b18-24, 1111a19-20; also notes 5 and 20 in chap. 2).

14. See 3. 1. 1110b25-29.

15. See 3. 5. 1113b30-33.

16. See 3. 5. 1113b34-1114a3.

17. See 2. 3. 1104b21-23; 3. 5. 1114a3-30; 5. 8. 1135a15-16, b24-25, 1136a1-4.

18. See 3. 4. 1113a15-26, 36-b2; 3. 5. 1114a3-30; 10. 5. 1176a16-23.

19. See 3. 1. 1110b27-33; 3. 5. 1114a12-22; 6. 9. 1142b17-20; 6. 12. 1144a35-36; 7. 3. 1146b22-23; 7. 8. 1151a5-20; 10. 9. 1179b10-31.

20. 3. 1. 1110b28-34; see 3. 5. 1113b6-1114b5. Note again that the ignorance involved here is *moral* ignorance. Aristotle is not discussing here either the young person in the process of learning the right moral principles nor the morally good person unsure about how to act in a totally unfamiliar situation. Aristotle believes that, if a person has been decently endowed by nature with the potentiality for sound practical judgment and if he has grown up within the educational structures of society, he can hardly be unaware of the right moral principles; and if he does not know them, it is a sign of defective moral character. Here Aristotle may be open to criticism for not distinguishing more clearly between moral goodness and moral enlightenment; it surely seems possible for a person to want to do what is morally right while at the same time, through no fault of his own, having a

defective conception of what *is* morally right. But Aristotle collapses the distinction. For example, he writes that "the stupid man [does wrong] because he has misguided notions of right and wrong," and he lists stupidity as a kind of morally defective character, along with self-indulgence and cowardice (*Rh.* 1. 10. 1368b22; Roberts). He defines the man of practical excellence as a person who both loves the *kalon* and knows how to achieve it (see, e.g., 6. 9. 1142b7-8; 6. 5). Although stupidity is never a virtue, it is not necessarily a moral vice. On the topic of moral enlightenment, see Vinit Haksar. "Aristotle and the Punishment of Psychopaths," *Philosophy*, 39 (1964), pp. 323-340.

21. See, e.g., 9. 8. 1169a4-17. The morally evil person is not one who is at the mercy of every emotion, for emotions, if not subjected to some control, seek their own satisfaction, making life too chaotic. Therefore, although the morally evil person goes to excess in some ways, he cannot do so in every way. "That would be impossible, for evil destroys even itself, and when it is present in its entirety it becomes unbearable" (4. 5. 1126a12-13).

22. See 2. 8. 1109a13-18; 3. 4. 1113a35-b2; 3. 10-12; 7. 7. 1150a24-33. There are other kinds of wickedness, of course. Often a person will not be completely wicked but only in certain ways; see 4. 1. 1119b21-27; 5. 11. 1138a16-17. "The wrongs a man does to others will correspond to the bad quality or qualities that he himself possesses" (*Rh.* 1. 10. 1368b15-16; Roberts).

23. 3. 11. 1118b25-27, 30-1119a5; cf. 3. 10. 1118a3-b7; 7. 4. 1148a16-22.

24. See 3. 10; 3. 11. 1119a11-20; 7. 12. 1153a33-35; 7. 14. 1154a8-20.

25. See 7. 8. 1150b33-36, 1151a12-20.

26. See 3. 5. 1114a12-23; 4. 2. 1121b13-17; 7. 4. 1148a16-17; 7. 7. 1150a18-31; 7. 8. 1150b29-35, 1151a11-15; 10. 9. 1179b17-18.

27. 7. 8. 1151a11-12; cf. 3. 10. 1118a23-26; 7. 3. 1146b18-21; 7. 4. 1147b23-28, 1148a7-15, b10-14; 7. 7. 1150a8-16.

28. See 7. 3. 1146b18-23; 7. 4. 1148a15-17; 7. 8. 1150b29-36, 1151a11-13; 7. 9. 1152a4-7.

29. 9. 4. 1166b7-9, 19-24; cf. 1. 13. 1102b13-24; 3. 2. 1111b13-15; 5. 9. 1136b6-8; 7. 3. 1146b23-24; 7. 8. 1151a5-13, 21-27.

30. *De an.* 3. 10. 433b5-10 (Hett); cf. 3. 11. 434a10-14. There are serious problems with the available Greek text of Book 7 of *Eth. Nic.*, but it is still possible, I think, to discern Aristotle's main themes about moral weakness with the help of remarks, such as this citation, from other books. In this citation Aristotle is not contradicting what he says in *Eth. Nic.* 3. 2. 1111b16: "Appetite [*epithumia*] can be opposed to choice [*proairesis*], but not

appetite [*epithumia*] to appetite [*epithumia*]." Sensual appetite is always for a particular object promising pleasure or away from an object promising pain, and this specificity keeps such appetites from opposing one another.

31. See 7. 3. 1146b18-23; 7. 7. 1150a25-30; 7. 8. 1150b29-36, 1151a11-13, 21-27; 7. 10. 1152a13-23; also chap. 5, note 51.

32. See 6. 5. 1140b4-6, 20-30; 6. 13. 1144b14-1145a2; 7. 10. 1152a7-9. It is not merely a logical point to say that it would be a contradiction for the man of practical wisdom to be also morally weak (see 7. 2. 1146a3-8). The contradiction holds only if Aristotle's analyses of the nature of practical wisdom and the nature of moral weakness are correct. The contradiction does not hold in the case of the merely clever man. He can at the same time be both clever and morally weak, i.e., he can cleverly deliberate about how to get a morally unacceptable pleasure (see 6. 12. 1144a23-32; 7. 10. 1152a9-13). See also Mortimore, *Weakness of Will*, p. 12: A person may also fail to act effectively *because* he is a morally weak person.

33. See 5. 9. 1136b6-8; 6. 9. 1142b17-20; 7. 3. 1147a37-b2.

34. 7. 2. 1145b27; cf. 21-30. See also "Practical Wisdom and Moral Philosophy" in chap. 6.

35. Aristotle's claim here is remarkably close to the pragmatic thesis that a genuine belief must have an effect on and make a difference in our actions. Ross confuses the issues when he writes, "[Aristotle] takes a decided stand against the Socratic view that no one is willingly bad, that actions follow necessarily on our state of belief" (Sir David Ross, *Aristotle*, 5th ed. rev., p. 201). The two clauses are not synonymous, and Aristotle gives Socrates a split decision on the first while agreeing with him on the second (see 3. 5. 1113b15-17; 7. 3. 1147b11-19). Ross seems to see this later in his book; see p. 224. For a careful and detailed examination of Aristotle's doctrine concerning the nature of moral weakness, see James Jerome Walsh, *Aristotle's Conception of Moral Weakness*.

36. A person may succumb to his appetites because he has only tentative beliefs about how he should act, but we cannot adequately explain moral weakness by distinguishing between knowledge and belief. People can be just as convinced of their beliefs as they are of their knowledge. We need to address ourselves to cases in which a person apparently acts contrary both to his own convictions and to his own wishes (see 7. 2. 1145b32-1146a3; 7. 3. 1146b24-30).

37. This is not an *ad hoc* distinction; it appears in many other places and is used to discriminate both between potentiality (*dunamis*) and actuality (*energeia*), and, as here, between two degrees of actuality. See 1. 5. 1095b31-1096a1; *Ph.* 8. 4. 255a30-b4; *De an.* 2. 1. 412a10-11, 22-28; 2. 5. 417a9-b2, 30-418a2. See also the first condition for living the good life, in "The Good Life," in chap. 9.

38. See 7. 3. 1146b31-35, 1147a10-18, b11-12; *De an.* 2. 1. 412a22-28.

39. 7. 3. 1147a7-8.

40. See 7. 3. 1146b36-1147b18. Somewhat different interpretations of these lines are offered by Anthony Kenny in "The Practical Syllogism and Incontinence" (*Phronesis*, 11 [1966], pp. 163-184), and by C. J. Rowe in *The Eudemian and Nicomachean Ethics: A Study in the Development of Aristotle's Thought*, pp. 115-120. The Greek text is problematic, and there may be room for more than one plausible interpretation.

41. An analysis in terms of the practical syllogism tends to emphasize the intellectual aspect of practical reasoning, but the appetitive side cannot be ignored. Alternatively, Aristotle could have analyzed moral weakness in terms of moral dispositions which, although they are fundamentally correct, are not always strong enough to move the morally weak person to act as he should.

42. See 7. 13. 1147a14-23. The claim that the morally weak person acts in ignorance but not due to ignorance (he acts as he does due to his morally weak character) is consistent with Aristotle's insistence on the freedom and moral responsibility of such a person. Cf. 7. 4. 1148a2-4, b5-6; 7. 10. 1152a15-16. In light of Aristotle's doctrine concerning the nature of moral judgment (*aisthēsis;* see chap. 6), the word *aisthētikēs* in 1147b17 should be translated, not as "sensory knowledge" (as Ostwald does) nor as "sense-perception" (as Rackham does), but as "moral perceptiveness" or "moral judgment." The difference in meaning is substantial.

43. Although morally weak actions are due to appetite, they still can involve reasoning. Aristotle admits that morally weak people follow "the guidance of reaon" and "deliberate" so that they attain their pleasures "as the result of calculation" (7. 10. 1152a13; 7. 7. 1150b19; 6. 9. 1142b18; cf. 12-20). In the third case (7. 3. 1147a32-b5) it surely seems that the morally weak person acts from choice, albeit a morally defective one. However, Aristotle repeatedly insists that the morally weak person acts "contrary to his wish. . . . against his choice and thinking. . . . [he does] not exercise choice" (5. 9. 1136b7; 7. 4. 1148a9, 17; cf. 3. 2. 1111b9-18; 3. 5. 1113b13-18; 5. 8. 1136a1; 7. 3. 1146b23-24; 7. 7. 1150a18-32, b19-21; 7. 8. 1150b29-1151a7; 7. 10. 1152a13-23). As far as I can see, Aristotle is forced to suffer some inconsistency here. He cannot admit that a person can genuinely wish for something he also judges to be bad; he is unwilling to accept an explanation which permits irrational desire (*epithumia*) to over-power and corrupt right reason, even temporarily. Allowing the morally weak person to wish for rather than simply desire morally unacceptable pleasure seems to leave no way in which to differentiate between him and the genuinely evil person. G. E. M. Anscombe tries, unsuccessfully I think, to

extricate Aristotle in "Thought and Action in Aristotle," in *New Essays on Plato and Aristotle*, pp. 143-158.

44. See 7. 8. 1150b30-36, 1151a11-15, 21-27; 7. 10. 1152a-13-33.

45. See "Pleasure and Kinds of Pleasure" in chap. 3; also notes 42 and 43 in chap. 3.

46. See 3. 10; 7. 4. 1148a23-b14; 7. 14. 1154b16-17.

47. See 7. 12. 1153a17-20; also "Instrumental and Intrinsic Practical Good" in chap. 3.

48. See 3. 10; 7. 4. 1147b20-1148a17, 23-b14; 7. 5. 1149a21-23; 7. 6. 1149a24-b31; 7. 9. 1151b17-22; 7. 14. 1154b16-17.

49. 7. 7. 1150b22; cf. 7. 2. 1145b28-30; 7. 6. 1149a24-b26; 7. 7. 1150b18-28; 7. 8. 1151a1-4.

50. See 1. 13. 1102b13-27; 3. 2. 1111b15-16; 7. 2. 1146a9-16; 7. 4. 1147b20-23; 7. 5. 1150a8-16; 7. 7. 1150a8-16, 33-35; 7. 8. 1151a26-28; 7. 9. 1151b27-1152a3.

51. See 7. 2. 1146a16-17; 7. 9. 1151b4-17.

52. See 7. 1. 1145a31-33; 7. 4. 1148a24-25; 7. 5. 1148b17-1149a20; 7. 6. 1149b27-35, 1150a1-7.

53. 7. 5. 1148b35.

54. See 7. 1. 1145a24-33; 7. 6. 1149b31-1150a5; 7. 14. 1154a31-b1. If a person has monstrous appetites by some catastrophic calamity of nature, Aristotle calls him brutish in an unqualified way (see 7. 5. 1148b32-1149a4). Morbidity is a special form of brutishness caused by some childhood trauma which generated perverse habits or by some physical or psychological disorder (see 7. 1. 1145a30-32; 7. 5. 1148b24-31, 1149a5-12).

55. See 6. 13. 1144b18-21, 28-30; 7. 2. 1145b22-27; 7. 3. 1147b9-17.

56. See Plato *Republic* 431b-435c, 441c-445b.

57. See 10. 3. 1173a18-22.

58. See, e.g., Lawrence Kohlberg, "Education for Justice: A Modern Statement of the Platonic View," in Gustafson, et al., *Moral Education: Five Lectures*, pp. 56-83. Kohlberg unfortunately parodies Aristotle, claiming Aristotle holds that "moral character . . . consists of a bag of virtues," like the "Boy Scout bag . . . a Scout should be honest, loyal, reverent, clean, brave" (p. 59).

59. See, e.g., 3. 9. 1117a28-35; 4. 1. 1119b21-26.

60. 5. 1. 1130a8-11; cf. 6. 13. 1144b32-1145a1.

61. Without the control of practical wisdom, courage, for example, can turn into rashness and impetuosity and become a vice rather than a virtue; see, e.g., 1. 3. 1094b17-18.

62. 6. 13. 1145a2-3. It is interesting to compare the ideal moral personality proposed by contemporary psychologists with Aristotle's ideal person, the man of practical wisdom.

9

Morality and the Good Life

We will conclude the exposition of Aristotle's ethics with an examination of the place of moral activity within the totality of human life. Situating this topic at the very end is, in some ways, a very un-Aristotelian move. Since "the end is the cause of all that comes under it," we would expect Aristotle to argue that we should have gotten ourselves clear about finalities at the start.[1] But Aristotle himself waits until the tenth and final book of the *Nicomachean Ethics* before presenting his conclusions about the constituents of the good life. His reason for doing so is apparently the same as ours: we would not have been able to appreciate the nature of man's total final good until now. That good consists in both practical and theoretical activities, and the elucidation of those activities has actually been a gradual unfolding of the final good. What remains to be done is to gather together and unify the doctrines already presented.

The two-dimensional character of human action once again offers us an admirable way to organize Aristotle's views, and it coincides with his own doctrine that "the good has two aspects: it is both an activity and a characteristic."[2] Under the first title we will see why it is that practical and theoretical activities constitute the good life, and under the second we will consider the kind of person who has the right kinds of characteristics. Although our final, total good consists in both, the connection between the best activities and the best men has already been examined in previous chapters.

THE GOOD LIFE

All human activity is teleological, aimed at some goal or end-state seen as good in some sense. Many of the things we call "good" are good only instrumentally; they help us get something else. Some things which are intrinsically good, valuable for their own sakes, can also be instrumentally good when they are part of a more comprehensive activity. But it is not possible for all goods to be instrumentalities.[3] There are some good things which are so final that they are always worth pursuing for their own sake, so that their attainment, taken as a whole, can constitute a better life than any other we might have as men.[4]

Most men have thought there is some such ideal "good life" and, Aristotle writes, the name they generally have given it is *eudaimonia*, that is, "the good life" (*agathos bios*), or "living well" (*eu zēn*), or "faring well" in the sense of having a life full of good things (*agatha*), or doing well (*eupraxia*).[5] We cannot be rational without wishing for the best life possible for ourselves, but merely saying there is such a life and giving it a name is not enough. We need to be clear about the qualities and constituents of that life.

Socrates had been shocked to see how many people fail to examine their goals and determine what kind of life is genuinely worth living, and how many people, as a consequence, live empty and meaningless lives, feeling cheated and disillusioned. Clearly, "not to have one's life organized in view of some end is a mark of much folly."[6]

Some people have thought it meaningless to search for some *one* good life; they have thought that each person is so unique and the various possibilities for constructing a good life too rich to fit into a single mold. However, Aristotle contends that we are not that plastic. We all share fundamentally the same nature, the form of humanness. Although we can and do differ among ourselves in many ways, we still all share the same basic potentialities and the same general kinds of fulfillments. Our commonalities allow us to construct an ideal—a delineation of the best and most pleasant life—which can hold, in general terms, for us all.[7]

As Socrates saw, people tend to derive their notions of the good life from the pleasures they know, and since they also have the most diverse views about what the best life is like, we need to proceed dialectically to decide what is the right view.[8]

Aristotle sets out the qualities of the best life mainly in the first book of the *Ethics*. Stated in the most general terms, that life must consist in the best possible activities done in the best possible way. This is not only a general description; it also helps rule out inadequate, confused, and simply mistaken opinions. More specifically, Aristotle lists five qualities the good life must have.

First, the best life possible to us must consist of *activities we can and do perform*. The good life must be attainable by us, for it is not rational to adopt goals which are completely unattainable. Moreover, it is not enough for a person simply to be alive nor simply to have certain potentialities (*dunameis*) or abilities (*hexeis*) or excellences (*aretai*). When we are inactive, as when we are asleep, we are not doing anything of human significance, much less living the good life. Consequently, the good life must consist in our own activities.[9]

Aristotle repeats this point again and again, because then, as now, men were deeply attracted to the view that the good life is either a life of idleness or it is something which luckily happens *to* us. But, Aristotle argues, the good life is neither doing nothing nor is it something which happens to us; it is something we *do*.[10]

Secondly, the activities comprising the good life must be *the best activities open to us, activities of what is best in us, performed well*.[11] We are neither plants nor brute animals, though we share the fact that we are alive with plants, and the fact that we have bodies and their drives and needs with other animals. What sets us off from all other living creatures is our ability to reason; its power and pervasive presence radically affect our nature so that we can engage in activities and pursue goals not open to nonrational beings.[12] Aristotle regards our reason, therefore, as "the best part of us," "our most sovereign part," and even "this divine element."[13] Since "the business [*ergon*] of that which is most divine is to think and to be intelligent," the activities constituting the good life must be, above all, rational through and through.[14] When Aristotle defines the good life as "an activity of the soul in conformity with a rational principle. . . . [and] with excellence," he is simply saying that that life consists in rational activities done as well as possible.[15]

This quality of the good life rules out the view of "the common run of people" who think only in terms of sensual pleasures. That is a kind of life more suitable for cattle than for men; it simply has no specifically human significance.[16]

The third quality of the good life is its very finality. It is not merely one among several good ways of living, for then it would lack

good things included in those other alternatives. The good life, as
Aristotle writes of it, is uniquely the best. Other, lesser goods are
always qualified in the sense that they stand under the judgment of
this final end for man, which is so ultimate and comprehensive, so
unconditionally and absolutely good (teleion) that there can be no further
standard(s) by which it might be judged.[17] Eudaimonic activities
must be not only intrinsically good but so complete and self-
sufficient that all other activities, including those of intrinsic but
limited value, can be done for their sake.[18] They must be so
fulfilling that they can make life desirable, and nothing else can
significantly add to the desirability of such a life.[19]

This third quality makes it clear that our final good cannot be
something apart from the activities by which it is achieved.[20] So, for
example, people are mistaken who value wealth and material goods
for their own sake. As we shall see in the next section, possessions
are only extrinsically good, valuable only for what they help us do,
and they therefore cannot themselves be our final good.[21] Again,
the good life does not consist in what we possess but in what we do,
including what we do with what we have.

The fourth quality of the good life is that the activities constituting it must normally be pleasurable or at least not devoid of
pleasure.[22] Pleasure naturally accompanies the unimpeded use of
our abilities, and since the best activities are those of our best
abilities, they will not only be pleasurable but normally the *most
pleasurable of all possible activities*.[23] As we have seen, different kinds
of pleasures naturally accompany different kinds of processes and
activities. Three of these—brutish, remedial, and simply recre-
ational pleasures—cannot be part of the essence of the good life.[24]
We have already discussed the first two; it is important to consider
the third briefly, because people often think that those with the
leisure to engage in recreation have the best life possible. If this
really were true, Aristotle contends, the significance of our life
(along with all the difficulties attending it) would be reduced to
triviality, for its most significant activities would be no more than
the pleasures enjoyed by children. The right view is to think of
recreation as primarily a form of rest, enabling us to return re-
freshed to activities worth taking seriously, which, as we will see in
a moment, are theoretical activities and morally good activities.[25]

The fifth and last quality of the good life is this: since the best life open to us should not suffer from the significant imperfection of precarious uncertainty, it must have an inherent permanence. The activities constituting it must be ones which can be *practiced throughout a man's life*, and the time in which we engage in them should also be complete—normally a lifetime.[26] "One swallow does not make a spring, nor does one sunny day."[27] This condition rules out activities appropriate or possible only in one age of adulthood.

These, then, are the five qualities of the good life. There are also certain conditions which must be present if we are to be able to live that life. Among these necessities must be counted a minimal amount of material goods. So, Aristotle writes that a person should be "sufficiently equipped with external goods, not simply at a given moment but to the end of his life."[28] Before discussing the activities which actually constitute the good life, we need to detour for a moment, to discuss the place of nonmoral goods in the good life. Both in Aristotle's time and in our own, many people have thought that such goods are crucial to living well, and people commonly expend immense effort to attain them.

THE PLACE OF NONMORAL GOODS IN THE MORALLY GOOD LIFE

We have seen again and again that practice is a matter of acting on, with, for, or against others, and we have also seen that, as a consequence, good character requires the right exercise of our power of agency both for its development and its expression. Morality is possible to us because we are agents, and moral judgments concern, in the most ultimate and comprehensive way, the exercise of our power and might. Children, for example, do not possess sufficient power to attain moral excellence, but they also are protected by that same fact from being morally evil.

The exercise of our power and the living of a morally good life require not only intelligence but also the help of others and the use of various instrumentalities.[29] These 'external goods' are not only important for learning how to act morally well; many of them are also normally essential to living morally well. "A generous man will need money to perform generous acts, and a just man will need it to meet his obligations. . . . and a courageous man will need strength if he is to accomplish an act that conforms with his virtue, and a man of self-control the possibility of indulgence."[30]

Our dependency on external goods creates very serious problems for any moral theory. So many natural goods, the instrumentalities of morality, are distributed unevenly among men. And so often are they gotten and kept only through luck that Aristotle calls them "gifts of fortune." Disasters can strip us of them, and then we seem to be "a kind of chameleon," sometimes having the instruments necessary to the morally good life and then, without warning, losing them. It does not seem right for our character (and the good life) to depend so much upon them, nor does precarious uncertainty seem compatible with the inherent stability and permanence of good character.[31] Nor, finally, does it seem right that some have a better chance at moral goodness than others, simply because they are born under better circumstances.

Problems such as these led Immanuel Kant centuries later to construct a morality of intentions in which he interpreted our power of agency to consist essentially in our ability to form our character through good resolutions (if we also have the power to carry them out, doing so is the best sign of the sincerity of our intentions). But Aristotle resists this move, not only because it is incompatible with his analysis of human agency but also because he thinks it is simply untrue to the facts in our experience. The inside and outside of human life are too closely interwoven.

Although it is true that "in the realm of nature, things are naturally arranged in the best way possible," not every person is guaranteed he will encounter no impediments or frustrations in living his life rightly and fully, any more than every acorn is assured of becoming a mighty oak.[32] Through defects of nature or because of unfortunate contingencies, many men lack some, perhaps nearly all, the conditions necessary for achieving moral excellence.[33] Experience shows that children who are deprived genetically, nutritionally, medically, or culturally are stunted, often irrevocably, in their possibilities, including their moral possibilities.

The importance of natural goods to the morally good life creates another problem. For they can be misused. Like the products of making, "they are not always good for a particular person."[34]

(This is true even for things genuinely good when considered *haplos*, in abstraction.) How then can they be part of that which is unconditionally, absolutely good?

Aristotle's main response is to point out that such goods are not part of the good life in the sense of being identifiable with it.[35] The morally good life consists in a person's characteristically acting excellently, which is a matter not of chance but of character.[36] The man of good character is a person who will do the best he can, making use of what he has, however much or little it may be.[37] Briefly, such a person will not misuse external goods; he will always use them rightly.[38]

This is not true of lesser men. For them, the natural good is not subordinated under and subsumed by the moral good but remains distinct from it and in potential conflict with it, and this is why both morally strong and morally weak men feel an attraction to violate their moral standards. But this conflict is not an ineluctable part of human morality. Even morally imperfect men do not always experience it, and the ideal toward which we are to grow is a resolution of the conflict by reason so that we desire nothing which is not morally acceptable.

The fact that morally imperfect men experience conflicts between the moral and the nonmoral good should not obscure the importance of external goods to the moral life. They are, as a general rule, either necessary conditions for or instruments in generating and living a good moral life. The fact that not all men have the same chance to develop and express their character fully according to the moral ideal continued to be an enormous problem for Aristotle, and long sections of the *Politics* are devoted to discussions about how the state might be organized so as to minimize the vagaries of stepmotherly chance. Because of our power of agency, we are not completely helpless, and many undesirable contingencies can be alleviated or removed through political (i.e., moral) activity, by the manner in which economic, eugenic, medical, social, and educational matters are arranged.[39]

Still, despite their importance, external goods are not and should not be regarded as part of the essence of the morally good life. So, Aristotle writes,

Only the morally good man ought to be given honor,
although people regard a man who has both moral excellence
and the gifts of fortune as being still more worthy of honor.
. . . If a man possesses the gifts of fortune without being
morally excellent, he is not justified in claiming high worth.
. . . since neither genuine worth nor true integrity can exist
without moral excellence. . . . [The merely wealthy try to]
imitate the man of integrity whenever they can, but they are
not really like him at all.[40]

LIVING THE GOOD LIFE

The best life possible to us consists, as we have seen, in our
participation in activities which are always intrinsically valuable.
The good life, therefore, is both an active life and a life consisting
preeminently in leisure activities. To call the good life "leisure
activity" is to call attention to the difference, as Aristotle sees it,
between two very general kinds of lives, a difference which divides
those who are living the good life from those who are not.[41] The
difference between them is precisely the difference between intrinsically good activities and merely instrumentally good activities first
discussed in Chapter 3.

To briefly recapitulate that discussion, instrumentally good
activities are valuable only for what they produce as their effect or
product, and those products are not, simply because they are the
end of making, intrinsically good. They may need to be put to some
use, as instrumentalities either in other extrinsically good activities
or in intrinsically valuable activities. For example, music and poetry
can be used to develop good moral character or they can simply give
pleasure, and reading and writing are necessary for many intrinsically good activities.[42] But how instrumentalities can contribute to
the good life is the concern of the user, the good man, not the
producer.

Technical skills typically involve *some* practical reasoning, but
when Aristotle considers the excellences of our deliberative faculty
(*to logistikon*), occasionally he does not even mention skillfulness.[43]
Although he refers to *technē* frequently, it is often only to clarify

something else, usually either natural changes or moral practical reasoning.[44]

His reasons for doing so are to be found in his analysis of making and his conviction of the close relation between kinds of activities and kinds of persons. Men engaged in poietic activities are best described as busy; they always have some end in view which they have not yet attained, and their activities are occupations with no real value of their own, involving long and tedious hours in striving to attain something which is generally only valuable for something else. Aristotle uses emotive terms such as "vulgar" (*banausos*) and "illiberal" (*aneleutheros*) to describe such striving, and if he seems excessively harsh in doing so, we need to remember how, today, we prefer machines to men in most cases of production, not merely for economic gain but because mere tasks, whether they be ditchdigging or working on an assembly line, can, as Aristotle argues, be dehumanizing. Men are used in such tasks as animate tools, and their value is determined by their productivity.

Since the modern industrial revolution, serious attempts have been made to minimize the dehumanizing effect of productive work, through labor laws and labor unions. Aristotle does not consider the possible ameliorating effects of such efforts. Living in a slave culture which he does not challenge, he is concerned only with the relation between kinds of activities and kinds of persons, and he regards all those who engage in production as living a slavish existence, even if they are not actually slaves. They are too preoc-cupied with striving to have either the leisure or the disposition to engage in intrinsically valuable activities.[45]

Leisure is not of itself a good, but it is a necessary condition for the good life, for then we are freed from striving for the things outside of ourselves that we need to live.[46] Today we no longer rely upon a slave system to free us from all toil, but technology also enables the vast majority of people who must work to have more time for leisure activity than they need to give to their work. Some men, confirming Aristotle's doctrine, become so preoccupied with their work that their entire life becomes one of striving, of making, and of accumulating to the point where it is difficult to find much humanity or human significance in their lives. But most men sense the rightness in Aristotle's contention that what really counts is what we *do* with what we have. They find the ultimate meaning of their lives, if they find it at all, in what Aristotle called "leisure activity."

Even today many people still think of the best leisure activity as consisting mainly in what Aristotle termed 'low level' pleasures—merely sensual pleasures and forms of recreation. Aristotle did not try to rule these out of the good life; instead he recommends that, if our leisure activity is to have genuine significance (necessary if we are to retain an enduring sense of personal dignity and worth), we should devote our leisure time mostly to two kinds of activities—intellectual accomplishment and moral accomplishment.

We have spent so much time following Aristotle's arguments for the value of morally excellent activity that we now need to balance that claim against his conviction that the most perfect activity possible to us is not moral but theoretical—understanding and appreciating reality and its laws.[47] "Knowing," he writes, "by its very nature, concerns what is inherently best; and knowing in the truest sense concerns what is best in the truest sense."[48] The best and most pleasurable activities are those which are the most rational: "What is by nature proper to each thing will be at once the best and most pleasant for it."[49] And by studying reality and its laws, things which are necessarily and eternally what they are, the scientist exercises his reason on "things which by their nature are valued most highly."[50] Since it is better and more pleasurable to exercise a capacity than to develop it, Aristotle is here describing not the process (*kinēsis*) of learning but the exercise (*energeia*) of our knowledge, once learned.[51]

Because the objects of scientific knowledge have a durability not enjoyed by the contingent, changing objects involved in practice, scientific knowledge can achieve standards of precision and universality that practical reason cannot hope to attain.[52] Aristotle did not anticipate the role of technology as a bridge between theory and practice, and he thought that scientific knowledge shows its superiority by the very fact that it can not be used for practical purposes. It is valuable solely for its own sake.[53]

There are other reasons to support the claims of *theoria*. It does not depend on a person's having power but only on his being intelligent, so that it is in itself not dependent on external goods and it is almost immune from ill fortune.[54] Those (like Aristotle) who have engaged in scientific activity tell of the incomparable pleasure it can give, a pleasure which continues to intensify throughout a person's life.[55] Such a life, Aristotle writes, enables a human being to transcend the limitations of his own composite nature, to lead a life blessed even to the gods, since it so closely resembles the kind of activity proper to them.[56]

Since scientific activity is the most perfect way in which a man can spend his leisure, the statesman must, above all, aim to provide the leisure necessary for citizens to live this kind of life.[57] And men with leisure, as rational beings, should naturally tend to engage in this kind of intellectual activity.[58]

Despite its superiority to moral practice, the theoretical life is still but "one portion of excellence in its entirety [*holē aretē*]."[59] We are not by nature pure intelligences; we are a synthesis (*sunthesis*) of mind and body, and we are also social and political beings.[60] Even if theoretical activity is the highest possible, good practice has its own independent value, and the good life for us must consist both of scientific activity and of morally good practice.[61]

To put the same point another way, Aristotle has argued that there are two fundamental ways in which we are in the world—the way of agency and the way of spectator. The way of agency has temporal priority, for we are first appetitive beings: as children we exercise the power we have long before we develop our ability to think in the full sense. When our ability to reason emerges and develops, it is from both what we have done and what others have done to us that we derive the materials on which to reflect. Eventually, when we have the leisure, our wonder leads us to inquire into and reflect at length on the nature of reality.[62] We want to know for the sake of knowing, not because we want to alter anything. We are spectators, content only to understand.

Even so, we cannot renounce the way of agency. Aristotle is so enamored with theoretical contemplation that he writes:

We must not follow those who advise us to have human thoughts, since we are (only) men, and mortal thoughts, as mortals should; on the contrary, we should try to become immortal as far as that is possible and do our utmost to live in accordance with what is highest in us.[63]

Try as we might to follow this advice, we can not escape from the continuing insistencies of other agents who do not cease to act upon us, and we have no choice about responding to them, one way or another. Moreover, our power to affect others is not something we can turn on and off at will. Because we have power, we always have it, and the only option open to us is how we shall direct and channel it. We can leave theoretical inquiries for a while and then come back to them, but we cannot leave our agency. We are irrevocably social beings, and we persist in existence, not by reflecting on what we know, but by exercising our agency. Because we are not self-sufficient, we are almost always in some need or other. We may postpone the satisfaction of our needs for a while, but in the end they win out. Still, even the postponement is a way of using our power.

Theoretical activity and practical activity are each a partial dimension of what it is to live as a human being; we are both thinkers and agents, and we cannot avoid either. Consequently, the best life for us consists in doing both kinds of activities, and doing them well, and in proper balance.[64]

A FINAL PROBLEM

The exposition of the foundations of Aristotle's moral philosophy is now complete. A final problem remains, which we can best introduce by sketching the general structure which Aristotle gives to the *Nicomachean Ethics*.

The first book of the *Ethics* is devoted almost entirely to an examination of the characteristics of the good life—the same topic to which the first section of this chapter is devoted. Aristotle makes it clear that he is concerned with *human* excellences and with the best life for *man*.[65] He also makes it clear that, since he is concerned with that life which is best (*ariston*), it must be, in the most unequivocal way, the most final, complete, and perfect (*teleiotaton*) end possible.[66] He avoids discussing the theoretical life, which he barely mentions, but implies the good life must consist of both moral and theoretical activity. This presumption gains weight when, in the thirteenth chapter of Book 1, Aristotle sets out his philosophic psychology and lists both theoretical wisdom and moral wisdom and goodness as human excellences.[67]

The next eight books of the *Nicomachean Ethics* are devoted almost exclusively to discussions of the practical life. Book 6 is a notable exception. There Aristotle repeats in outline the psychological picture which first appeared in 1. 13; he defines practical wisdom as the excellence of calculative reason, and theoretical wisdom as the excellence of scientific reason, and then devotes the next nine chapters to a discussion of the differences between these two intellectual excellences.[68] In the final two chapters of Book 6, he discusses the value of each excellence and the place of each in the good life. He makes four distinct points:

(1) both "are necessarily desirable in themselves. . . . for each of them is the virtue of a different part of the soul";[69]

(2) theoretical wisdom is "one portion of virtue in its entirety";[70]

(3) "a man fulfills his proper function only by way of practical wisdom and moral excellence";[71]

(4) since theoretical wisdom is superior to practical wisdom, practical wisdom neither uses theoretical wisdom nor has authority over it.[72]

In Books 7, 8, and 9 and the first five chapters of Book 10, Aristotle returns to topics within the province of practice—kinds and goodness of moral personalities, of pleasures, and of friendships. In 10. 6 he returns for the first time to his claims in Book 1 about the characteristics of the good life; and in 10. 9, the last chapter of the *Nicomachean Ethics*, he discusses the role of the state in moral education as an introduction to the *Politics*. The general structure and direction of the *Ethics* seems relatively clear and unproblematic.

But all is not clear and unproblematic, for in chapters 7 and 8 of Book 10, Aristotle completely contradicts a number of the most fundamental claims about moral practice which he had so carefully constructed and defended throughout the rest of the *Ethics*. In 10. 7-8 he concludes that theoretical activity and the good life are *coextensive;* "the activity of our intelligence [*nous*] constitutes the complete happiness [*eudaimonia*] of man, provided it encompasses a complete span of life"; and excellent practice, insofar as it has any claim at all on the good life, is a part of that life only "in a secondary sense."[73]

Given the fact that Aristotle has insisted both that practical wisdom is intrinsically good and that excellent moral character and its actions are "the best of ends," given his insistence in 1. 7. that the good life must lack nothing significant (be *teleiotaton*), given the enormous effort he has made to explicate the life of practice, what reasons can he offer to support this extraordinary claim?[74] He offers three reasons. The first is an appeal to those with experience, the theoreticians who have felt the pleasure and value of scientific thinking.[75] This appeal has only limited cogency. It shows the possibility, even the probability that the theoretical life is a good candidate for part of the good life, but it does not support the claim that such a life is the *only* candidate.

Aristotle's second argument is that only theoretical activity fully satisfies the criteria for the good life.[76] It is the most self-sufficient, the least dependent on external conditions, the most free from toil and striving, the activity of the best part of man (his reason), and valuable only for its own sake. What now becomes apparent is that the qualities of the good life for man (based on valuative experiences with human psychology and human actions) are being transformed into the qualities of a life which is not human at all but divine. Contemplative activity is the only kind of activity appropriate to divinity, and Aristotle's delineation of the best life in 10. 7-8 is not derived from his examination of the potentialities and entelechies of human nature; rather, it is modeled after divine activity. Men should live, insofar as they can, as gods! Aristotle in fact finally makes this appeal explicit, and elaborates it further by speculating that, if the gods care at all about human affairs, they surely must love and will reward those who are most like them.[77]

He makes a rather tortured effort to argue for this view in a passage in 10. 7. First he defines humanness as he had defined it, as a synthesis of *psuchē* and body, and admits that the kind of life he is recommending is "more than human," but advises us to think of ourselves only as our intelligence (*nous*), which is a "divine element" in us.[78] He still admits that it is not our full nature, but says that we might "regard it as each man's true self," and think of its activity as our "own life," as the best life for us even as humans.[79]

Aristotle's third argument begins with the admission that a person cannot live on this exalted plane continually; "insofar as he is human and lives in the society of his fellow men," each person will still have to engage in practice.[80] But even then practice is part of the good life only "in a secondary sense, since its active exercise is confined to man" as a composite being; such activity, however well done, is "peculiarly human."[81] The paradigm of divine activity ends up by condemning specifically human activity for being *human* activity. But Aristotle is not through yet. He also contends that practical activities are all "unleisurely, aim at an end [beyond themselves], and are not chosen for their own sake."[82] Since he had maintained that the doing of right actions for some further reason subordinates their moral value to another value, thereby destroying their moral value, Aristotle is willing to try to make his case by reducing all moral practice to production.[83]

If we are to understand how Aristotle could so desperately contradict himself, we need to retrace our steps and think again about two problems which have recurred in the course of the *Ethics*. One concerns his view of the nature of practical reason and of its objects, actions; the other, the relation within man between his reason and his emotions. Both of these problems can be traced to positions Aristotle held early in his career when he was closer to Plato in philosophic beliefs. First, he had held that theoretical and practical reason are essentially one; "the only difference is one of end; practical thinking aims at something outside itself, speculative thinking does not."[84] Secondly, he had held a kind of dualistic psychology, in which the soul—reason—inhabits an alien body teeming with desires needing suppression and direction.[85]

The *Nicomachean Ethics*, as we have seen, is not totally free of either of these beliefs, even though there are many passages, presumably written by Aristotle later in his career, which totally reject both beliefs. His problematic analysis of practical excellences analyzed in Chapter 6, his tendency to regard all actions as instrumentalities, and his tendency to analyze all actions in terms of means and ends, all reflect an earlier view of practice.[86] Likewise,

Aristotle's failure to take a more positive stand on the relation between reason and desire causes severe problems for his delineation of practical reason as a distinct faculty.[87] During his discussion of the internal conflicts caused by appetition and characterizing moral weakness, and perhaps influenced by that analysis, Aristotle seems to revert to a more dualistic position, denigrating the physical and emotional side of man. It is that part of us which makes us subject to decay, which makes our nature not only inferior to the divine but also "evil."[88] It is in these same pages that he begins to stress again his earlier belief that the essence of man *is* his mind. Reinforcing this tendency is a carry-over from his days with Plato, when Aristotle held the 'replenishment' theory of pleasure he later renounced, thinking of nonintellectual pleasures (involving the nutritive and appetitive parts of the soul) as only "incidentally pleasant"; the only thoroughly good pleasures are those connected with activities like thinking.[89] The implication, which Aristotle does not explicitly draw until 10. 7-8, is that the moral virtues, which regulate these second-rate pleasures, are also excellences in a "secondary," "peculiarly human" way.

Directly related to the tensions in Aristotle's treatment of pleasures and moral qualities is the manner in which he draws the distinction between intrinsically good activities (*energeiai*) and those which are only instrumentally good (*poiēseis*).[90] In the background of that discussion lies a hidden paradigm for intrinsically good activities—the activity proper to God, who does not change and so who exists outside of time, who lacks nothing and therefore whose activities involve no striving but are all immanent. This is an ideal inappropriate for humans, whose existence is ineluctably bound up with temporalities, with change, and with striving. Aristotle says little about the actual nature of theoretical contemplation, but from what he does say, we know it is the activity of a person who has left learning behind and who has reached a position of understanding that allows him to simply gaze in appreciative wonderment (in apparently nondiscursive thought) at reality and its laws.[91] This is an implausible ideal for humans; for one of the "facts of life" surely is the fact that in science striving never ceases, for no one has reached, nor does anyone believe they can reach, a substantially final understanding of reality. Another "fact of life" is that, contrary to Aristotle's claim, striving (research) is often far more pleasurable than the contemplation of knowledge already learned. Once an inquiry has been successfully completed, we generally lose interest in it. Further, since we are not perfect beings, we always have new prospects, new possibilities, and new challenges; our limits are not just given, and we can always continue to grow and stretch the present limits.

The force of this objection is to show that Aristotle's distinction between intrinsically good and instrumentally good activities should not have been made to depend so heavily on the presence or absence of striving and of temporal considerations. Because he used divine activity as his paradigm, Aristotle also was unable to develop a more adequate moral doctrine concerning actions which have an end beyond the actions themselves. This also kept him from examining more closely the relationships between morality and productive activities, which in turn allowed him to claim that those who are engaged mainly in productive activities have no personal moral quality of significance.

Aristotle's claim in 10. 7-8 that the good life is composed entirely of theoretical activity, therefore, is not something isolated from the rest of the *Nicomachean Ethics;* it rather is the logical outcome of doctrines Aristotle was in the process of growing away from but doctrines from which, at least in the text we have, he had not been able fully to emancipate himself. The heritage of his training at Plato's school was both his greatest good fortune and his heaviest philosophic burden.

We know he was growing toward a resolution of many of the problems mentioned in this section, because, after he distinguished between theoretical and practical wisdom, he depicted practical wisdom in terms which finally would not have allowed him to have excluded it and its functions from the good life for man. Put negatively, practical wisdom and its exercise cannot be reduced, on Aristotle's own doctrines, to the status of an instrumentality serving theoretical activity. For the activities which produce an excellence must be the same kind of activities which the excellence, when developed, produces.[92] Consequently, only theoretical activities can produce theoretical wisdom. Moreover, practical (political) wisdom may make leisure possible, but leisure is only a condition for, not a means to, theoretical contemplation, just as leisure is also a condition for the possibility of many morally good activities.

Positively, the delineation of the nature of the good life and of its components is produced, on Aristotle's own doctrine again, by practical reason, not by theoretical reason. Practical reason does not have the right to say *how* theorizing itself should be done; theorizing does have its own rights on which practical reason may not intrude.[93] But it is practical wisdom which determines that theoretical activity should be part of the good life for man; and it is political wisdom, "the most sovereign and most comprehensive master science [*architektonikē*]" which decides which activity, practical or theoretical, should take precedence in the particular situations of life.[94] Political wisdom, Aristotle writes,

> determines which sciences ought to exist in states, what kind of sciences each group of citizens must learn, and what degree of proficiency each must attain. . . . its end seems to embrace the ends of the other sciences.[95]

Despite the fact that theoretical activity is the more perfect (on this Aristotle never seemed to waver), both *theōria* and *praxis* must be parts of the good life for man. The good life is not possible without either. This, then, is the support for presenting, in the previous section of this chapter, Aristotle's final view of the good life as a composite of both moral and theoretical activities.

A Personal Note

It is very tempting, when discussing a philosopher like Aristotle, to become a propagandist on his behalf, to minimize or ignore problems he did not resolve. One can rationalize that, if serious problems are brought to light, a man who deserves careful thought may not be given that consideration. But if we learn anything at all from Aristotle, it is that we follow wherever the truth may lead. The very meaning of our lives is in the balance.

It also can be immensely exciting to get to know the mind of a person like Aristotle, to see him tugged in various directions and torn by the allurements of different views. This should not be totally unexpected, for, as Trond Eriksen writes, "philosophical thought is often nourished by tensions between positions that cannot be reconciled. For a thinker is a man who has a problem, not a man who has got rid of them all."[96] Like his teacher Plato, and like Plato's teacher Socrates, Aristotle leaves us with questions, but they are far better questions than we had when we first came to him. In the first chapter of this book, he was described as neither the first nor the last word in moral philosophy. His heritage is not a neat set of doctrines to be memorized and filed away, but the example of what it is to wrestle with the problems involved in trying to make sense out of what it is to be a human being. If he helps us do that better than we could by ourselves, then he is a mentor worth choosing and a friend worth having.[97]

Notes to Chapter 9

1. *Eth. Eud.* 1. 8. 1218b16 (Solomon); cf. *Eth. Nic.* 1. 2. 1094a19-26; 3. 5. 1114b15-16; also "Third Contrast" in chap. 2.

2. 7. 12. 1152b33.

3. See 1. 2. 1094a18-22; 1. 7. 1097a26-28; *Metaph.* 2. 2. 994a1-10, b13-16. See also Patterson Brown, "Infinite Causal Regression," in *The Philosophical Review*, 75 (1966), pp. 510-525.

4. On a first reading Aristotle may seem to make an illicit transition from "All men act for the sake of some end" to "There is some one end for the sake of which all men act." A careful reading, however, bears out the presumption that the father of logic would not fall into so primitive an error. The general line of Aristotle's argument can be stated as follows: Not all our activities are instrumentalities; we must regard some as final or consummatory. If there are any ends which are absolutely final, they must have certain qualities or characteristics. Since there are, in fact, activities with those qualities and in which we can engage, they are also the activities which comprise the good life for man and in which men *should* preeminently engage. See also note 6 below.

5. See 1. 4. 1095a17-19; 1. 8. 1098b20-21; 6. 2. 1139b3-4; also note 7 in chap. 5. The best translation of the term *eudaimonia* is the noncommittal "the good life." The usual translation, "happiness," unduly emphasizes our sentient nature and obscures Aristotle's insistence that the good life consists in activity, that it is not merely a pleasurable disposition, although pleasure normally naturally accompanies it. On this see H. H. Joachim, *Aristotle, "The Nicomachean Ethics": A Commentary*, p. 28; also Sir David Ross, *Aristotle*, 5th ed. rev., p. 190. Joachim also notes that the Greek ordinary usage of *eudaimonia* suggested not only a man's internal contentment but also his genuine prosperity; see also Arthur W. H. Adkins, *Merit and Responsibility: A Study in Greek Values*, pp. 254, 257n12. On this point see also the next section below, "The Place of Nonmoral Goods in the Morally Good Life." J. L. Austin criticizes misinterpretations of Aristotle caused by translating *Eudaimonia* as "happiness," but curiously still concludes that " 'happiness' is probably after all to be preferred as a translation, partly because it is traditional, and still more because it is fairly colourless;" see his "*Agathon* and *Eudaimonia* in the Ethics of Aristotle," in *Aristotle: A Collection of Critical Essays*, pp. 261-296. The first reason Austin alleges is an irrelevancy, the second simply false. Since Kant, the term 'happiness' has taken on primarily nonmoral connotations and is not equivalent to Aristotle's *eudaimonia*. So, for example, Aristotle's claim that all men wish for the best life possible for them is not translatable into the claim that all men take happiness to be the final and overriding purpose of their actions.

6. *Eth. Eud.* 1. 2. 1214b10 (Roberts); cf. *Eth. Nic.* 1. 2. 1094a23-26. This admonition, taken together with Aristotle's belief that moral weakness is rampant, indicates he may have thought most people do not organize their lives with a consistent view of what the best life might be for them.

7. Because we all share a common essence (*ousia*) or form (*eidos*), we all have a common function (*ergon*) or entelechy, that is, the actualization of our specifically human qualities and abilities. See 1. 7. 1097b22-1098a7; 2. 6. 1106a15-25; 10. 5. 1176a3-23; 10. 7. 1178a5-8; *Pol.* 1. 2. 1253a8-15; *Eth. Eud.* 2. 1. 1218b37ff.; *Metaph.* 7. 10. 1035b14-1036a12; 7. 11. 1036b22-33; 8. 2. 1043a12-28; *Part. an.* 1. 1. 640b1-4, 641a15-32; *Gen. an.* 1. 23. 731a24-34; *Ph.* 2. 8. As we have seen in chap. 2, Aristotle also claims that kinds of activities have their own objective natures. On the meanings of 'nature', see chap. 3, note 5.

8. See, e.g., 1. 4. 1095a20-26; 1. 7. 1097b21-22; 1. 8. 1098b22-29; 3. 5. 1113b15-16. For a discussion of the role and cogency of dialectical reasoning in explicating practical intuitions about ultimates (here man's ultimate goal), see chap. 6.

9. See 1. 5. 1095b31-1096a4; 1. 6. 1096b34; 1. 7. 1097b4-6; 1. 8. 1098b12-19, 29-1099a6; 1. 9. 1099b8-27; 1. 10. 1100a13-14; 1. 13. 1102b5-10; 7. 3. 1147a10-13; 9. 9. 1169b28-31; 10. 6. 1176a35-b2; *De an.* 2. 1. 412a22-27; 2. 5. 417a22-b25; *Pol.* 7. 3. 1325a32-b22; *Poet.* 6. 1450a16-19. Acting exhibits a power not shown by being acted upon; see *De an.* 3. 5. 430a17-18. In 1. 5. 1095b33, when Aristotle writes that "even excellence [*aretē*] proves to be imperfect as an end," he is referring to good qualities which are not being actualized.

10. See 4. 1. 1120a12-13; 8. 8. 1159a17-27. The good man still deserves honor, of course; see 4. 3. 1123b17-35. This quality of the good life rules out the view that our final good is radically beyond our own power to attain. Aristotle understood Plato to be holding for some such transcendent good, and he argues against that position in 1. 6; see also 1. 4. 1095a27-28; 6. 7. 1141a23-24; *Eth. Eud.* 1. 8. 1217b2-16; *Metaph.* 1. 9. 991a19-32; 7. 14.

11. See 1. 7. 1098a7-17; 1. 13. 1102a12-17.

12. See citations in chap. 2, note 34.

13. See, e.g., 3. 3. 1113a6-7; 9. 4. 1166a17-23; 9. 8. 1168b30-31; 10. 6. 1177a4-6; 10. 7. 1177a12-16, b26-29; *Part. an.* 2. 10. 656a7-8.

14. *Part. an.* 4. 10. 686a28-29 (Peck); cf. *Eth. Nic.* 1. 7. 1098a3-17; 1. 8. 1098b12-19; 1. 9. 1099b25-27; 2. 2. 1103b32-33; 6. 5. 1140b4-5; 10. 7. 1177a12-16.

15. 1. 7. 1098a7-8, 16-17; cf. 1097b22-35; 1. 8. 1098b17-19, 31; 1. 9. 1099b25-27; 1. 13. 1102a5-6.

16. See 1. 5. 1095b16-22; 1. 7. 1097b30-1098a3; 1. 13. 1102a16-17; 7. 13. 1153b25-36; 10. 6. 1177a7-10. Most of the moral virtues are concerned

with the 'necessary' pleasures. What distinguishes our agency is not just our ability to reason effectively about how to attain pleasure, but our ability to enjoy such pleasures only when they are morally acceptable.

17. See 1. 1; 1. 2. 1094a18-27; 1. 7. 1097a25-b20; 1. 12. 1101b35-1102a3; 6. 5. 1140b5-6; 6. 9. 1142b29-31; 10. 3. 1173a28-29; 10. 6. 1176b1-8; *Metaph.* 5. 16. When the notion of the good life is left indeterminate, its value cannot be questioned nor can it be desired merely or also as an instrumental good (see 1. 7. 1097b5-6). But when we become more definite, then men can and do err by valuing intrinsic goods, including those constituting the good life, merely as instrumentalities, or by not valuing them at all. Aristotle does not contest this fact; he does insist, however, that when men do so, we can and ought to say they are wrong (see, e.g., 1. 5. 1096b7-10).

18. See 1. 1. 1094a15-17; 1. 2. 1094a18-22; 1. 7. 1097a15-b6; 10. 6. 1176b30-31.

19. See 1. 7. 1097b7-20; 10. 2. 1172b30-35; 10. 6. 1176b5-6.

20. See 1. 7. 1098a30-b7; 6. 2. 1139b3-4; 6. 5. 1140b5-7; 10. 6. 1176b1-8. The good life should be honored, since it is an absolutely intrinsically good standard; see 1. 12. (There are also serious problems with 1. 12; see chap. 6, note 96.)

21. See 1. 5. 1096a6-10; *Pol.* 1. 9. 1257b23-1258a17; 7. 13. 1331b39-1332a3. But a moderate amount of material possessions normally is a necessary condition for living the good life.

22. See 1. 8. 1099a7, 13-16, 21; 7. 13. 1153b7-17.

23. See 7. 12. 1152b38-1153a7; 7. 13. 1153b7-18, 1154a1-7; 10. 5. 1176a3-29; 10. 6. 1177a18-23.

24. Remedial processes and their pleasures have been discussed in "Pleasure and Kinds of Pleasure" in chap. 3, and brutishness in chap. 8.

25. See 10. 3. 1174a1-3; 10. 6. 1176b8-1177a10; *Pol.* 8. 3. 1337b30-1338a9; 8. 5. 1339b15-1340b19. Some activities, Aristotle holds, can be desirable both for their own sake and for the sake of something else; see 1. 1. 1094a7-14.

26. See 1. 7. 1098a17-19; 1. 9. 1100a3-5; 1. 10. 1100a31-b17; 10. 7. 1177b23-26. As usual in matters of practice, there can be exceptions; see 9. 8. 1169a18-26. Most commentators think that, at least sometime during his philosophic career, Aristotle entertained the possibility of the immortality of at least part of man's *psuchē*, his *nous*. On this, see 10. 7. 1177b25-33; *De an.* 1. 1. 403a5-12; 1. 4. 408b18-32; 2. 1. 413a3-7; 2. 2. 413b24-33; 3. 4. 429a10-26; 3. 5; *Gen. an.* 2. 1. 731b23-732a6; 2. 3. 736b27-29; see also Joachim, pp. 61-68, 288-291. But this is irrelevant to the eudaimonic life, which is the final end of man, who as a composite being, consists of a whole

psyche and body. There is no indication that the mature Aristotle believed individual persons are immortal; see 1. 10. 1100a10-30; 3. 2. 1111b20-23.

27. 1. 7. 1098a18; see also 17-19; 1. 10. 1100b17-18.

28. 1. 10. 1101a14-16.

29. See 1. 8. 1098b12-13, 1099a31-b8; 1. 9. 1099b27-28; 4. 3. 1124a12-16; 7. 13. 1153b10-24; 8. 1. 1155a3-10; 9. 9. 1169b3-1170a19; 10. 7. 1177a28-32; 10. 8. 1178a29-b3, 33-1179a17; *Pol.* 2. 6. 1265a35-37; 4. 11. 1295a35-38; 7. 1. 1323a22-27, b40-1324a2; 7. 12. 1331b39-1332a3; *Metaph.* 5. 5. 1015a20-24; *Rh.* 1. 5. 1360b4ff. Gifts of fortune include both 'external goods' and goods of the body; among the latter are physical health and personal attractiveness; among the former, friends (the best), honor (the next best), reputation, power, and wealth.

30. 10. 8. 1178a29-33; cf. 8. 1. 1155a16; 8. 5. 1157b21-24; also citations in note 29 above.

31. See 1. 5. 1095b32-1096a2; 1. 9. 1100a3-8; 1. 10. 1100b1-7; 10. 6. 1176a33-36; *Ph.* 2. 5. 197a8-36; 2. 6. 197b1-13.

32. 1. 9. 1099b21-22; cf. 1. 10. 1100b28-30.

33. See 1. 5. 1096a1-2; 1. 9. 1100a5-9; 1. 10. 1101a1-16; 7. 4. 1148b23-35; *Pol.* 7. 13. 1331b39-1332a2; *Ph.* 2. 8. 199a33-b7. Achieving the good life, then, is not an all-or-nothing matter but does admit of degrees. Aristotle says as much in 3. 9. 1117b9-13; 10. 3. 1173a17-28; 10. 8. 1179a23-33; and *De an.* 2. 4. 415b3-8. Moreover, as we saw in chap. 8, some people may achieve moral goodness only in a "mixed way," by being morally strong.

34. 5. 1. 1129b3; cf. 2-7; see also 1. 3. 1094b15-18; 4. 1. 1120a4-5; 5. 6. 1134a34-35; 5. 9. 1137a26-30; *Pol.* 7. 13. 1332a8-18; *Rh.* 1. 1. 1355b3-8.

35. See 1. 6. 1096a6-10; 1. 8. 1098b13-19; 4. 1. 1120a35-b2; 4. 3. 1124a20-b7; 9. 8. 1168b15-27; *Pol.* 7. 1; 7. 13. 1332a26-27.

36. See 1. 10. 1100b8-13; 4. 1. 1120b2-4; *Pol.* 7. 1. 1323b21-29; 7. 13. 1332a30-32; also chaps. 5-6.

37. See 3. 6. 1115a15-23; 4. 1. 1120a4-13, b7-19; 4. 3. 1124a13-16. In fact, misfortunes may provide opportunities in which the nobility of a person's character can shine in all its purity; see 1. 10. 1100b12-1101a13; *Pol.* 7. 13. 1332a18-20. Aristotle also holds that a man deserves external goods only insofar as he is morally good, but a good man's generosity makes it difficult for him to accumulate much wealth; see 1. 10. 1100a24-25; 2. 7. 1108b1-3; 4. 1. 1120b14-19, 1121b4-6; 4. 3.

38. See *Pol.* 2. 5. 1265a29-37; 7. 1. 1323a22-b21; 7. 13. 1332a8-25; *Eth. Nic.* 10. 8. 1178b33-1179a17.

39. See, e.g., *Pol.* 2. 6. 1265a38-b18; 7. 13. 1331b39-1332a8, 27-32; 7. 16. 1335b20-27.

40. 4. 3. 1124a25-b3 (translation mine).

41. See 10. 8. 1177b4-5, 21-23; *Pol.* 7. 14. 1333a30-38; 7. 15; 8. 3. 1337b30-1338a13.

42. See 6. 2. 1139b3-4; 6. 5. 1140b5-7; also chap. 7, note 16.

43. See, e.g., 1. 13. 1103a4-10; 6. 6. 1141a3-8; 6. 11. 1143b14-16; 6. 13. 1144b14-15. "Life is action [*praxis*] and not production [*poiēsis*]" (*Pol.* 1. 4. 1254a7 [Jowett]; see *Eth. Nic.* 10. 4. 1175a12).

44. See, e.g., 2. 1. 1103b7-25; *Part. an.* 1. 1. 640a10-b4; *Gen. an.* 2. 1. 734b20-735a29.

45. See *Pol.* 1. 4. 1253b23-1254a17; 1. 5; 1. 6. 1255b4-15; 1. 7; 1. 11. 1258b35-38; 1. 13; 3. 4. 1277a33-b7; 3. 5. 1277b33-1278a21; 3. 9. 1280a32-1281a12; 7. 5. 1326b27-32; 7. 9. 1328b33-1329a2, 19-26; 7. 14. 1333a16-b3; 7. 15. 1334a11-39; *Eth. Nic.* 5. 6. 1134b8-15; 8. 11. 1161a35-b5; 9. 7. 1168a6-8; 10. 6. 1177a7-9. Aristotle's attempts to justify slavery are both embarrassed and embarrassing. He simply refused to admit his own doctrine that making is a uniquely human activity demanding the exercise of practical (calculative) reason, for the consequence of this doctrine is that all men necessarily are moral agents, with a moral character. Instead, he claims that some people (slaves) can have skills with no faculty of deliberation (see *Pol.* 1. 13. 1260a12). His own analysis of the nature of practical reason shows it is not possible for any rational being to live in such a way as not to lead a particular kind of life, so that the meaning of a man's life can never be caught completely by a listing of or history of his capacities and skills. Not only does the exercise of skills take place within a larger context of (moral) ends, but the exercise of skills need not be a mere instrumentality, as even Aristotle was forced to admit (see, e.g., 7. 12. 1153a24-27; *Pol.* 8. 2. 1337b3-23; 8. 6. 1340b33-1341a16). Aristotle neglected also to recognize the unique and intrinsic value present in the consummatory creative activity of the artist. But admitting all this would have meant he would also have had to condemn slavery. Moreover, the distinction between the primarily useful and the consummatory is far more fluid than Aristotle thought, as constantly changing views about the contents of liberal arts curricula indicate. For an inportant critique of Aristotle's distinction between poietic and moral kinds of activities, see J. L. Ackrill's "Aristotle's Distinction between *Energeia* and *Kinesis*," in *New Essays on Plato and Aristotle*, pp. 159-174. A refutation of Aristotle's contention that there is but one right valuative description of kinds of activities may have serious consequences for Aristotle's claim that there is but one right general description of the good life for men.

46. See *Pol.* 8. 3. 1337b30-1338a7; *Eth. Nic.* 10. 7. 1177b22-26; *Metaph.* 1. 2. 982b20-27.

47. See 6. 7. 1141b12-b7; 6. 12. 1143b33-1144a6; 6. 13. 1145a7-12; 10. 7; *Metaph.* 1. 1. 982a1-4; 1. 2. 982a5-b10; *De an.* 3. 4 and 5. Since First

Philosophy or Theology is the best kind of theorizing, the criteria for the good life apply most perfectly to it; see "Fourth Contrast" in chap. 2.

48. *Metaph.* 12. 7. 1072b18-20 (Hope); cf. *Eth. Nic.* 6. 7. 1141a20-21, 28-b3.

49. 10. 7. 1178a5-6; cf. 6. 12. 1144a3-7; 10. 7. 1177a18-27, b18-27; *Part an.* 1. 5. 644b32-645a19. *Theōria* involves neither the pain of deprivation nor the striving typical of appetition; see 7. 12. 1152b37-1153a1; 7. 14. 1154b17-20; 10. 3. 1173b16.

50. 6. 7. 1141b3; cf. 1141a19-21; 10. 7. 1177a18-22.

51. See 1. 7. 1098a6-18; 6. 3. 1139b25-35; 6. 7. 1141a16-21; 10. 7. 1177a25-26; *Metaph.* 12. 7. 1072b24-25; also chap. 2, note 59.

52. See 6. 1. 1139a5-13; 6. 3. 1139b17-24; 6. 5. 1140a33-b3; 6. 6. 1140b31-1141a3; 6. 7. 1141a17-18; *Metaph.* 1. 2. 982a24-b10; 2. 1. 993b20-30; 12. 7. 1072b14-26.

53. See "Practical Reasoning and Theoretical Reasoning" in chap. 4; also chap. 2, note 59; also 6. 7. 1141b4-8.

54. See 10. 7. 1177a27-b1, 21-23; 10. 8. 1178a23-b7; *Pol.* 2. 7. 1267a10-12; also chap. 2, note 50 above. Because he models *theōria* on divine activity, Aristotle tends to portray scientific activity as a radically individualized enterprise. He neglects its nature as the activity of a historically evolved community with its own special norms, traditions, and initiations. He also ignores his own claims that the best life for man must include friends with whom to share one's thoughts; see, e.g., 8. 6. 1168a22-27.

55. See 10. 7. 1177a23-27, b21-26; 10. 8. 1177b18-22.

56. See 1. 9. 1099b11-17; 7. 14. 1154b24-28; 10. 7. 1177a12-22, b26-1178a3; 10. 8. 1178a19-23, b7-32, 1179a23-33; *Pol.* 7. 2. 1324a23-b2; 7. 3; 7. 14. 1333a17-37; *Metaph.* 1. 2. 982b28-983a11; 12. 7. 1072b14-30; 12. 9. 1074b14-33. The divine already possesses perfection; since change could only be for the worse, attribution of practical activity to the divine is obviously inappropriate; see 10. 8. 1178b8-23; *Metaph.* 9. 9. 1051a3-21.

57. See *Pol.* 2. 9. 1269a34-35; 2. 11. 1273a32-b7; 7. 9. 1328b33-37.

58. See *Metaph.* 1. 1. 981b13-25; 1. 2. 982b11-28.

59. 6. 12. 1144a5; cf. 1-10.

60. See 10. 7. 1177b27-29; 10. 8. 1178a7-23, b4-7, 33-1179a9; *Metaph.* 8. 3. 1043a29-b32. We are also psychologically incapable of sustaining the same kind of activity indefinitely; see 7. 14. 1154b21-31.

61. See, e.g., 6. 1. 1138b35-1139a17; 6. 12. 1144a1-8; *Pol.* 7. 1. 1323b21-26.

62. See *Metaph.* 1. 1. 981b20-23; 1. 2. 982b12-27.

63. 10. 7. 1177b32-35; cf. *De an.* 2. 4. 415b3-8. But in 1. 10. 1101a20, Aristotle had defined the good life (*eudaimonia*) as making us "blissful only as human beings," and in 9. 4. 1166a 18-23, he says that, since we are human,

none of us would want to become divine in order to live a divinely perfect life. This wide vacillation between two incompatible positions, each set out with the same earnestness, causes the problem discussed in the final section of this chapter.

64. Because Aristotle delineates theory and practice as radically distinct exercises of our rationality, each with its own unique domain, he does not and cannot describe how one is to construct a single, unified life, doing both well and in proper balance. Theory and practice, it seems, must remain separate compartments in a person's life, each virtually sealed off from the other.

65. See 1. 9. 1099b13, 26; 1. 13. 1102a13-17; see also the citations in chap. 5, note 8; also Aristotle's description of political wisdom in 1. 2; 1. 4. 1095a16; 6. 8. 1141b23-1142a11.

66. See 1. 7. 1097a28-30, 1098a15-17; 1. 9. 1099b13, 16-17, 29-30, 1100a4; 1. 10. 1101a13-15.

67. See 1. 13. 1103a4-7; see also 1. 9. 1099b31-32; 1. 10. 1100b17-19.

68. "We have now completed our discussion of what practical and theoretical wisdom are . . . and we have shown that each is the excellence of a different part of the soul" (6. 11. 1143b14-16).

69. See 6. 12. 1144a1-3; 6. 13. 1145a3-4.

70. See 6. 12. 1144a3-6. In this passage and in 6. 13. 1145a7-11, Aristotle in fact first explicitly states what he also may have implied in 1. 7. 1097a28-30 and 1098a16-18, that theoretical activity *is* the good life (for it is its formal or defining cause). For the sake of simplicity, however, I have focused my attention on 10. 7-8.

71. See 6. 12. 1144a7-8.

72. See 6. 13. 1145a7-11; see also 1. 2. 1099b25-31.

73. 10. 7. 1177b23-25 and 10. 8. 1178a8; cf. 10. 8. 1178b7-8.

74. As an examination of those reasons shows, they are a methodological disaster. Yet, strangely enough, right in the middle of them appears a brief reflection on the methodology proper to moral philosophy, including the statement, "truth is judged by the actual facts of life" (10. 8. 1179a18; cf. 17-22). Aristotle himself raises the question of whether he has properly supported his claim. But then he immediately plunges into speculations about the activities of the gods.

75. See 10. 7. 1177a23-24.

76. See 10. 7. 1177a12-b5, 17-23; 10. 8. 1178a23-28.

77. See 10. 8. 1178b8-32, 1179a23-33. It would seem that Aristotle is here guilty of the charge he had leveled against Plato, of proposing as a human good something radically inappropriate to man.

78. See 10. 7. 1177b26-33.

79. See 10. 7. 1177b33-1178a3.

80. 10. 8. 1178b4-5. Insofar as practical activities are pursued merely as expediencies and not because they are noble, living the theoretical life does not presuppose or require practical excellence at all (see 2. 4. 1105a28-33).

81. 10. 8. 1178a13.

82. 10. 7. 1177b17-18.

83. "Anyone struck by the distinction between *poieseis* and *praxis* would conclude that the value to be realized in virtuous conduct can be subordinated to no other value without changing its entire nature. . . . [In 10. 7-8] the heart of the distinction between *poiesis* and *praxis* is torn out, as even *praxeis* are reduced to the status of means to contemplation." From J. Donald Monan, *Moral Knowledge and its Methodology in Aristotle*, pp. 85-86, 114.

84. C. J. Rowe, *The Eudemian and Nicomachean Ethics: A Study in the Development of Aristotle's Thought*, p. 67. See chap. 4, note 39; also the introduction to chap. 6.

85. See the introduction to chap. 6.

86. See chap. 3, notes 10, 12, 54; chap. 4, notes 1, 15, and 16; chap. 6, and note 3.

87. See chap. 4, note 1; chap. 6.

88. See, e.g., 7. 14. 1154b21-32.

89. See chap. 3, notes 35, 36, and 42.

90. See chap. 2, note 76; also chap. 3, "Instrumental and Instrinsic Practical Good," "*Poïesis* and *Praxis:* Making and Doing," and note 13.

91. See note 51 above; also chap. 2, note 59.

92. See 2. 1-2.

93. See 6. 7. 1141a22-b9; 6. 12. 1143b33-35; 6. 13. 1145a7-11.

94. 1. 2. 1094a27-28. Note that the observation in 7. 12. 1153a20 that theoretical activity can be overdone and be detrimental to one's health is a practical, not a theoretical, judgment; as also is the implication that in this case of conflict between theoretical and practical concerns it is best to quit theorizing for a while.

95. 1. 2. 1104a28-b6; cf. 1. 9. 1099b30; 6. 7. 1141b2-23.

96. Trond Berg Eriksen, *Bios Theoretikos*, p. 11.

97. Aristotle reveals many facets of his personality in his writings; for a portrait of Aristotle the man, see Anton-Hermann Chroust, *Aristotle*, 1: 232-248.

Glossary of Greek Terms

This list contains some of the most important technical terms or most frequently used words in Aristotle's vocabulary. They are listed according to the English, not the Greek, alphabet.

agathos (ἀγαθός): good; *ta agatha* (τὰ ἀγαθά): good things

agnoia (ἄγνοια): ignorance; lack of moral perceptiveness

aidōs (αἰδώς): shame, sense of shame

aisthēsis (αἴσθησις): sense perception; sensation; moral sense or perception of the particulars in one's situation

aitia (αἰτία): source, cause

akinēsis (ἀκίνησις): unchanging, involving no alteration

akolasia (ἀκολασία): self-indulgence, licentiousness; *akolastos* (ἀκόλαστος): a self-indulgent person

akousion (ἀκούσιον): involuntary; *akōn* (ἄκων): unwillingly

akrasia (ἀκρασία): moral weakness, incontinence; *akratēs* (ἀκρατής): a morally weak person

archē, archai (pl.) (ἀρχή,–αί): source, origin, cause; fundamental principle

aretē, aretai (pl.) (ἀρετή,–αί): excellence or best state of something, enabling the possessor to function well; when translated as "virtue" does not necessarily mean moral excellence—the sense depends on the context

atuchēma, atuchēmata (pl.) (ἀτύχημα,–ατα): mishap, accident, misfortune

autotelēs (αὐτοτελής): complete, self-contained; containing its own end, and so intrinsically good

bios (βίος): life, lifetime

blabera, ta (τὰ βλαβερά): the harmful or disadvantageous, opp. to *ta sumpheronta*, the beneficial

boulēsis, boulēseis (pl.) (βούλησις,–εις): wish, aim, desire

186

bouleusis, bouleuseis (pl.) (βούλευσις,–εις): deliberation, calculation about how to act (an activity of *to logistikon*)

deinotēs (δεινότης): cleverness in practical matters

dianoia (διάνοια): reason, intelligence; discursive thinking

dialektikē, hē (ἡ διαλεκτική): the dialectic; the art of reflectively analyzing, discussing, and arguing from purported evidence for a position

dikaiosunē (δικαιοσύνη): justice; *dikaios* (δίκαιος): just

dunamis, dunameis (pl.) (δύναμις,–εις): power, force, ability; potentiality, capacity to change or be changed

eidos (εἶδος): form, i.e., that which makes a thing to be the sort of thing it is

endoxa (ἔνδοξα): opinions, esp. generally accepted opinions

energeia, energeiai (pl.) (ἐνέργεια,–αι): activity, active exercise; actualization of a potentiality (a *dunamis*); activity involving no change, as opp. to kinetic activity

enkrateia (ἐγκράτεια): moral strength, strong character; *enkratēs* (ἐγκρατής): a morally strong person

entelecheia (ἐντελέχεια): actuality; fulfilment, attainment of an end-state; having an end-state which is the actualization of a potentiality (*dunamis*) or set of potentialities

epagōgē (ἐπαγωγή): inductive thinking; inductive argument

epieikeia (ἐπιείκεια): equity, fairness; the corrective to strict legalism

epistēmē (ἐπιστήμη): knowledge or science; strictly, theoretical knowledge; *to epistēmonikon* (τὸ ἐπιστημονικόν): scientific or theoretical reason

epithumia, epithumiai (pl.) (ἐπιθυμία,– αι): appetite, desire, yearning; nonrational desire as contrasted with rational desire or wish (*boulēsis*)

ergon, erga (pl.) (ἔργον,–α): work, function; deed, act; the nature of a thing is defined by its function, which is also the excellence of that thing

eschatos (ἔσχατος): uttermost or ultimate in time, place, or value; perfect; *ta eschata* (τὰ ἔσχατα): the ultimate, particular facts of a situation

ethos (ἔθος): habit engrained through practice; *ethismos* (ἐθισμός): habituation

ēthos (ἦθος): moral character

eudaimonia (εὐδαιμονία): the good life, living well; traditionally translated as 'happiness'; *eudaimonein* (εὐδαιμονεῖν): to live the good life

eupraxia (εὐπραξία): good action, good practice, living morally well

eu zēn (εὖ ζῆν): the good life; synonymous with *eudaimonia*

genesis (γένεσις): beginning, coming into being

gnōmē (γνώμη): judgment, good sense, insight

hamartēma (ἁμάρτημα): mistake, error; simple error as opp. to moral error

haplōs (ἁπλῶς): absolutely, unqualifiedly; generally; abstractly or in itself as opp. to in the particular situation

hē (ἡ): the (fem. gender)

hekastos (ἕκαστος): particular; *ta kath' hekasta* (τὰ καθ' ἕκαστα): individuals, groups of particulars

hēdonē (ἡδονή): pleasure

hekousion (ἑκούσιον): voluntary; *hekōn* (ἑκών): willingly, voluntarily

hexis, hexeis (pl.) (ἕξις,–εις): characteristic state, habitual quality; intelligent disposition; *hexis proairetikē* (ἕξις προαιρετική): moral disposition, character trait

ho (ὁ): the (masc. gender)

holōs (ὅλως): generally, entirely, wholly, absolutely

horos (ὅρος): limit, definition, norm

hupothesis (ὑπόθεσις): hypothesis; *ex hupotheseōs* (ἐξ ὑποθέσεως): conditionally, hypothetically

kai (καί): and

kakia (κακία): moral evil, vice, wickedness

kalon, to (τὸ καλόν): the noble; the morally good

kinēsis, kinēseis (pl.) (κίνησις,–εις): change, motion, movement; process involving stages and taking time to complete, as opposed to *energeia*, which is *akinēsis*. involving no movement

logismos (λογισμός): thinking involving logical stages, concluding to a judgment

logistikon, to (τὸ λογιστικόν): calculative, deliberative, practical reason

logos, logoi (pl.) (λόγος,–οι): literally, speech or statement; reason in the sense of the ability to think abstractly, using principles; reason in the sense of the rational basis for something—its plan, theoretical explanation or support; a principle given by reason; *orthos logos* (ὀρθὸς λόγος): right reason, correct rule

meson, to (τὸ μέσον): the mean or middle position between two extremes

mesotēs, hē (ἡ μεσότης): syn. with *to meson*

metabolē (μεταβολή): any kind of change or movement

mnēmē (μνήμη): memory

noēsis (νόησις): intelligence, intellect; thinking; *noein* (νοεῖν): to think

nous (νοῦς): intelligence; highest part of the rational soul; intuitive thought; *orektikos nous* (ὀρεκτικὸς νοῦς): lit., desiring thought; choice

orexis, orexeis (pl.) (ὄρεξις,–εις): desire; with *dianoētikē* or *bouleutikē* choice, rational deliberate desire

organon (ὄργανον): instrument, object used as an instrument

ou, ouk, ouch (οὐ, οὐκ, οὐχ): not (the form used depends on the word following the negative)

ousia (οὐσία): being, substance; essence

panourgia (πανουργία): slyness, wiliness

pathēsis, pathēseis (pl.) (πάθησις,–εις): capacity to be acted on by others; or state of being affected by others; a suffering or enduring; contrasted with *poiēsis*, acting on others

peras, perata (pl.) (πέρας,–ατα): limit, edge

phainomena, ta (τὰ φαινόμενα): the appearances of things, the data of experience

phantasia (φαντασία): imagination; ability to have mental images

philia (φιλία): friendship, social relations

phronēsis (φρόνησις): practical or moral wisdom; sometimes translated as "prudence"; the excellence of calculative reason (*to logistikon*); *ho phronimos* (ὁ φρόνιμος): the man of practical wisdom

phusis (φύσις): nature; *phusei* (φύσει): by nature, naturally

poiēsis, poiēseis (pl.) (ποίησις,–εις): action, movement; agency as contrasted with *pathēsis*; making or production, as contrasted with *praxis; poiein* (ποιεῖη): to act, to make, to produce

politikē (πολιτική): political wisdom; expertise on sociopolitical matters

praktikos (πρακτικός): practical; *ho praktikos bios* (ὁ πρατικὸς βίος): the active life

praxis, praxeis (pl.) (πρᾶξις,–εις): the exercise of agency; action or practice, as contrasted with theoretical activity; action in the sense of morally significant conduct, as contrasted with *poiēsis*

proairesis, proaireseis (pl.) (προαίρεσις,–εις): choice, efficacious intention, purpose

propeteia (προπέτεια): impetuosity

psuchē (ψυχή): life principle; form of a living being; soul

sophia (σοφία): wisdom, esp. theoretical or philosophic wisdom; the excellence of scientific reason (*to epistēmonikon*)

sōphrosunē (σωφροσύνη): moral excellence; self-control; sometimes translated as "temperance"; the best state of moral character; *ho sōphrōn* (ὁ σώφρων): the morally excellent man

spoudaios, ho (ὁ σπουδαῖος): the person of high (esp. high moral) standards; the person who takes living seriously; the good man

sullogismos (συλλογισμός): deductive thinking; deductive argument

sumpheronta, ta (τὰ συμφέροντα): things beneficial or advantageous, as opp. to *ta blabera*—the harmful; either syn. with or opp. to the morally good—see context

sunesis (σύνεσις): correct understanding in practical matters; roughly equivalent to 'conscience'

sungnōmē (συγγνώμη): emphathetic judgment; considerateness; forgiveness

sunthesis (σύνθεσις): synthesis, combination

technē, technai (pl.) (τέχνη,–αι): art, skill, productive ability or know-how

telos, telē (pl.) (τέλος,–η): end, goal, consummatory state; *teleios* (τέλειος) and *teleiotatos* (τελειότατος): perfect, complete, final; *ta pros to telos* (τὰ πρὸς τὸ τέλος): that done for the sake of the end, the means

thēriotēs (θηριότης): brutishness

theōria (θεωρία): scientific, theoretical thought; contemplation; *theorein* (θεωρεῖν): to engage in theoretical enquiry, thinking, or contemplation

thumos (θυμός): spirit, courage, anger

timē (τιμή): honor

to (τό): the (neuter gender)

zōon, zōa (pl.) (ζῷον,–α): living being

Works Cited

Ackrill, J. L. "Aristotle's Distinction between *Energeia* and *Kinesis*." In *New Essays on Plato and Aristotle*, ed. Renford Bambrough, pp. 121-141.

Adkins, Arthur W. H. *Merit and Responsibility: A Study in Greek Values*. Oxford: The Clarendon Press, 1960.

Allan, D. J., "Aristotle's Account of the Origin of Moral Principles." In *Proceedings of the 11th International Congress of Philosophy*, 12: 120-127. Amsterdam: North-Holland Publishing Company, 1953.

————. "The Practical Syllogism." In *Autour de'Aristote: Recueil d'études de philosophie ancienne et médievale, offert à Monseigneur A. Mansion*, pp. 325-340. Louvain: Publications Universitaires de Louvain, 1955.

————. *The Philosophy of Aristotle*. 2d ed. Oxford: Oxford University Press, Oxford Paperbacks University Series, 1970.

Ando, Takatura. *Aristotle's Theory of Practical Cognition*. 3d rev. ed. The Hague: Martinus Nijhoff, 1971.

Anscombe, G. E. M. *Intention*. 2d ed. Oxford: Basil Blackwell, 1963.

————. "Thought and Action in Aristotle." In *New Essays on Plato and Aristotle*, ed. Renford Bambrough, pp. 143-158.

Austin, J. L. "*Agathon* and *Eudaimonia* in the *Ethics* of Aristotle." In *Aristotle: A Collection of Critical Essays*, ed. J. M. E. Moravcsik, pp. 261-296.

Bambrough, Renford, ed. *New Essays on Plato and Aristotle*. International Library of Philosophy and Scientific Method, edited by A. J. Ayer. London: Routledge & Kegan Paul, 1965.

Brand, Myles, ed. *The Nature of Human Action*. Glenview, Ill: Scott, Foresman & Co., 1970.

Brown, Patterson. "Infinite Causal Regression." *The Philosophical Review*, 75 (1966), pp. 510-525.

Burnet, John. *The Ethics of Aristotle*. London: Methuen & Co., 1900.

Chroust, Anton-Hermann. *Aristotle: New Light on his Life and on Some of his Lost Works*. 2 vols. Notre Dame: University of Notre Dame Press, 1973.

Cooper, John M. *Reason and Human Good in Aristotle*. Cambridge: Harvard University Press, 1975.

Dover, K. J. *Greek Popular Morality in the Time of Plato and Aristotle*. Berkeley: University of California Press, 1974.

Eriksen, Trond Berg. *Bios Theoretikos: Notes on Aristotle's "Ethica Nicomachea" X, 6-8*. Oslo: Universitetsforlaget, 1976.

Fortenbaugh, W. W. *Aristotle on Emotion*. London: Gerald Duckworth & Co., 1975.

Gauthier, R.-A. "On the Nature of Aristotle's Ethics." From *La morale d'Aristote*. Paris: Presses Universitaires de France, 1958. In *Aristotle's Ethics: Issues and Interpretations*, ed. & trans. Walsh and Shapiro, pp. 10-29.

Goldman, Alvin I. *A Theory of Human Action*. Englewood Cliffs, N. J.: Prentice-Hall, 1970.

Grant, Sir Alexander. *The Ethics of Aristotle, Illustrated with Essays and Notes*. 2 vols. London: Longmans, Green, and Co., 1885.

Greenwood, L. H. G. *Aristotle: "Nicomachean Ethics" Book Six with Essays, Notes, and Translation*. Cambridge: University Press, 1909.

Grene, Marjorie. *A Portrait of Aristotle*. London: Faber & Faber, 1963.

Haksar, Vinit. "Aristotle and the Punishment of Psychopaths." *Philosophy*, 39 (1964), pp. 323-340. Rpt. in Walsh and Shapiro, pp. 80-101.

Hamburger, Max. *Morals and Law: The Growth of Aristotle's Legal Theory*. New Haven: Yale University Press, 1951.

Hardie, W. F. R. *Aristotle's Ethical Theory*. Oxford: The Clarendon Press, 1968.

Hart, H. L. A. "The Ascription of Responsibility and Rights." *Proceedings of the Aristotelian Society*, 49 (1948-1949), pp. 171-194.

Jaeger, Werner. *Aristotle: Fundamentals of the History of his Development*. 2d ed. trans. Richard Robinson. Oxford: The Clarendon Press, 1948.

Joachim, H. H. *Aristotle, "The Nicomachean Ethics": A Commentary*. ed. D. A. Rees. Oxford: The Clarendon Press, 1951.

Kenny, Anthony. *Action, Emotion, and Will*. Studies in Philosophical Psychology, edited by R. F. Holland. London: Routledge & Kegan Paul, 1963.

————. "The Practical Syllogism and Incontinence." *Phronesis*, 11 (1966), pp. 163-184.

Kitto, H. D. F. *The Greeks*, 2d ed. rev. Baltimore: Penguin Books, 1957.

Kohlberg, Lawrence. "Education for Justice: A Modern Statement of the Platonic View." In Gustafson, James M., et al., *Moral Education: Five Lectures*, pp. 56-83. Cambridge: Harvard University Press, 1970.

Lloyd, G. E. R. *Aristotle: The Growth and Structure of his Thought*. Cambridge: Cambridge University Press, 1968.

Lloyd-Jones, Hugh. *The Justice of Zeus*. Berkeley: University of California Press, 1971.

Lynch, John Patrick. *Aristotle's School: A Study of a Greek Educational Institution*. Berkeley: University of California Press, 1972.

Michelakis, Emmanuel M. *Aristotle's Theory of Practical Principles*. Athens: Cleisiounis Press, 1961.

Milo, Ronald D. *Aristotle on Practical Knowledge and Weakness of Will*. The Hague: Mouton & Co., 1966.

Monan, J. Donald. *Moral Knowledge and its Methodology in Aristotle*. Oxford: The Clarendon Press, 1968.

Moravcsik, J. M. E., ed. *Aristotle: A Collection of Critical Essays*. Notre Dame: University of Notre Dame Press, 1968.

Mortimore, Geoffrey W., ed. *Weakness of Will*. Controversies in Philosophy, edited by A. G. N. Flew. London: MacMillan, 1971.

Oates, Whitney J. *Aristotle and the Problem of Value*. Princeton: Princeton University Press, 1963.

Peters, F. E. *Aristotle and the Arabs: The Aristotelian Tradition in Islam*. New York: New York University Press, 1968.

Rescher, Nicholas. "Aspects of Action." In *The Logic of Decision and Action*, ed. Nicholas Rescher, pp. 215-219. Pittsburgh: University of Pittsburgh Press [1967].

———. "On the Characterization of Actions." In *The Nature of Human Action*, ed. Myles Brand, pp 247-254.

Ross, Sir David. *Aristotle*. 5th ed. rev. (1949). London, Methuen & Co., 1964.

Rowe, C. J. *The Eudemian and Nicomachean Ethics: A Study in the Development of Aristotle's Thought*. Proceedings of the Cambridge Philological Society, Supplement 3. Cambridge: The Cambridge Philological Society, 1971.

Ryle, Gilbert. *The Concept of Mind*. London: Hutchinson & Co., 1949.

Simon, Yves R. "Introduction to the Study of Practical Wisdom." *The New Scholasticism*, 35 (1961) pp. 1-40.

Stewart, J. A. *Notes on the "Nicomachean Ethics" of Aristotle*. 2 vols. Oxford: The Clarendon Press, 1892.

Tracy, Theodore James. *Physiological Theory and the Doctrine of the Mean in Plato and Aristotle*. Chicago: Loyola University Press, 1969.

Urmson, J. O. "Aristotle on Pleasure." In *Aristotle: A Collection of Critical Essays*, ed. J. M. E. Moravcsik, pp. 323-333.

Veatch, Henry B. *Aristotle: A Contemporary Appreciation*. Bloomington: Indiana University Press, 1974.

Walsh, James J. *Aristotle's Conception of Moral Weakness*. New York: Columbia University Press, 1963.

———. and Shapiro, Henry L., eds. *Aristotle's "Ethics": Issues and Interpretations*. Belmont, Cal.: Wadsworth Publishing Co., 1967.

Index

Accidents (*atuchēmata*): 141. *See also* Mistakes, simple

Action, human (*praxis* in a broad sense): 17-42; awareness required for, 20-21, 23, 27, 31, 37n.31, 63-64, 67; a combination of affecting and being affected, 7, 19, 37n.31; a complex of facts, 20-21, 29-31; contrasted with events and processes, 7-8, 20-24; contrasted with passivity, 18-20, contrasted with theoretical activity, 21, 24-27; deliberation does not always precede, 63, 73n.13, 75n.28; description of, an exercise of practical reason, 42n.81; done only "incidentally," 40n.68, 41n.76, 44, 154n.13; an expression of character formed by similar actions, 41n.76, 113, 122n.96; final cause of, is also its first principle, 22; intrinsically and instrumentally good, 43-46, 56n.6, 60n.54, 80-81, 115n.3; may not reflect one's character, 41n.76; means-end distinction in descriptions of, 60n.54; necessary and sufficient conditions for, 27, 39n.65; not identical with behavior, 20, 29, 33; organic unity of, dependent on agent, 31, 67; "purposeless," 36n. 27; refraining and omission kinds of, 33, 35n.8; responsibility-assessments for, 19, 28; requires desire, 21-22, 63; requires power, 7, 18-19, 27, 65; source of, is an agent, 18, 23, 37n.31; teleological nature of 21-22, 31-32; term "action" can be used elastically, 17, 27-28, 40n.67; the two-dimensional character of, 28, 32-33, 41n.76-78, 112-114; voluntariness of, 20-21, 23-24, 38n.38. *See also* Choice; Deliberation; Desire; Facts of practice, the; Means; Power; Reason, practical

Action, theory of human: fundamental to moral philosophy, 17; delineation of, an exercise of practical reason, 103

Action-types: 29-30; Aristotle's two approaches to, 40n.76; difficulties in the delineation of, 31, 40n.76, 56n.13, 182n.45; an objective basis for moral evaluations, 43-46, 99, 103, 106, 171n.7; rightness in recognizing, can be influenced by character, 42n.81, 45-46, 110-111. *See also* Argumentation

Activity (*energeia*): 26, 45-46; contrasted with processes (*geneseis* and *kinēseis*), 26, 44-46, 60n.51, 80-81; divine, an "activity of immobility" (*akinēsis*), 46; divine model for, 174; intrinsically good (*autotelēs*) by nature, 44, 46, 56n.6; kinds of, 25-27, 48, 60n.51; life is, 122n.96, 182n.43;

195

normally pleasurable, 47-48; occasionally bad for an individual, 46, 185n.94. *See also* Activity, moral; Activity, theoretical

Activity, moral (*praxis* in the strict sense): 23, 26-27, 51; Aristotle's two approaches to, 51-52; behavioral descriptions of, 51; cannot be defined by an impersonal norm, 110; characteristic of the good person, 112-114; contrasted with making, 54, 80-81; contrasted with theoretical activity, 24-27, 112, 170-171; difficulties in determining how to do, 52, 110; its end inheres in, 86-88; a form of activity (*energeia*), 48; generates moral excellence, 109; norm for, is the good person, 81, 110-111; norm for, is the mean, 51-52, 81, 87, 110; normally pleasurable, 88; relation of, to character, 109, 112-114; social-political activity is, 51, 124-126. *See also* Excellence, the man of moral; Paradigms; Process, productive; Wisdom, man of practical

Activity, theoretical (*theōria*: 24-27, 68, 168-169; as activity (*energeia*), 25-26, 39n.63; contrasted with practical activity, 24-27, 168-169, 182n.45; description of, 7, 25, 39n.63, 57n.25, 168-169, 174; divine paradigm for, 172, 174-175; independence of, from somatic processes, 38n.50; involves no change, 25-26; most perfect activity possible, 116n.24, 168-169; perfected by truth, 116n.25; the process of learning and, 174-175; the proper activity of a philosopher, 25. *See also* Knowledge, thoretical; Wisdom, theoretical

Actualization (*energeia* in a wide sense): of a potentiality (*dunamis*), 45, 120n.65, 156n.37; two degrees of, 146-147, 156n.37; soul, the, of the body, 72n.1. *See also* End, the; Function

Advantageous, the (*ta sumpheronta*): pursued by the man of practical wisdom, 83, various senses of, 59n.45, 83, 132. *See also* Self-love; Wisdom, the man of practical

Agency, human: 18-24; a complex of reason and desire, 7-8, 21-24, 62-63, 73n.8; moral implications of, 129. *See also* Action, human

Anger, (*thumos*): impetuosity in, 115n.10; a species of desire, 98; restraint of, by reason, 115n.10; superior to sensual appetite, 115n.10; when provoked, not malicious, 92n.32, 142

Appetite, sensual (*epithumia*): 22: acts due to, 22-24, 74n.14; always directed to some end, 21; can oppose choice, 155-156n.30; cannot corrupt reason, 147, 149, 157n.43; the cause of moral evil, 23, 101, 140, 143; conforms to reason in moral excellence, 101, 117n.31; needs training and guidance by reason, 54, 101, 115n.4; a species of desire (*orexis*), 37n.32, 98. *See also* Desire

Argumentation: in moral matters often futile, 42n.81, 108-109, 121n.77, 129, 131, 136n.25

Aristotle: changes in his philosophic views, 78n.39, 96-97; influence of Plato on, 4, 127; regarded as a moral aristocrat, 130-131, 134n.6, 137n.34; neither a dogmatic absolutist nor a complete relativist, 6, 9-11, 16n.5, 50, 110, 130-132; not a hedonist, 59n.49; personality of, 185n.97; life of, 3-4

Art. *See* Process, productive; Skill

Beneficial, the. *See* Advantageous, the

Brutishness (*thēriotēs*): 149

Calculation. *See* Deliberation

Calculative reason. *See* Reason, practical

Capacity (*dunamis*): 91n.5; contrasted with activity (*energeia*), 120n.65; developed by practice, 127; distinguished from character, 91n.5; for initiating or undergoing change, 57n.18; moral neutrality of, 135n.14. *See also* Actualization; Power

Character, moral (*ēthos*): 86, 98-102; consists of dispositions (*hexeis*), 82, 86-87, 91n.5, 135n.16; determines how skills are used, 7, 50-51, 103; developed through actions, choices, and habituation, 8, 12, 41n. 76, 74n.15, 86-87, 100, 104, 113, 128; distinguished from behavior, feelings, and sufferings, 34n.6, 86-87, 91n.5; emotions are docile to reason in good, 101; individual traits and, 150; kind of, depends on relations between reason and desire, 100-102; kinds of, 100-102; kinds of, generated by kinds of actions and experiences, 8, 86, 108, 113; not a capacity for opposites, 82; not developed merely through instruction, 8, 136n.25; not merely conditioned desires, 98; permanence of, 86-87, 92n.32&34, 144; practical reason and, 98; responsibility for one's 73n.13, 100, 120n.66, 143; revealed by actions, 41n.78, 86, 93n.41, 112-113, 116n.23, 122n.96, 155n.22; revealed by pleasures and pains, 41n.78, 86-87, 113, 142; role of emotions in, 100-102; self-awareness and, 100; simple errors

do not reflect, 100-102, 141-142; a synthesis of reason and desire, 98, 117n.31; unrelated to a person's theoretical opinions, 74n.15, 140, 175-176, 185n.80; voluntary nature of, 24. *See also* Characteristics; Desires

Characteristics (*hexeis*): 63, 86, 91n.5; defined by actions they cause, 123n.96, excellence and, 62; exercise of, pleasurable, 49; kinds of, generated by kinds of actions, 71, 100, 104, 127-128, 136n.25; mere possession of, 35n.9, 122-123n.96, 146-147. *See also* Character

Children: actions of, 7, 20, 22-23, 27, 37n.31; appetites of, need training, 101, 127-128, 135-136n.16; born with morally neutral nature, 13, 127, 135n.14. *See also* Education, moral

Choice (*proairesis*): 64-67, 74n.14-15, 75n.25; the aim and conclusion of deliberation, 65; contrasted with wishing, conjecturing, opining, 74n.15, 98-99; correctness of, 74n.15, 85, 99; deliberation does not always precede, 63, 73n. 13, 75n.28; an exercise of practical reason, 74n.15; frustrated, 22, 33, 75n.25; normally issues in action, 75n.25, 112-113, 164; objects of, 22, 99; reveals character 74n.15, 116n.23. *See also* Deliberation; Desire

Citizenship: 126-127, 130, 133n.2, 3, 5

Cleverness (*deinotēs*): 83-84; moral weakness and, 147, 156n.32

Coercion (*bia*); 18; deliberation and, 24; two ways of understanding, 23-24; voluntariness destroyed by, 20, 32

Constitution: 134n.5; criteria for acceptability of, 130-132; form of government determined by the, 133-134n.5; kinds of, 129-130, 137n.29

Constraint. *See* Coercion

Contemplation. *See* Activity, theoretical

Continence. *See* Moral strength

Data of moral philosophy. *See* Methodology in moral philosophy, the

Deductive thinking (*sullogismos*): 39n.61. *See also* Induction; Syllogism, practical

Deliberation: 63-68, 74n.15, 75n.21; conditions necessary for, 64-65; excellence in, characteristic of practical wisdom, 84; a function of practical reason, 63-65, 76n.28; influenced by character, 76n.28; limited to consideration of contingent means, 64-65, 68, 115n.3; logical form of, 66-68, 75n.28; norm of effectiveness in, 83; when successful, ends in choice, 64. *See also* Choice; Cleverness; Reason, practical; Syllogism, practical; Wisdom, practical

Desire (*orexis*): 37n.32, 62, 73n.8, 116n.15; cannot corrupt reason, 147, 149, 157n.43; is necessary for action, 21-22; may not yield to arguments, 121n.77, 131; needs to be led by reason, 54, 95, 99-101, 116n.14, 117n.31, 128, 130-131, 134n.7, 143, 150; needs to be trained, 135n.16; ontological status of, 62, 72, 97, 116n.14, 176; role of state in regulating, 126-129, 134n.7, 137n.36; three kinds of, 37n.32, 98; wayward, corrected by pain, 101, 137n.36. *See also* Appetite; Choice; Wishes

Dialectical method, the (*hē dialektikē*) 106-109; Aristotle's use of,

118n.56, 119n.60. *See also* Induction; Methodology in moral philosophy, the

Dispositions. *See* Characteristics

Doing (praxis). *See* Activity, moral

Education, moral: 126-132; induction, habituation, and experience in, 119n.61; instructor's character in, 121n.74, 126; nature, nurture, and instruction in, 127-129, 135n.12, 150-151; not merely training, 100; paradigms and, 111, 122n.86, 126; political nature of, 125-132; practice precedes instruction in, 100, 128-129. *See also* Character, moral; Paradigms, moral; Socrates

Egotism. *See* Self-love

Emotions: 34-35n.6, 86. *See also* Desire

End, the (*to telos*): 21-22, 31; defines the nature of an action done for its sake, 22, 27, 29, 33, 155; "inheres" in intrinsically good actions, 44; is distinct from instrumentalities, 44; is the object of desires and wishes, 98; practical ignorance of right, is a moral fault, 139-143; predetermined by nature, 99. *See also* Action, human; Activity; Function; Good, the; Process, productive

Equity (*epieikeia*): 78n.44

Excellence (*aretē*): 62; function is, 62, 72n4, 95; human, 62; intellectual, 62-63; moral, 112-114. *See also* Excellence, moral; Reason; Wisdom, practical, Wisdom, theoretical

Excellence, moral (*ēthikē aretē*): 85-90; achievement of, not always pleasurable, 128; consists in harmony between reason and desire, 63, 100-102; egotism and, 14; an extreme, 93n.47; generated by actions, 128; good citizenship and, 126-127, 130; identical to one form of justice, 131-132; judged by actions, choices, and pleasures, 113; the mean for moral qualities, 87; motivation in, 85-88; not merely a matter of habituation, 95, 98, 128; not reducible to right behavior, 87, 128; not widely achieved, 130; practical wisdom, cannot exist without, 63, 88, 95, 98, 116n.14; requires reason rule over emotions, 100-101, 128; results in harmony between character and actions, 112-114; self-control (*sōphrosunē*) the paradigmatic form of, 87-88, 143-144; unconditionally good, 88. *See also* Character, moral; Desire; Education, moral; Mean, the; Wisdom, practical

Excellence, the man of moral (*ho sōphrōn*): 13-14, 86-90; autonomy of, 87-88, 121n.82; best judge of pleasures, 49, 87; comparison of, with modern psychological ideals, 13; effectiveness of, 13; emotions of, follow the mean, 60n.59, 87-88, 101; has sensitive intelligent habits of conduct, 13, 43, 87; internal integrity of 13, 101-102; life of, is full of pleasure, 88. *See also* Excellence, moral

Experience: 119n.62; found in the laws of the state, 124; involves induction, perception, and habituation, 107, 119n.61; judgments of people of, 111-112; an objective basis for moral knowledge, 10, 104, 124-125; the ultimate defense of moral claims, 77n.35. *See also* Methodology in moral philosophy, the

Explanation, teleological: 21-23, 29-33, 55n.5. *See also* Action, human

Facts of practice, the (*ta phainomena, ta erga, ta eschata*): 29-31; action-types and, 29; determine outer side of an action, 29; error about, 139, 141-143; found in experience, 104; fundamental data in moral inquiry and moral knowledge, 103-109; six, sometimes seven, kinds of, 29-30; theories must account for, 6, 106; use of, in moral judgments 104-106. *See also* Action, human; Knowledge, moral; Methodology in moral philosophy, the; Sensitivity, moral

Faculty. *See* Capacity; Power

Feelings: 86. *See also* Desires

Friendship (*philia*): 8, 89, 124, 126, 181n.29

Function (*ergon*): defined by end, 72n.2, 95; the excellence of a thing is its proper, 62, 72n.4, 95; of the intellect, 62-63; of man, 72. *See also* Actualization; End, the; Excellence

Gifts of fortune: the good life and, 163-166; treasured too highly, 89

Good (*agathon*): all men wish for what is, 83: both an activity and a characteristic, 43, 112-114, 122-123n.96, 159; definition of, 20, 43; genuine and merely apparent, 102, 117n.35; instrumental and intrinsic, 43-44, 80-81; the object of desires and wishes, 21, 98; practical and theoretical, 21; recognition of practical, depends on character, 122n.82; relation of, to the advantageous, 59n.45, 83; what is abstractly (*haplōs*), distinguished from what is for a particular person or circumstance, 46, 49-50, 55n.5, 60n.58, 78n.43, 148, 164-165. *See also* Action, human; Advantageous, the

Good life, the (*hē eudaimonia*): 159-

177; based on nature, 103; consists of activities rather than characteristics, 122-123n.96, 161, 179n.9; constituents of 168-170; delineated by practical reason, 103; denied to slaves, 166-167, 175, 182n.45; general description of, 160-163; "happiness" a misleading term for, 14-15, 178n.5; honored, not just praised, 123n.96; instruments necessary for, 163-166; leisure activities and, 166-168; a life of psychological health and fulfillment, 13; not an all-or-nothing affair, 181n.33; only one right general view of, 160; the place of moral activity in, 59n.42; problems with Aristotle's doctrine of, 170-176; productive processes not a part of, 166-167; the state as an expression of, 125; theoretical activity the best part of, 170-172; various ways of constructing, 130
Goods, external. See Gifts of fortune

Habituation (ethismos): behavioral objectives of, 127-128, 131, 136n.18; compatibility with voluntariness, 24, 73n.13; role in moral education, 41n.76, 100, 127-128, 131, 136n.25. See also Character, moral; Characteristics; Education, moral
Happiness. See Good life, the
Harmful things (ta blabera). See Advantageous, the
Honor (timē): 123n.96, 166; among the best gifts of fortune, 181n.29

Ignorance (agnoia): 139-140; distinction between actions done "in" and "due to," 36n.21, 143, 147, 152-154n.7, 157n.42; intentional, non-intentional, and unintentional, 31, 42n.82; moral, caused

by wayward desires, 139-140, 146-148; moral, characteristic of morally defective character, 140; moral, culpability for, 142; simple, 20, 139, 141-142. See also Accidents; Mistakes, simple; Moral evil; Moral weakness; Sensitivity, moral
Immortality: Aristotle's position on, 180n.26
Impetuosity (propeteia): 22, 148. See also Anger; Moral weakness
Incompetence. See Stupidity
Incontinence. See Moral weakness
Induction (epagōgē): 39n.61; nature of, 107, 119-120n.63; role of, in moral judgments, 107-109; use of, in the Ethics, 109. See also Dialectical method, the; Methodology of moral philosophy, the; Reason, intuitive; Reason, practical; Sensitivity, moral
Insensitivity. See Ignorance, moral
Integrity. See Morality
Intellect. See Reason
Intelligence (nous). See Reason, intuitive
Involuntary, the (to akousion): 21, 34n.5, 36n.20, 154n.13. See also Coercion; non-Voluntary, the; Voluntary, the; Suffering

Judgment, moral (gnōmē): 52, 106-112, 129; an affective-intuitive exercise of practical reason, 74n.13, 76n.29, 107-108, 111; cannot be schematized in universal rules, 68-71, 77n.33, 103, 110, 129; concerns both generalities and particulars, 66; developed through practical experience, 69-71, 77n.33, 107-109, 129; of good person is reliable, 42n.81; influence of character on, 11-12, 61n.70-71, 105-106, 108, 111, 119n.57; of many people is suspect, 42n.81, 105; a matter of sensitivity to particulars, 68, 70-71, 105-112, 120n.64, 129, 157n.42; about matters of justice (*sungnōmē*), 120n.66; morally evil, 140; no rules of relevancy in, 108; objects of, 17; presupposes endowment by nature, 107, 127; when inefficacious, is "understanding" (*sunesis*), 84. *See also* Choice; Deliberation; Facts of practice, the; Reason, practical; Sensitivity, moral; Understanding

Justice (*dikaiosunē*): 52; a criterion for the acceptability of constitutions, 131-132; equity (*epieikeia*) and 78n.44; the fundamental virtue of a good state, 130, 137n.29; good judgment in matters of (*sungnōmē*), 120n.66; in the sense of laws of a state, 131; in the sense of moral excellence, 89-90, 131-132, 150-151; in the sense of treating equals equally, unequals unequally, 131; rules of, will vary from state to state, 57n.28, 130. *See also* Constitution; State, the

Knowledge, moral: 10-12, 68-71, 103-112; an instrumentality in practice, 8, 12, 121n.72; involves factors both interior to and independent of the knower, 121n.82; learned from affective experience, 69-71, 104-112; may be studied philosophically, 79n.50; not applied theoretical knowledge, 68-71; skill and, 68-69, 81-83. *See also* Experience; Facts of practice, the; Induction; Judgment, moral; Methodology in moral philosophy, the; Reason, practical; Rules, moral; Sensitivity, moral; Understanding

Knowledge, theoretical (*epistēmē*): 25, 68-71, 168-169; developed through instruction and experience, 79n.55; an excellence of theoretical reason, 72n.4; independence of, from moral character, 74n.15; not concerned with what is good or bad for individuals, 70; not directly useful to practice, 68-70, 170; objects of, 25, 68, 170; qualities of, 68, 170; three kinds of, 25, 182n.47. *See also* Philosophy, First; Reason, theoretical; Wisdom, practical

Law: distinguished from the constitution, 134n.5; an expression of practical wisdom, 105-106, 109-110, 124, 131; importance of the rule of, 54, 61n.70, 131; moral rules and, 110; promotes good conduct, 127, 131, 134n.5; a safeguard of justice, 61n.70. *See also* State, the

Leisure: activities are the good life, 166-170; must be promoted by the state, 124, 135n.8, 169; a prerequisite for the good life, 124, 175-176

Making. *See* Process, productive

Man: agent, patient, and spectator, 7, 18, 24-26, 169-170; common form of, among individuals, 10, 160, 179n.7; contrasted with brute animals, 22-23; defined as a complex, 72n.1; defined in terms of reason alone, 72n.1, 172-173; endowment of, by nature, 107, 127; immortality of, 182n.26; inherently neither good nor evil, 13, 127, 135n.14; nature of, 10, 135n.13; proper function (*ergon*) of, 135n.14, 179n.7; a social and political being, 13, 124. *See also* Reason

Man, Aristotle's psychological picture of: 12, 96-97; influence of, on his delineation of the good life, 72n.1, 173-174; parts of the soul in, 72n.1, 95-96; problems caused by, 72n.1, 97; produced by practical reason, 120-121n.72; support for, 105. *See also* Reason, practical; Soul

Mean, the (*to meson*): 51-52; exemplified in the moral paradigm, 60n.59; the goal of dispositional training, 136n.16; limitations of the notion of, 60n.58; the measure of both actions and character, 51-52, 87; moral sensitivity and, 52; norm for, is right reason, 81, 110; not to be confused with moderation, 60n.58; origin or idea of, in physiological theory, 60n.59; relative to the individual, 110. *See also* Activity, morally good; Excellence, moral

Means: 56n.10; as a constituent part of an end, 56n.10; as distinct from the end of an action, 44, 115n.3; price of the, relative to the value of its product, 50

Metaphysics. *See* Philosophy, First

Methodology in moral philosophy: 10-12, 103-112; appeal to affective experience in 10, 68-71, 77n.33, 104-112, 125; appeal to "common sense" in, 118n.46; appeal to good, experienced people in, 69, 100, 105, 111-112; inevitable circularity involved in, 120-121n.72; influence of character on, 100, 104, 119n.57, 121n.74; problems with ordinary language in, 105-106; requirements of reason in, 105-106; ultimate data in, consists in moral facts, 9-10, 44, 104-108, 125, 145-146, 150; use of counter-examples in, 77n.35; use of the dialectical method in, 106-109, 118n.56, 119n.60-61, 160;

use of ordinary moral language in, 17-18, 25, 28, 34n.2, 38n.40, 39n.65, 55n.4-5, 105, 109, 125; use of previous theories in, 106, 145-146, 150. *See also* Dialectical method; Facts of practice, the; Judgment, moral; Philosophy, moral

Mishaps. *See* Accidents

Mistakes, simple (*hamartēmai*): 141-142. *See also* Ignorance

Moral evil (*kakia*): 142-144; caused by malformed desires, 102, 127, 130-131, 139, 142-144; causes blindness to what is genuinely good, 111, 121n.77, 140, 143; destroys itself, 155n.21; not a necessary feature of the universe, 135n.14; paradigmatic form of, is self-indulgence (*akolasia*), 143-144

Moral strength (*enkrateia*): 102, 148-149, 165

Moral weakness (*akrasia*): 144-148; Aristotle's analysis of, 24, 145-148, 165; choice and, 24; cleverness and, 147; difficulties in understanding, 145-146; distinguished from completely evil character, 92n.16, 145; inferiority of, to moral excellence 94n.51; the most common kind of moral personality, 181n.6; in nonsensual pleasures, 148; shame caused by, 93-94n.51; Socrates' analysis of, 23, 106, 145-146; sphere of, in proper sense, 59n.42, 148; understanding (*sunesis*) and, 92n.16; voluntary character of, 24. *See also* Pleasures, necessary; Socrates

Morality: 105; aims at integrity, 8, 112-114, 125, 129, 150-151; both individual and social aspects to, 8, 89-90, 105; concerns both actions and character, 112-114; effectiveness and, 9, 13, 141, 154-155n.20;

may be studied philosophically, 79n.50; not reducible to right rules of conduct, 110; political nature of, 99, 126

Movement (*kinēsis* and *metabolē*): 35n.15; actualization and, 45; contrasted with activity (*energeia*), 45; two kinds of, 34n.4. *See also* Power

Nature (*phusis*): provides objective basis for morality, 10, 44, 47-49, 99, 103, 106, 179n.7; role of, in moral education, 127; various senses of the term, 55-56n.5, 95, 135n.13; what is by, may be changeable, 58n.28

Necessity: 24, 38n.47

Noble, the *(to kalon):* 46; an absolute ideal, 10-11, 80-81, 110, 160-162, 164-165, 168-169; can be apprehended only by reason, 95, 115n.4; includes both moral and theoretical activity, 46-48; includes only activities (*energeiai*), 46

Nonvoluntary, the *(to ouch hekousion)*: 34n.5, 36n.20, 154n.13. *See also* Involuntary, the: Voluntary, the

Nutritive faculty: 62; irrelevant to specifically human practice 72n.2

Obstinancy: 149

Omissions: 35n.8

Opinions (*endoxai*), moral. *See* Methodology in moral philosophy.

Opinions (*endoxai*), theoretical: not affected by character, 74n.15, 140

Pain. *See* Pleasure

Paradigms, moral: difficulties in choosing proper, 53-54, 111, 133n.4; the mean exemplified by,

53, 87-88; the norm for truth in moral matters, 53; the role of, 53, 111, 122n.86, 126; states as, 126. *See also* Education, moral; Mean, the

Philosophy, First: the best of the theoretical sciences, 25-26, 182-183n.47; theoretical wisdom and, 26. *See also* Knowledge, theoretical; Reason, theoretical; Wisdom, theoretical

Philosophy, moral: 7-8, 103-112; aim of, is practical, 8, 12, 104, 121n.72, 130; concerns both character and actions, 112-114, 122-123n.96; influence of character on doing, 10-11, 99, 119n.57; itself an exercise of practical reason, 8, 11-12, 103-104; limitations of, 11-12, 52-53, 71, 78n.43, 104, 136n.25; not a theoretical science, 11, 68-71, 121n.72; objective basis for, in nature, 10-11, 99, 103; religious belief not presupposed by, 8-9, a study of pleasure and pain, 47. *See also* Education, moral; Good, the; Methodology in moral philosophy, the; Morality; Nature; Reason, practical; Wisdom, practical

Philosophic wisdom. *See* Wisdom, theoretical

Plato: Aristotle and, 4, 115n.10

Pleasure *(hēdonē):* 47-50; accompanies activity (*energeia*), 47-48; the best clue to a person's character, 113; the cause of moral evil, 127, 140; different activities are accompanied by different, 47-49; the end of sheer appetite is, 22; ethics is a study of, 47; of friendship, 124; the good life for man must include, 162; moral education and, 127, 135-136n.16, 137n.36; noble, 48; not a process, 47; not a sufficient criterion of moral good, 49; not the ultimate good, 59n.49; an objective standard for the value of, 49; opinions about the nature of, 43-44, 58n.32; replenishment theory of, 58n.36, 174; sought as an intrinsic good, 47; two discussions of in the *Ethics*, 5, 58n.32; two general kinds of, open to humans, 48, 176. *See also* Activity; Education, moral; Pleasures, necessary

Pleasures, necessary: 48; accompany processes, 48-50, 58n.36; moral excellence and, 87; need to be controlled, 135n.16; not paradigmatically human pleasures, 58n.36; only incidentally pleasurable, 47, 59n.42; second-rate, 59n.42; the state and, 134n.7. *See also* Desires; Excellence, moral; Mean, the; Process, productive

Potentiality (*dunamis*). See Capacity

Power (*dunamis*): 35n.9, 45, 55-56n.5; either innate or acquired by practice, 120n.65; the fundamental notion in the notion of agency, 7, 18, 37n.31, 65; related to one sense of "nature," 55-56n.5. *See also* Capacity; Movement

Process (*kinēsis*): 35n.15, 45; caused either mechanically or by agents, 34n.4; contrasted with action, 20-24, 44-46; kinds of, 35n.15. *See also* Activity; Movement; Process, productive

Process, productive (*poiēsis*): 50-51; contrasted with moral activity (*praxis*), 54, 80, 103; contrasted with theoretical activity, 70; description of, 44-45, 50-51; end of, not intrinsically good, 50-51; instrumentally good by nature, 46; judged by norm of effectiveness, 44, 50, 80; kinds of, 45, 50; kinds

of men, and, 167; not all practical goods can be, 160; occasionally may be intrinsically good, 182n.45; requires a rational characteristic in its agent-cause, 54. *See also* Activity, moral; Cleverness; End, the; Good, the; Process; Skill

Prudence: a misleading translation of *phronēsis*, 73n.6. See also Wisdom, practical

Punishment: 131; primarily rehabilitative, 137n.36. See also Education, moral; State, the

Reason (*logos*), 22-25; the best part of man, 117n.33, 161, 172; by itself does not initiate action, 21; by nature, meant to rule the emotions, 117n.33; the emotions cannot corrupt, 147, 149, 157n.3; excellences of, 72n.4; practical and theoretical functions of, 62. *See also* Induction, Reason, intuitive; Reason, practical; Reason, Theoretical; Skill; Understanding

Reason, intuitive (*nous*): 39n.61, 107-108; common to both theoretical and practical reason 72n.4, 107, 119n.63; contrasted with discursive thought, 39n.61, 107; an eye or vision, 108, 112; the highest and best power humans possess, 117n.33, 172-173; an intellectual excellence, 72n.4; operation of, 107-108; role of, in moral judgment, 74n.13, 107-111. *See also* Judgment, moral; Sensitivity, moral

Reason, practical (*to logistikon*): 62-79, 95-123; action is the end of, 67-68, 70-71; changes in Aristotle's views about, 78n.39, 96-97, 175; a complex of thought and desire, 21-24, 27, 63-64, 98; contrasted with theoretical reason,

24-25, 66-67, 71, 80, 96, 112; a creative faculty in judging particulars, 66, 103, 106-109; a critical faculty in forming practical rules, 66-67, 103; deliberation a function of, 64, 76n.28; deliberation not the only function of 68, 74n.16, 77n.33, 95-96, 99; developed through experience, 68-69; excellences of, 62-63, 72n.4, 120n.70; failures of, 143, 146-147; an imperative faculty making wishes efficacious, 65-67, 104; intuition in the functioning of, 76n.29, 107-108, 119n.63; logical form of 66-68, 77n.36; moral and non-moral functions of, 80-84; not applied theoretical reason, 68-70, 76n.28; perfected by the attainment of truth, 63, 67, 106, 116n.25; problems with Aristotle's delineation of 95-97; relation of, to theoretical activity, 175-176; role of rules formulated by, 27, 52, 68; two general kinds of errors possible to, 139; wishes and, 63-99. *See also* Choice; Deliberation; Methodology in Moral Philosophy, the; Skill; Syllogism, practical; Wisdom, practical

Reason, right (*orthos logos*): 81, 110. *See also* Mean, the; Wisdom, the man of practical

Reason, theoretical (*to epistēmonikon*): 62; contrasted with practical reason, 24-25, 62-63, 66-68, 112, 116n.14; end of, 67; excellences of, 62, 72n.4; logical form of, 67; objects of, 68, 170; perfected by the attainment of truth, 116n.25; role of intuition in functioning of, 107, 119n.63. *See also* Knowledge, theoretical; Wisdom, theoretical

Recreation; 162

Refrainings. *See* Omissions

Relativism, moral: 9-11, 43-44, 131

Responsibility, moral: agent's, for both good and bad practice, 23; animals and children have limited, 23; assessments of, difficult to make, 32-33, 34n.6; assessments of, presuppose a theory of action, 19, 39n.65; diminished or destroyed by coercion and provocation, 19, 32, 92n.32, 142; for one's own character, 73n.13, 100, 120n.66, 143; for simple errors, 141-142; lies with each individual, 11, 129; the need to assign, is the rationale for a theory of action, 19-20, 28; requires rational examination of the ends of action, 100; Socrates' view about, 23, 139, 149-150, 156n.35. *See also* Ignorance; Voluntary, the

Rules, moral (*logoi*): hold only generally, 11, 51-53, 68, 70-71, 77n.33&35, 78n.43, 103, 110; originate from experience and reflection on experience, 77n.33; role of the state in promulgating, 124-127, 130; societal context of, 125. *See also* Good, the; Methodology in moral philosophy, the; Wisdom, the man of practical

Scientific knowledge. *See* Knowledge, theoretical

Self-control (*sōphrosunē*): the paradigmatic form of moral excellence, 87-88, 143-144. *See also* Excellence, moral

Self-indulgence (*akolasia*): the paradigmatic form of moral evil, 143-144. *See also* Moral evil

Self-love: 14, 88-90. *See also* Wisdom, the man of practical

Sensitivity, moral (*aisthēsis*): 52, 77n.31, 106-109; articulation of, a separate skill, 67, 77n.15; a combination of objective and subjective factors, 121-122n.82; concerns facts of moral life, 66, 103, 105-106, 120n.64; developed through affective experience, 107-108, 111-112, difficulty in attaining, 52; a distinctive operation of practical reason, 103, 110-111; distinguished from sensory perception, 108, 120n.68; an eye or vision, 108, 112; involves inductive thinking, 107-108; involves intuitive thought (*nous*), 107-108. See also Insensitivity; Judgment, moral; Methodology in moral philosophy, the; Reason, practical; Wisdom, practical

Sex. *See* Pleasures, necessary

Shame (*aidōs*): 93-94n.51, 147-148

Skepticism, moral: 9-10

Skill (*technē*): 81-83; Aristotle's denigration of, 91n.3, 166-170; a capacity for moral opposites, 82-84, 91n.5; cleverness a kind of, 83; conditioned by morality, 50-51; descriptions of persons in terms of, always incomplete, 7, 82-83, 182n.45; distinguished from practical wisdom and good character, 41n.76, 84; the ends of, are of limited value, 82; an "excellence" of practical reason, 72n.4; exercise of, occasionally intrinsically good, 182n.45; an exercise of practical reason, 81; importance of knowledge in, 81-82; judged by norms of effectiveness, 81-82; a kind of wisdom, 81; learned from experience, 68-69, 81; a rational characteristic (*hexis*), 81, 91n.5; rules for, are not absolute, 81; similarities of, to moral knowledge, 68-69, 81-85. *See also* Action, human; Process, productive

Slavery, Aristotle's treatment of: 126, 167, 182n.45

Slyness (*panourgia*): 83. *See also* Cleverness; Skill

Socrates: intellectualism of, 84, 97, 115n.8, 140, 150; on moral education, 70, 135n.12, 136n.25, 160; on moral weakness, 23, 106, 145-146; on practical error, 23, 139, 149-150, 156n.35

Soul (*psuchē*): 72n.2; the actuality or form of the body, 55n.5, 72nn.1 & 2; excellences of the, 73n.6; immortality of the, 180n.26; parts of the 72nn.1 & 2, 95-97, 115n.10 116n.14. *See also* Desires; Man; Man, Aristotle's psychological picture of; Reason

State, the (*hē polis*): 124-138, 133n.5; an association based on exchange, 133n.2; the citizen of, 130, 133n.3, 133n.5; the constitution of 130, 133-134n.5; distinction between the best and the best possible, 129-130; the excellence of, 126-127; the function of, 126; the good life and, 125-126; justice the chief virtue of, 131; justice different in different forms of, 130; kinds of governments of, 130, 137n.29; leisure, should promote, 124, 135n.8; a macrocosmic counterpart of man, 134n.6; moral criteria regulating, 131-132; as moral educator, 124-127, 130; moral nature of, 13; a natural society, 13, 124, 126, 133n.2; negative utilitarianism and, 133n.2. *See also* Constitution; Law

Stupidity: 154-155n.20; a fault, 141

Suffering (*pathēsis*): contrasted with acting, 18; distinguished from character, 34n.6; either a capacity for or a state of being acted upon, 18; involuntary and nonvoluntary, 34n.6; may be affected by one's character, 34n.6; a quality, 91n.5; responsibility assessments in cases of, 34n.6. *See also* Capacity; Potentiality

Syllogism, practical: 66-67, 77n.33, 115n.3; an "after the fact" schematization, 76n.28, 108; error in, 143, 146-147; interpretations of, 75n.28, 77n.33, 157n.40; major premise in, enunciates what is good, 77n.33; major premise in, the expression of dispositions, 76n.29; major premise in, has truth value, 100; minor premise in, enunciates what is relevant and possible, 77n.33; minor premise in, involves sensitivity, 66; may have several premises, 76n.30. *See also* Choice; Deliberation, Judgment, moral

Theoretician, the: cannot abandon the life of practice, 169-170, 173; lives a life like that of God, 169, 172-173; often is inept in practical matters, 79n.49

Ultimate particulars. *See* Facts of practice, the

Understanding (*sunesis*): 79n.57, 84; contrasted with practical wisdom, 79n.57, 84; an intellectual excellence, 72n.4; moral weakness and, 91-92n.16

Vegetative soul. *See* Nutritive faculty

Virtue. *See* Excellence

Voluntary, the (*to hekousion*): 21; coercion excluded from, 23-24, 32; difficulties with Aristotle's use of the term, 36nn.20&21; habituation and, 24; two ways of understanding, 23-24; outside influence not excluded from,

23-24. *See also* Action, human; Involuntary, the; Nonvoluntary, the

Wisdom, the man of practical (*ho phronimos*): autonomy of, 121-122n.82; the best judge in moral matters, 83, 100, 111; the best judge of the value of pleasure, 49; characterized by moral sensitivity, 106-107, 111, 145; characterized by right actions, 113; an egotist in the best sense, 14, 83, 88-90; epitomizes right reason, 81, 110; the norm, in a sense, of morality, 110-111. *See also* Excellence, moral; Paradigms, moral; Sensitivity, moral; Wisdom, practical

Wisdom, practical (*phronēsis*): 83-85, 103-114; change in Aristotle's views about 78n.39; characterized by experienced sensitivity, 106-110; description of 73n.6, 84, 113, 145, 151; end and function of, 73n.6, 74n.13, 84-85; the ends of action and, 95-100; an excellence of practical reason, 63, 72n.4, 83, 129, 171; incompatible with moral wrongdoing, 84, 88; moral excellence, cannot exist without, 84-85, 95, 98, 116n.14, 129; not applied theoretical wisdom, 68-70; not merely a rational characteristic, 84; not merely skill, 84, 152n.1; not merely understanding, 84; requires habituation and instruction, 74n.13, 129; a synthesis of right reason and right desire, 110, 117n.31. *See also* Reason, practical; Sensitivity, moral

Wisdom, political (*politikē*): 176, 184n.65; aim of, 99, 126, 169, 176; and practical wisdom, 134n.6

Wisdom, theoretical (*sophia*): 26, 39n.59, 62-63; the excellence of theoretical reason, 62, 72n.4, 171; generated from theoretical activity, 175; problems with Aristotle's delineation of, 170-176; superiority of, to practical wisdom, 171. *See also* Knowledge, theoretical; Reason, theoretical

Wishes (*bouleseis*): 98-99, 116n.15; change in Aristotle's view about, 117n.35; choice and, 74n.15, 98-99; correctness of, 99; an exercise of practical reason, 99, 116n.22, 117n.35; a form of desire, 98; judged by actions, 112-113, not merely appetite, 98-99; role of, in practical reasoning, 63-64; a synthesis of desire and reason, 98; wayward, the cause of moral evil, 101-102. *See also* Choice; Deliberation; Desire; Reason, practical